OXFORD Junior Illustrated Thesaurus

Compiled by
Alan Spooner

Illustrated by
Peter Visscher

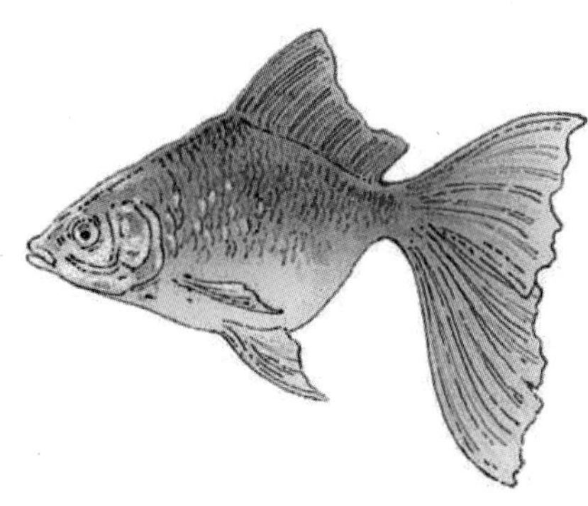

OXFORD
UNIVERSITY PRESS

Great Clarendon Street, Oxford OX2 6DP

Oxford University Press is a department of the University of Oxford.
It furthers the University's objective of excellence in research, scholarship, and education by publishing worldwide in

Oxford New York

Auckland Bangkok Buenos Aires Cape Town Chennai Dar es Salaam Delhi Hong Kong Istanbul Karachi Kolkata Kuala Lumpur Madrid Melbourne Mexico City Mumbai Nairobi São Paulo Shanghai Taipei Tokyo Toronto

Oxford is a registered trade mark of Oxford University Press in the UK and in certain other countries

First published 1999
This edition 2003

British Library Cataloguing in Publication Data available

ISBN 0-19-910858-7 Hardback
ISBN 0-19-910859-5 Paperback

5 7 9 10 8 6

Typeset by Pentacor PLC, High Wycombe

Printed by Gráficas Estella, Spain

PREFACE for teachers and parents

This thesaurus contains two main types of entry.

1 There are entries which give *synonyms* for the common words in a child's vocabulary. Where appropriate, opposites are also given. Example sentences or phrases put each word in a meaningful context.

2 There are *topic entries* which give lists of words which are not synonyms but which are related to the headword. For example, various kinds of animal are listed under **animal**; musical terms are given under **music**; and so on. These entries will be helpful to individual children who just need a jog to the memory to find the word they were looking for; they also provide opportunities for them to explore and discuss the vocabulary of a particular topic.

The arrangement of the thesaurus is simple and user-friendly. Each entry is self-explanatory: there are no abbreviations or cryptic devices. The headwords, which comprise all the words children are likely to look up as starting-points for a word-search, are arranged in simple alphabetical sequence, avoiding the need for a separate index (a common but awkward and confusing feature of some other thesauruses). The more discussable entries - topic entries, and entries for headwords with a particular complex range of senses or usages - are boxed in a blue outline. This will encourage young readers to browse.

The English language is infinitely variable and adaptable. Ultimately, children's awareness of this variety and adaptability will come not from a book like this, but from their experience of language in use. I hope, therefore, that they will be encouraged to see the thesaurus not just as a book to refer to, but as a book which raises questions about vocabulary - and about language in general - which they will want to discuss with teachers, parents, and other experienced users of our language.

The headword list in this thesaurus is derived from that of the *Oxford Junior Illustrated Dictionary*, to which this book will make an ideal companion volume.

Alan Spooner

USING THIS THESAURUS

A thesaurus helps you find words to make your language more interesting, and to help you say exactly what you want to say. It gives you words which have the same meaning as the word you thought of. These are called *synonyms*.

It may give you words which mean the *opposite* of the word you thought of.

It will often give you words which are useful when you are talking or writing about a particular *topic*.

Remember that a thesaurus does not give you explanations or definitions of what words mean. If you want to know what a word means, you need to look it up in a dictionary like the *Oxford Junior Illustrated Dictionary*.

IN THIS THESAURUS YOU WILL FIND...

Headwords
The words you look up are printed in heavy black type, so that they are easy to find.

Examples
Sentences or phrases showing how you might use the word are printed in ordinary type.

Related words
Sometimes we give lists of words which are specially interesting. These entries are in the boxes. Many of these are not lists of synonyms, but lists of words related to a topic.

bolt *verb*

1 Remember to bolt the back door.
OTHER VERBS YOU MIGHT USE ARE **to bar** **to fasten** **to lock**

2 The horse bolted.
OTHER VERBS ARE **to escape** **to run away**
For other words, see **run**

3 Don't bolt down your food!
OTHER VERBS ARE **to gobble** **to gulp**

book *noun*
VARIOUS KINDS OF BOOK ARE
album **annual** **atlas** **diary** **dictionary** **directory** **encyclopedia** **hymn book** **novel** **paperback** **story book** **thesaurus**

bottom *noun*

1 the bottom of a wall.
OTHER WORDS YOU MIGHT USE ARE **base** **foot** **foundation**
The opposite is **top**

2 the bottom of the sea.
ANOTHER WORD IS **bed**
The opposite is **surface**

Synonyms
Words which mean the same as the word you look up are the synonyms. These are words you might use instead of the word you look up. They are printed in bold black type.

Numbers
When a word has more than one meaning, or if it is used in more than one way, we number the different uses.

Antonyms
If the word you look up has a useful opposite, it comes after the synonyms.

Aa

a b c d e f g h i j k l m n o p q r s t u v w x y z

abandon *verb*

1 It's cruel to abandon a pet.
OTHER VERBS YOU MIGHT USE ARE **to desert** **to forsake** **to leave**

2 We abandoned the game when it rained.
OTHER VERBS ARE **to cancel** **to give up** **to postpone**

able *adjective*

1 Are you able to play tomorrow?
OTHER WORDS YOU MIGHT USE ARE **allowed** **free**

2 Jo is an able tennis player.
OTHER WORDS ARE **capable** **clever** **skilful** **talented**

abolish *verb*

I wish they would abolish tests.
OTHER VERBS YOU MIGHT USE ARE **to end** **to get rid of** **to remove**

accept *verb*

1 Please accept this gift.
OTHER VERBS YOU MIGHT USE ARE **to receive** **to take**

2 I accept that it was my fault.
OTHER VERBS ARE **to admit** **to agree** **to believe**

accident *noun*

1 OTHER WORDS YOU MIGHT USE ARE **collision** **crash** **mishap**
WORDS YOU MIGHT USE FOR A VERY SERIOUS ACCIDENT ARE **calamity** **catastrophe** **disaster**

2 We met by accident.
OTHER WORDS ARE **chance** **coincidence**

accompany *verb*

Dad accompanied us to school.
A PHRASE YOU MIGHT USE IS **to go with**

account *noun*

Jo wrote an account of the match.
OTHER WORDS YOU MIGHT USE ARE **description** **report** **story**

accurate *adjective*

1 Is your watch accurate?
OTHER WORDS YOU MIGHT USE ARE **correct** **right**

2 Give me an accurate account of what happened.
OTHER WORDS ARE **exact** **precise** **true**

ache *verb* and *noun*

For other words, see **pain**

achievement *noun*

It was a great achievement to win by four goals.
OTHER WORDS YOU MIGHT USE ARE **accomplishment** **feat** **success**

act *verb*

1 She acted quickly to put out the fire.
PHRASES YOU MIGHT USE ARE **to do something** **to take action**

2 Jo likes to act in plays.
OTHER VERBS YOU MIGHT USE ARE **to appear** **to perform**
To act without using words is **to mime**

3 He was acting like an idiot.
ANOTHER VERB IS **to behave**

action *noun*

1 The film was full of action.
OTHER WORDS YOU MIGHT USE ARE **activity** **excitement**

2 It was a kind action to dig Mr Brown's garden.
OTHER WORDS ARE **act** **deed**

active *adjective*

1 Our puppy is very active.
OTHER WORDS YOU MIGHT USE ARE **energetic** **lively**

2 Mum is active in charity work.
OTHER WORDS ARE **busy** **involved** **working**

activity *noun*

1 What activities do you enjoy?
OTHER WORDS YOU MIGHT USE ARE **hobby** **job** **project** **task**

2 The shops are full of activity when the sales are on.
OTHER WORDS ARE **action** **bustle** **excitement**

actual *adjective*

Is that the actual tree Robin Hood lived in?
OTHER WORDS YOU MIGHT USE ARE **genuine** **real**

add *verb*

1 Add the milk and the sugar.
OTHER VERBS YOU MIGHT USE ARE **to combine** **to mix** **to put together**

2 We added the numbers together.
For other words you might use when you do maths, see **mathematics**
The opposite is **subtract**

additional *adjective*

OTHER WORDS ARE **extra** **more**

admire *verb*

1 We admired the firemen's skill.
OTHER VERBS YOU MIGHT USE ARE **to praise** **to respect** **to wonder at**

2 I admired the view.
OTHER VERBS ARE **to appreciate** **to enjoy** **to like**

admit *verb*

1 Jo admitted that she was wrong.
OTHER VERBS YOU MIGHT USE ARE **to accept** **to confess** **to own up**

2 They only admit you if you have a ticket.
OTHER VERBS ARE **to allow in** **to let in**

adore *verb*

Jo's dog adores her.
OTHER VERBS YOU MIGHT USE ARE **to idolize** **to love** **to worship**

adult *noun*

ANOTHER WORD IS **grown-up**

advance *verb*
As the army advanced, the enemy ran away.
OTHER VERBS YOU MIGHT USE ARE **to approach** **to come near** **to move forward** **to progress**
The opposite is **retreat**

advantage *noun*
It's an advantage to have the wind behind you when you run.
ANOTHER WORD IS **help**

advertise *verb*
They advertised a new car on TV.
OTHER VERBS YOU MIGHT USE ARE (*informal*) **to plug** **to promote** **to publicize**

advertisement *noun*
OTHER WORDS YOU MIGHT USE ARE (*informal*) **ad** or **advert** **commercial** **poster**

advice *noun*
My advice is to save your money.
OTHER WORDS YOU MIGHT USE ARE **recommendation** **suggestion**

advise *verb*
What did the doctor advise?
OTHER VERBS YOU MIGHT USE ARE **to recommend** **to suggest**

aeroplane *noun*
For other machines that fly, see **aircraft**

affect *verb*
The weather affects my mood.
OTHER VERBS YOU MIGHT USE ARE **to alter** **to change** **to influence**

afraid *adjective*
The dog is afraid of thunder.
OTHER WORDS YOU MIGHT USE ARE **frightened** **scared** **terrified**

aggressive *adjective*
That dog looks rather aggressive.
OTHER WORDS YOU MIGHT USE ARE **hostile** **rough** **violent**
The opposite is **friendly**

agree *verb*
1 Mum agreed that I was right.
OTHER VERBS YOU MIGHT USE ARE **to accept** **to admit**
2 We agreed to go shopping.
OTHER VERBS ARE **to arrange** **to consent** **to decide**

a b c d e f g h i j k l m n o p q r s t u v w x y z

aim *verb*

1 Aim the gun at the target.
OTHER VERBS YOU MIGHT USE ARE **to direct** **to point**

2 We aimed to arrive by teatime.
OTHER VERBS ARE **to intend** **to plan** **to try** **to want**

aircraft *noun*

VARIOUS KINDS OF AIRCRAFT ARE
aeroplane **airliner** **balloon** **glider**
helicopter **jumbo jet** **jet plane**

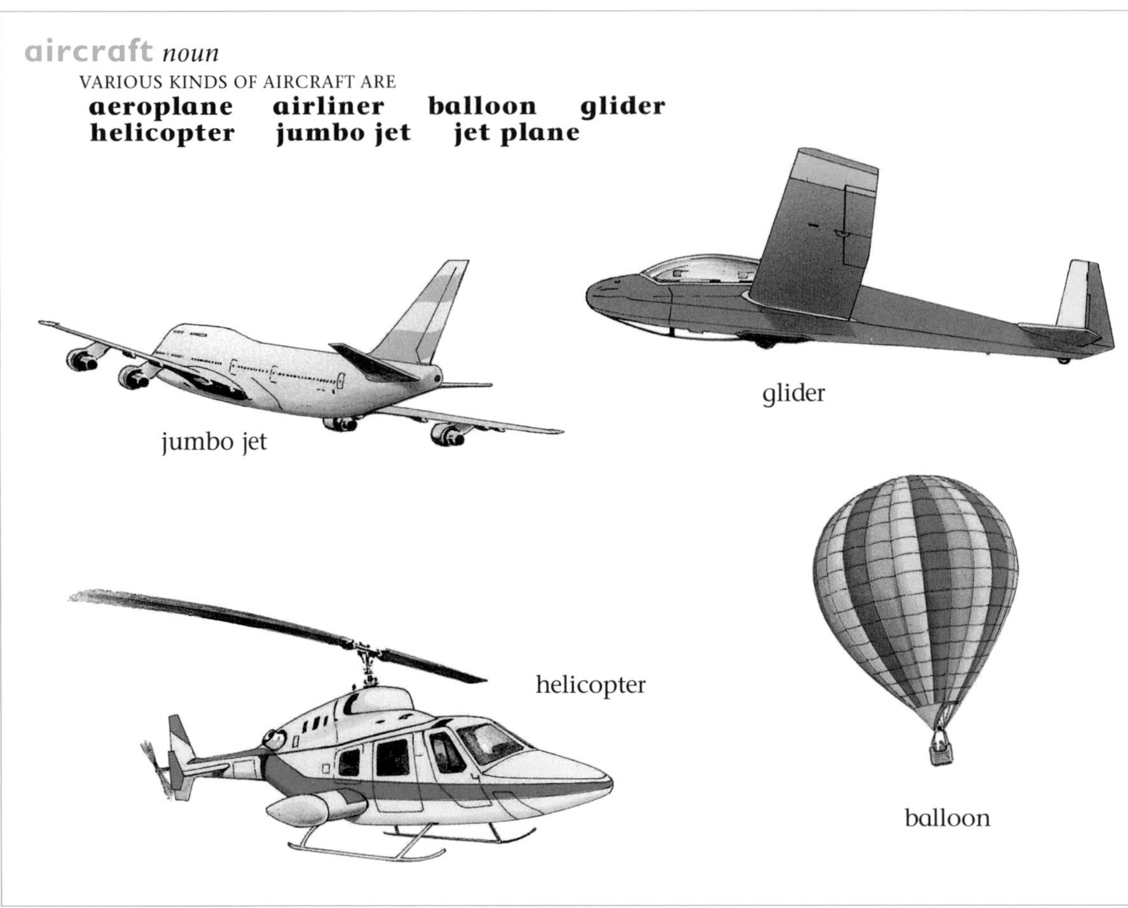

alarm *noun*

1 An alarm goes if there is a fire.
OTHER WORDS YOU MIGHT USE ARE **signal** **siren** **warning**

2 The storm was so bad that the animals were filled with alarm.
OTHER WORDS ARE **dismay** **fear** **fright** **panic** **terror**

alarm *verb*

The thunder alarmed the animals.
OTHER VERBS YOU MIGHT USE ARE **to frighten** **to scare** **to upset**

alert *adjective*

A sentry must be alert.
OTHER WORDS YOU MIGHT USE ARE **attentive** **awake** **observant** **watchful**

allow *verb*

You are allowed to drive when you have passed a test.
OTHER VERBS YOU MIGHT USE ARE **to authorize** **to license** **to permit**

amaze *verb*
The conjuror's tricks amazed us.
OTHER VERBS YOU MIGHT USE ARE **to astonish** **to astound** **to surprise**

amazing *adjective*
For other words, see **extraordinary**

ambition *noun*
Sam's ambition is to be a pilot.
OTHER WORDS YOU MIGHT USE ARE **aim** **goal** **objective** **wish**

ambush *verb*
The soldiers ambushed the enemy.
OTHER VERBS YOU MIGHT USE ARE **to attack** **to jump out on** **to take by surprise** **to trap**

ammunition *noun*
KINDS OF AMMUNITION ARE
bullet **cannonball** **hand grenade** **missile** **shell**
For other words, see **weapon**

amount *noun*
OTHER WORDS YOU MIGHT USE ARE **quantity** **total**

amuse *verb*
While we waited for the bus I tried to amuse the others.
OTHER VERBS YOU MIGHT USE ARE **to cheer up** **to divert** **to entertain**

amusing *adjective*
an amusing joke.
OTHER WORDS YOU MIGHT USE ARE **comic** **funny** **humorous** **witty**

ancient *adjective*
For other words, see **old**

anger *noun*
He showed his anger by slamming the door.
OTHER WORDS YOU MIGHT USE ARE **annoyance** **fury** **rage** **temper**

angry *adjective*
Mum was angry when Jo broke the window.
OTHER WORDS YOU MIGHT USE ARE **annoyed** **cross** **furious** **in a temper** **infuriated** **irate** (*informal*) **mad** **vexed**
The opposite is **pleased**

animal *noun*, see next page

announce *verb*
1 Jo announced that she was ready.
OTHER VERBS YOU MIGHT USE ARE **to declare** **to report** **to state**
2 The DJ announced our record.
ANOTHER VERB IS **to introduce**

announcement *noun*
The head read some announcements.
OTHER WORDS YOU MIGHT USE ARE **notice** **statement**

animal *noun*

OTHER WORDS YOU MIGHT USE ARE

beast **creature**

A word you might use for a big animal you don't like is **brute**

DIFFERENT CLASSES OF ANIMAL ARE

amphibian **bird** **fish** **mammal** **reptile**

ANIMALS THAT FARMERS KEEP ARE

bull **cow** **goat** **horse** **ox**
pig **sheep**

ANIMALS PEOPLE KEEP AS PETS ARE

cat **dog** **donkey** **ferret** **gerbil**
guinea pig **hamster** **horse** **mouse** **rabbit**
rat **tortoise**

WILD ANIMALS YOU MIGHT SEE IN BRITAIN ARE

badger **bat** **deer** **dormouse** **fox**
hare **hedgehog** **mole** **otter** **shrew**
squirrel **stoat** **vole** **weasel**

OTHER WILD ANIMALS ARE

antelope **ape** **baboon** **bear** **beaver**
bison **buffalo** **camel** **cheetah**
chimpanzee **dromedary** **elephant** **elk** **giraffe**
gorilla **grizzly bear** **hippopotamus** **hyena**
jackal **jaguar** **kangaroo** **koala** **leopard**
lion **llama** **mongoose** **monkey** **moose**
panda **panther** **platypus** **polar bear** **porcupine**
reindeer **rhinoceros** **skunk** **snake** **tiger**
wallaby **wolf** **zebra**

ANIMALS THAT LIVE IN THE SEA ARE

dolphin **fish** **octopus** **porpoise** **seal**
sea lion **turtle** **walrus** **whale**

annoy *verb*
The wasps were annoying me.
OTHER VERBS YOU MIGHT USE ARE **to bother** **to irritate** **to pester** **to torment** **to trouble** **to upset** **to worry**

answer *noun*
1 an answer to a question.
OTHER WORDS YOU MIGHT USE ARE **reply** **response**
2 the answer to a problem.
OTHER WORDS ARE **explanation** **solution**

anxious *adjective*
1 Mum gets anxious if I'm late.
OTHER WORDS YOU MIGHT USE ARE **concerned** **nervous** **worried**
2 We were anxious to start.
OTHER WORDS ARE **eager** **keen**

apologize *verb*
I apologized for being rude.
A PHRASE IS **to say sorry**

appeal *verb*
The sick man appealed for help.
OTHER VERBS YOU MIGHT USE ARE **to ask** **to beg** **to plead**

appear *verb*
1 He appeared out of the mist.
OTHER VERBS YOU MIGHT USE ARE **to arrive** **to come out** **to turn up**
2 You appear tired.
OTHER VERBS ARE **to look** **to seem**

appetite *noun*
1 an appetite for food.
OTHER WORDS YOU MIGHT USE ARE **greed** **hunger**
2 an appetite for adventure.
OTHER WORDS ARE **desire** **longing** **passion** **wish**

appointment *noun*
The head can't see us this afternoon because she has another appointment.
OTHER WORDS YOU MIGHT USE ARE **arrangement** **engagement** **meeting**

approach *verb*
I got nervous when the big dog approached me.
A PHRASE IS **to come near**

appropriate *adjective*
£10 was an appropriate price.
OTHER WORDS YOU MIGHT USE ARE **fitting** **proper** **right** **suitable**

approve *verb*
Did you approve of what I did?
OTHER VERBS YOU MIGHT USE ARE **to admire** **to like** **to praise**

approximately *adverb*
The trip costs approximately £10.
OTHER WORDS YOU MIGHT USE ARE **about** **nearly** **roughly**

a b c d e f g h i j k l m n o p q r s t u v w x y z

area *noun*

1 The playground is a large area.
OTHER WORDS YOU MIGHT USE ARE **expanse** **surface**

2 Uncle Tom lives in a nice area of London.
OTHER WORDS ARE **district** **neighbourhood** **part** **region**

argue *verb*

Jo and Sam are good friends: they don't often argue.
OTHER VERBS YOU MIGHT USE ARE **to disagree** **to quarrel**

argument *noun*

1 We had an argument about who was going to pay.
OTHER WORDS YOU MIGHT USE ARE **disagreement** **dispute** **quarrel**

2 There has been a lot of argument in the paper about a bypass.
OTHER WORDS YOU MIGHT USE ARE **controversy** **debate**

arm *noun*

For other parts of the body, see **body**

arrange *verb*

1 Jo arranged the books on the shelf.
OTHER VERBS YOU MIGHT USE ARE **to set out** **to sort** **to tidy**

2 We arranged a trip to the sea.
OTHER VERBS ARE **to decide on** **to fix** **to organize** **to plan**

arrest *verb*

The police arrested the suspect.
OTHER VERBS YOU MIGHT USE ARE **to capture** **to catch** **to detain** **to take into custody**

arrive *verb*

1 When will Granny arrive?
OTHER VERBS YOU MIGHT USE ARE **to appear** **to come** **to turn up**
The opposite is **depart**

2 We arrived home for dinner.
OTHER VERBS ARE **to come** **to get to** **to reach**

art *noun*

KINDS OF ART ARE
collage **drawing** **embroidery** **modelling** **needlework** **painting** **photography** **pottery** **sculpture** **sewing** **sketching** **weaving**

DIFFERENT ARTISTS ARE
painter **photographer** **potter** **sculptor** **weaver**

artificial *adjective*

1 Sam wore an artificial beard in the play.
OTHER WORDS YOU MIGHT USE ARE **false** **pretend**

2 This dress is made of artificial material.
OTHER WORDS ARE **man-made** **synthetic**
The opposite is **genuine**

ask *verb*

1 What did you ask?
OTHER VERBS YOU MIGHT USE ARE **to enquire** **to find out** **to inquire**

2 The criminal asked to be given another chance.
OTHER VERBS ARE **to beg** **to implore** **to plead** **to request**

3 My friends asked me to go out.
ANOTHER VERB IS **to invite**

assistant *noun*

You can't do that job on your own: you need an assistant.
OTHER WORDS YOU MIGHT USE ARE **helper** **partner**
Someone who helps a person with an official job is a **deputy**.
Someone who helps a person commit a crime is an **accomplice**.

assorted *adjective*

For other words, see **various**

astonish *verb*

The player's skill astonished us.
OTHER VERBS YOU MIGHT USE ARE **to amaze** **to astound** **to surprise**

athlete *noun*

OTHER WORDS YOU MIGHT USE ARE **sportsman** **sportswoman**
For various sports, see **sport**

attach *verb*

WAYS TO ATTACH THINGS ARE **to bind** **to connect** **to fasten** **to fix** **to glue** **to join** **to link** **to stick** **to tie**

attack *verb*

1 The soldiers attacked the enemy.
DIFFERENT WAYS TO ATTACK ARE **to ambush** **to assault** **to bomb** **to bombard** **to charge** **to raid**

2 Two men attacked him in the street.
OTHER VERBS YOU MIGHT USE ARE **to mug** **to set on**

The opposite is **defend**

attempt *verb*

Jo attempted to swim ten lengths.
OTHER VERBS AND PHRASES ARE **to endeavour** **to exert yourself** **to make an effort** **to try**

a b c d e f g h i j k l m n o p q r s t u v w x y z

attend *verb*

1 We attended the school concert.

PHRASES YOU MIGHT USE ARE **to be present at** **to go to**

2 Are you attending to me?

OTHER VERBS YOU MIGHT USE ARE **to listen** **to pay attention**

attract *verb*

The bright lights attracted us.

OTHER VERBS YOU MIGHT USE ARE **to appeal to** **to fascinate** **to interest**

attractive *adjective*

1 an attractive person.

OTHER WORDS YOU MIGHT USE ARE **beautiful** **charming** **glamorous** **good-looking** **handsome** **likeable** **pleasant** **pretty**

The opposite is **ugly**

2 an attractive idea.

OTHER WORDS ARE **appealing** **interesting** **pleasing** **tempting**

The opposite is **boring**

audience *noun*

The audience enjoyed the play.

OTHER WORDS YOU MIGHT USE ARE **listeners** **spectators**

author *noun*

ANOTHER WORD IS **writer**

For other words, see **write**

available *adjective*

Our magazine is now available.

OTHER WORDS YOU MIGHT USE ARE **on sale** **ready**

average *adjective*

It was an average kind of day.

OTHER WORDS YOU MIGHT USE ARE **middling** **normal** **ordinary** **typical** **usual**

The opposite is **extraordinary**

avoid *verb*

Sam avoided the washing-up.

OTHER VERBS YOU MIGHT USE ARE **to dodge** **to escape** **to get out of** **to shirk**

awake *adjective*

I was awake all night because of the storm.

OTHER WORDS YOU MIGHT USE ARE **alert** **conscious**

The opposite is **asleep**

award *noun*

Jo got an award for swimming ten lengths.

OTHER WORDS YOU MIGHT USE ARE **badge** **medal** **prize** **reward** **trophy**

aware *adjective*

Jo was aware that Mum would worry if she was late.

ANOTHER WORD IS **conscious**

awful *adjective*

For other words, see **bad**

awkward *adjective*

1 Ducks look awkward when they walk on dry land.
ANOTHER WORD IS **clumsy**

2 Are you trying to be awkward?
OTHER WORDS ARE **difficult** **uncooperative**

3 The visitors came at an awkward time.
ANOTHER WORD IS **inconvenient**

Bb

baby *noun*
ANOTHER WORD IS **infant**
A baby just starting to walk is a **toddler**

back *noun*
I had to wait at the back of the queue
OTHER WORDS ARE **end** **rear** **tail-end**
The opposite is **front**

back *verb*
Dad backed the car into the gate.
ANOTHER VERB IS **to reverse**

bad *adjective*, see next page

badge *noun*
a school badge.
OTHER WORDS YOU MIGHT USE ARE
crest **emblem** **sign** **symbol**

bad-tempered *adjective*
OTHER WORDS YOU MIGHT USE ARE **angry** **cross** **grumpy** **irritable** **short-tempered**
The opposite is **cheerful**

bag *noun*
For other words, see **container**

bake *verb*
For other ways to cook things, see **cook**

bad *adjective*

THIS WORD HAS MANY USES. HERE ARE SOME OF THE WAYS YOU CAN USE IT, AND SOME OTHER WORDS YOU COULD CHOOSE

1 a bad deed.
criminal cruel evil immoral sinful villainous wicked wrong

2 a bad child.
disobedient mischievous naughty

3 a bad player.
hopeless incompetent rotten useless

4 a bad accident.
appalling awful dreadful frightful horrible serious severe shocking terrible

5 a bad piece of work.
careless incorrect poor shoddy useless weak worthless

6 bad food.
decayed mouldy rotten smelly

7 a bad smell.
nasty objectionable offensive revolting sickening unpleasant

8 a bad habit.
dangerous harmful nasty unhealthy

9 I feel bad today.
feeble ill poorly sick unwell

The opposite is **good**

ball *noun*

THINGS SHAPED LIKE A BALL ARE **globe sphere**

For other shapes, see **shape**

ban *verb*

They banned smoking on the buses.

OTHER VERBS YOU MIGHT USE ARE **to forbid to make illegal to prohibit**

band *noun*

1 Robin Hood lived with a band of outlaws.
ANOTHER WORD IS **gang**

2 Jo plays the guitar in a band.
OTHER WORDS ARE **group orchestra**

For more words to do with music, see **music**

3 A wooden barrel has bands of metal round it.
OTHER WORDS ARE **hoop loop ring**

bang *noun*

1 We heard a loud bang.
OTHER WORDS YOU MIGHT USE ARE **blast boom crash explosion**

For other sounds, see **sound**

2 I got a nasty bang on the head.
OTHER WORDS ARE **blow bump hit knock**

banish *verb*

The traitor was banished from his country.

OTHER VERBS ARE **to exile to expel to send away**

bank *noun*

We sat on a grassy bank.

OTHER WORDS YOU MIGHT USE ARE **embankment slope**

banner *noun*
The people in the procession waved banners.
OTHER WORDS YOU MIGHT USE ARE **flag** **standard** **streamer**

banquet *noun*
OTHER WORDS ARE **dinner** **feast** (*informal*) **spread**
For other words, see **meal**

bar *noun*
1 a wooden bar.
OTHER WORDS YOU MIGHT USE ARE **beam** **rail** **rod**
2 an iron bar.
ANOTHER WORD YOU MIGHT USE IS **girder**
3 a bar of chocolate.
ANOTHER WORD IS **block**

bare *adjective*
OTHER WORDS YOU MIGHT USE ARE **naked** **nude** **unclothed** **uncovered** **undressed**

barely *adverb*
Sam was so tired that he could barely keep his eyes open.
OTHER WORDS YOU MIGHT USE ARE **hardly** **only** **just** **scarcely**

barren *adjective*
The desert was completely barren.
OTHER WORDS YOU MIGHT USE ARE **bare** **lifeless** **sterile**

barrier *noun*
They put up a barrier to keep the crowd off the field.
OTHER WORDS ARE **barricade** **fence** **railings** **wall**

base *noun*
1 Dad used cement to make a firm base for the shed.
ANOTHER WORD IS **foundation**
2 Don't sit near the base of the cliff.
OTHER WORDS YOU MIGHT USE ARE **bottom** **foot**
3 After a long march, the soldiers returned to their base.
OTHER WORDS ARE **depot** **headquarters**

bashful *adjective*
The little boy was too bashful to say 'thank you'.
OTHER WORDS YOU MIGHT USE ARE **modest** **shy** **timid**

basic *adjective*
I know the basic facts, but I've still got a lot to learn.
OTHER WORDS ARE **chief** **essential** **important** **main** **principal**

basin *noun*
OTHER WORDS ARE **bowl** **dish**

basket *noun*
For other kinds of container, see **container**

a b c d e f g h i j k l m n o p q r s t u v w x y z

bat *noun*
The special bat you use in tennis is a **racket**.
The stick you hit the ball with in golf is a **club**.

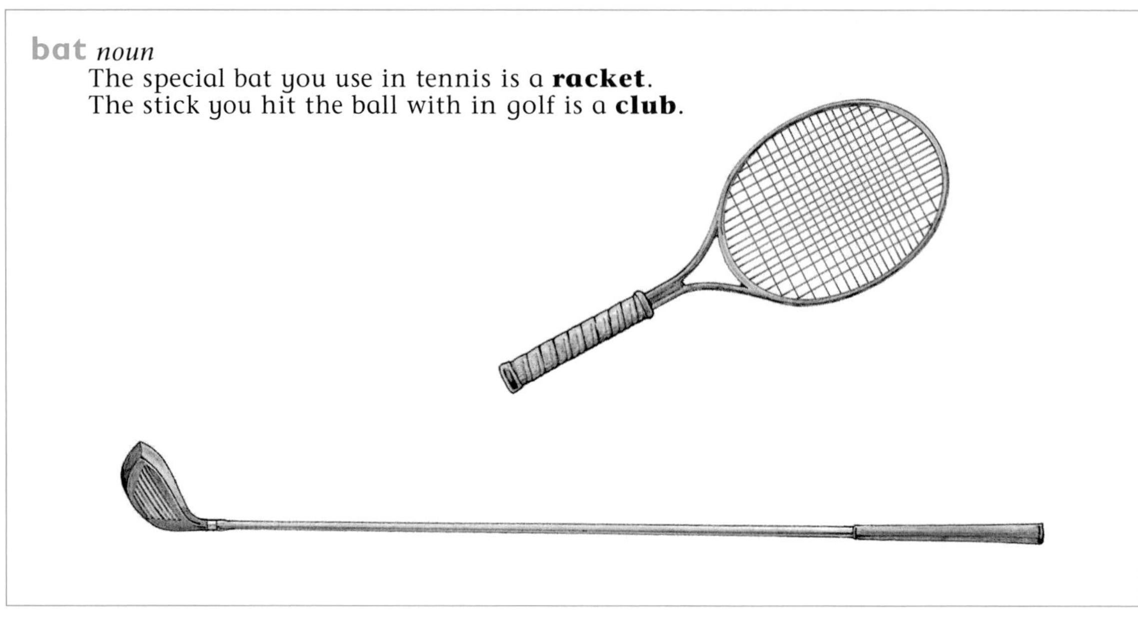

bath *noun*
SPECIAL KINDS OF BATH ARE
jacuzzi **sauna** **shower**

battle *noun*
For other words, see **war**

bay *noun*
OTHER WORDS YOU MIGHT USE ARE **cove** **estuary** **gulf** **inlet**

beach *noun*
Jo and Sam spent a happy day at the beach.
OTHER WORDS YOU MIGHT USE ARE **sands** **shore**
For other words, see **seaside**

beam *noun*
1 a beam of wood.
OTHER WORDS YOU MIGHT USE ARE **bar** **plank**
2 a beam of light.
OTHER WORDS ARE **ray** **shaft**

beam *verb*
He beamed when he heard my voice.
OTHER VERBS YOU MIGHT USE ARE **to grin** **to laugh** **to look happy** **to smile**

bear *verb*
1 Will this branch bear my weight?
OTHER VERBS YOU MIGHT USE ARE **to carry** **to hold** **to support**
2 She bore the pain bravely.
OTHER VERBS ARE **to endure** **to put up with** **to stand** **to suffer**

beast *noun*
OTHER WORDS YOU MIGHT USE ARE **animal** **creature**
ANIMALS THAT MAKE YOU AFRAID ARE **brute** **monster**

beat *verb*

1 We beat our opponents 6–0.
OTHER VERBS YOU MIGHT USE ARE **to conquer** **to defeat** **to outdo** **to overcome** (*informal*) **to thrash**

2 It's cruel to beat animals.
For other verbs, see **hit**

3 Dad beat some eggs to make an omelette.
OTHER VERBS ARE **to mix** **to stir** **to whisk**

4 When I run my heart beats fast.
OTHER VERBS ARE **to knock** **to pound** **to throb**

beautiful *adjective*

1 a beautiful bride.
OTHER WORDS YOU MIGHT USE ARE **attractive** **charming** **elegant** **glamorous** **good-looking** **gorgeous** **handsome** **lovely** **pretty**
The opposite is **ugly**

2 beautiful weather.
OTHER WORDS ARE **enjoyable** **fine** **good** **nice** **pleasant**

beckon *verb*

Sam beckoned to me to join him.
OTHER VERBS YOU MIGHT USE ARE **to make a sign** **to signal**

become *verb*

In time the little shoot will become a big tree.
PHRASES YOU MIGHT USE ARE **to change into** **to grow into** **to turn into**

bed *noun*

PARTS OF A BED ARE
base **headboard** **mattress**
A bed with a base and a mattress is a **divan**.
Two beds one above the other are **bunks**.
A bunk on a ship is a **berth**.
An old-fashioned bed with curtains round is a **four-poster**.

THINGS YOU USE TO MAKE A BED ARE
bedclothes or **bedding**

DIFFERENT KINDS OF BEDCLOTHES ARE
bed linen **bedspread** **blanket** **counterpane** **coverlet** **duvet** **eiderdown** **pillow** **pillowcase** **quilt** **sheet**

bee *noun*

KINDS OF BEE ARE **bumble-bee** **drone** **queen bee**

begin *verb*

When does the film begin?
OTHER VERBS YOU MIGHT USE ARE **to commence** (*informal*) **to get going** **to start**
The opposite is **end**

behave *verb*

1 Sam behaved strangely today.
ANOTHER VERB IS **to act**

2 Our teacher told us to behave.
A PHRASE IS **to be good**

a b c d e f g h i j k l m n o p q r s t u v w x y z

behaviour *noun*

Our teacher praised our good behaviour.

OTHER WORDS ARE **conduct** **manners**

belief *noun*

1 It's my belief that ghosts don't exist.

OTHER WORDS YOU MIGHT USE ARE **opinion** **view**

2 We had a special service where people with different religious beliefs said prayers together.

OTHER WORDS ARE **creed** **faith** **religion**

believe *verb*

1 You can't believe all he says.

OTHER VERBS YOU MIGHT USE ARE **to accept** **to rely on** **to trust**

2 I believe he cheated.

OTHER VERBS ARE **to consider** **to feel sure** **to think**

bell *noun*

DIFFERENT WAYS BELLS SOUND ARE

chime **clang** **jangle** **jingle** **peal** **ping** **ring** **tinkle** **toll**

belongings *noun*

Be sure to take your belongings when you get off the train.

OTHER WORDS YOU MIGHT USE ARE **possessions** **property** **things**

bench *noun*

1 a bench to sit on.

OTHER WORDS YOU MIGHT USE ARE **form** **seat**

2 a carpenter's bench.

ANOTHER WORD IS **table**

bend *noun*

a bend in the road.

OTHER WORDS YOU MIGHT USE ARE **corner** **curve** **turn** **twist**

bend *verb*

1 The blacksmith bent the metal into fantastic shapes.

OTHER VERBS YOU MIGHT USE ARE **to coil** **to curl** **to curve** **to distort** **to fold** **to twist** **to wind**

2 He was so tall that he had to bend to go through the door.

OTHER VERBS ARE **to bow down** **to crouch** **to duck** **to stoop**

bet *verb*

ANOTHER VERB IS **to gamble**

KINDS OF BETTING ARE **the lottery** **the pools**

bewildered *adjective*
We were bewildered by all the different traffic signs.
OTHER WORDS YOU MIGHT USE ARE **confused** **muddled** **puzzled**

bewitched *adjective*
I was bewitched by the magical music.
OTHER WORDS ARE **charmed** **enchanted** **spellbound**

biased *adjective*
The referee was biased.
OTHER WORDS YOU MIGHT USE ARE **one-sided** **prejudiced** **unfair**

big *adjective*
1 a big person. a big thing.
OTHER WORDS YOU MIGHT USE ARE **colossal** **enormous** **fat** **giant** **gigantic** **great** **huge** **large** **massive** **monstrous** **tall**
2 a big hall.
OTHER WORDS ARE **roomy** **spacious** **vast**
3 a big event.
OTHER WORDS ARE **grand** **impressive** **spectacular**
4 a big decision.
OTHER WORDS ARE **important** **serious**
The opposite is **small**

bill *noun*
Keep the bill to prove how much you paid.
OTHER WORDS YOU MIGHT USE ARE **account** **receipt**

bind *verb*
They bound the prisoner's hands.
OTHER VERBS YOU MIGHT USE ARE **to secure** **to tie**

bird *noun*, see next page

bit *noun*
1 I don't want it all, only a bit of it.
OTHER WORDS YOU MIGHT USE ARE **chunk** **crumb** **dollop** **fraction** **morsel** **part** **piece** **portion** **section**
2 Mum told Jo to sweep up every bit of the broken mug.
OTHER WORDS ARE **chip** **fragment** **speck** **splinter**
3 I picked up the bits of paper and put them in the rubbish bin.
ANOTHER WORD IS **scrap**

bite *verb*
The dog tried to bite me!
OTHER VERBS YOU MIGHT USE ARE **to nip** **to snap at**
For other words, see **eat**

bitter *adjective*
1 a bitter taste.
OTHER WORDS YOU MIGHT USE ARE **acid** **harsh** **sharp** **sour**
2 a bitter wind.
OTHER WORDS ARE **biting** **piercing**
For other words, see **cold**
3 a bitter quarrel.
OTHER WORDS ARE **angry** **resentful** **spiteful**

black *adjective*
OTHER WORDS ARE **dark** **inky** **pitch-black** **sooty**

bird *noun*

swan

A male bird is a **cock**.
A female bird is a **hen**.

WORDS FOR A YOUNG BIRD ARE

chick **fledgling** **nestling**

SOME BIRDS KEPT AS PETS ARE

budgerigar **canary** **cockatoo** **macaw**
parakeet **parrot**

pheasant

BIRDS KEPT ON A FARM ARE

poultry

KINDS OF POULTRY ARE

chicken **duck** **goose** **turkey**

COMMON BRITISH GARDEN BIRDS ARE

blackbird **bullfinch** **chaffinch** **goldfinch**
greenfinch **robin** **sparrow** **starling** **thrush**
tit **wren**

SOME BIRDS YOU MIGHT SEE OR HEAR IN THE BRITISH COUNTRYSIDE ARE

crow **cuckoo** **curlew** **dove** **grouse**
jackdaw **jay** **lapwing** **lark** **linnet**
magpie **martin** **nightingale** **partridge** **peewit**
pheasant **pigeon** **raven** **rook** **skylark**
swallow **swift** **wagtail** **warbler**
woodpecker **yellowhammer**

SOME BIRDS OF PREY ARE

buzzard **eagle** **falcon** **hawk** **kestrel**
kite **osprey** **owl** **sparrowhawk**

BIRDS THAT LIVE NEAR WATER ARE

coot **duck** **flamingo** **goose** **grebe**
heron **kingfisher** **moorhen** **pelican** **swan**

SOME SEA BIRDS ARE

cormorant **puffin** **seagull** **tern**

OTHER BIRDS ARE

ostrich **peacock** **penguin** **stork** **vulture**

blade *noun*
THINGS WITH A SHARP BLADE ARE
axe **dagger** **knife** **razor** **scissors** **shears** **sword**

blame *verb*
When she saw the mess, Mum blamed me!
OTHER VERBS YOU MIGHT USE ARE **to accuse** **to criticize** **to scold**

blank *adjective*
1 a blank piece of paper.
OTHER WORDS YOU MIGHT USE ARE **clean** **unmarked** **unused**
2 Fill in the blank spaces.
ANOTHER WORD IS **empty**

blast *noun*
1 a blast of cold air.
For other words, see **wind**
2 the blast of a bomb.
OTHER WORDS ARE **bang** **boom** **explosion**

blaze *verb*
OTHER VERBS YOU MIGHT USE ARE **to burn** **to flame** **to flare up**
For other words, see **fire**

bleak *adjective*
a bleak hillside.
OTHER WORDS YOU MIGHT USE ARE **bare** **cold** **exposed** **miserable** **windswept** **windy**

blend *verb*
Dad blended the ingredients to make a cake.
OTHER VERBS YOU MIGHT USE ARE **to beat** **to combine** **to mix** **to stir together** **to whisk**

blessed *adjective*
OTHER WORDS ARE **holy** **sacred**

blind *adjective*
OTHER WORDS YOU MIGHT USE ARE **sightless** **visually handicapped**

block *noun*
a block of concrete.
OTHER WORDS ARE **chunk** **lump** **slab**

a **b** c d e f g h i j k l m n o p q r s t u v w x y z

block *verb*
1 A flock of sheep blocked the road.
ANOTHER VERB IS **to obstruct**
2 The roads were blocked with traffic.
OTHER VERBS YOU MIGHT USE ARE **to clog** **to jam**

bloom *verb*
Roses bloom in the summer.
OTHER VERBS YOU MIGHT USE ARE **to blossom** **to flower**

blossom *noun*
In spring we have masses of blossom on our apple tree.
OTHER WORDS ARE **blooms** **flowers**

blow *noun*
Sam got a nasty blow on the head.
For other words, see **hit**

blunt *adjective*
The opposite is **sharp**

blurred *adjective*
a blurred photograph.
OTHER WORDS YOU MIGHT USE ARE **cloudy** **faint** **fuzzy** **hazy** **misty** **unclear** **unfocused**
The opposite is **clear**

blush *verb*
She blushed when the teacher praised her work.
OTHER VERBS YOU MIGHT USE ARE **to flush** **to go red** **to redden**

boast *verb*
He boasted that he was best at everything.
ANOTHER VERB IS **to brag**

boat *noun*, see opposite page

body *noun*, see next page

bodyguard *noun*
OTHER WORDS YOU MIGHT USE ARE **guard** (*informal*) **minder** **protector**

bog *noun*
OTHER WORDS ARE **marsh** **quicksands** **swamp**

boil *verb*
1 Is the water boiling?
ANOTHER VERB IS **to bubble**
2 Jo put the potatoes on to boil.
For other ways to cook things, see **cook**

boat *noun*

OTHER WORDS ARE

craft **ship** **vessel**

DIFFERENT KINDS OF BOAT ARE

aircraft carrier **barge** **battleship** **canoe** **cruiser** **destroyer** **dinghy** **ferry** **galleon** **house boat** **junk** **launch** **lifeboat** **liner** **motor boat** **oil tanker** **paddle steamer** **punt** **raft** **rowing boat** **sailing boat** **speedboat** **steamer** **submarine** **tanker** **trawler** **tug** **warship** **yacht**

bold *adjective*

1 a bold deed.

For other words, see **brave**

2 bold handwriting.

OTHER WORDS YOU MIGHT USE ARE **big** **clear** **large**

bolt *verb*

1 Remember to bolt the back door.

OTHER VERBS YOU MIGHT USE ARE **to bar** **to fasten** **to lock**

2 The horse bolted.

OTHER VERBS ARE **to escape** **to run away**

For other words, see **run**

3 Don't bolt down your food!

OTHER VERBS ARE **to gobble** **to gulp**

bone *noun*

For other words you might use, see **body**

book *noun*

VARIOUS KINDS OF BOOK ARE

album **annual** **atlas** **diary** **dictionary** **directory** **encyclopedia** **hymn book** **novel** **paperback** **story book** **thesaurus**

a b c d e f g h i j k l m n o p q r s t u v w x y z

body *noun*

Another word for the body of a dead person is **corpse**.
Another word for the body of a dead animal is **carcass**.
The main part of your body, not including the head, arms, and legs, is the **trunk**.

PARTS OF YOUR TRUNK ARE

abdomen or **tummy** **back** **bottom** or **buttocks** **breast** **chest** **navel** or **tummy button** **nipples** **shoulders**

THE INNER ORGANS OF YOUR BODY INCLUDE

bladder **bowels** **glands** **heart** **intestines** **kidneys** **liver** **lungs** **ovaries** **stomach** **womb**

Your **arteries** take blood from the heart to other parts of the body, and your **veins** take blood back to the heart.
Your **muscles** are the parts you use when you move.
The **nerves** take messages to and from the brain.
Your **sexual organs** are your **penis** or **vagina**.

PARTS OF YOUR HEAD ARE

brain **cheeks** **chin** **ears** **eyes** **forehead** **gums** **hair** **jaw** **lips** **mouth** **nose** **nostrils** **scalp** **teeth** **throat** **tongue**

Your arms and legs are your **limbs**.

PARTS OF YOUR ARM ARE

elbow **hand** **shoulder** **wrist**

PARTS OF YOUR HAND ARE

fingers **fingernails** **knuckles** **palm** **thumb**

PARTS OF YOUR LEG ARE

ankle **calf** **foot** **knee** **shin** **thigh**

PARTS OF YOUR FOOT ARE

heel **instep** **toe** **toenails**

Your bones are your **skeleton**.

THE MAIN BONES OF YOUR HEAD ARE

jaw **skull**

IMPORTANT BONES IN YOUR BODY ARE

backbone or **spine** or **vertebrae** **pelvis** **ribs**

THE MAIN JOINTS IN YOUR BODY ARE

ankle **elbow** **hip** **knee** **knuckle** **neck** **shoulder** **vertebra** **wrist**

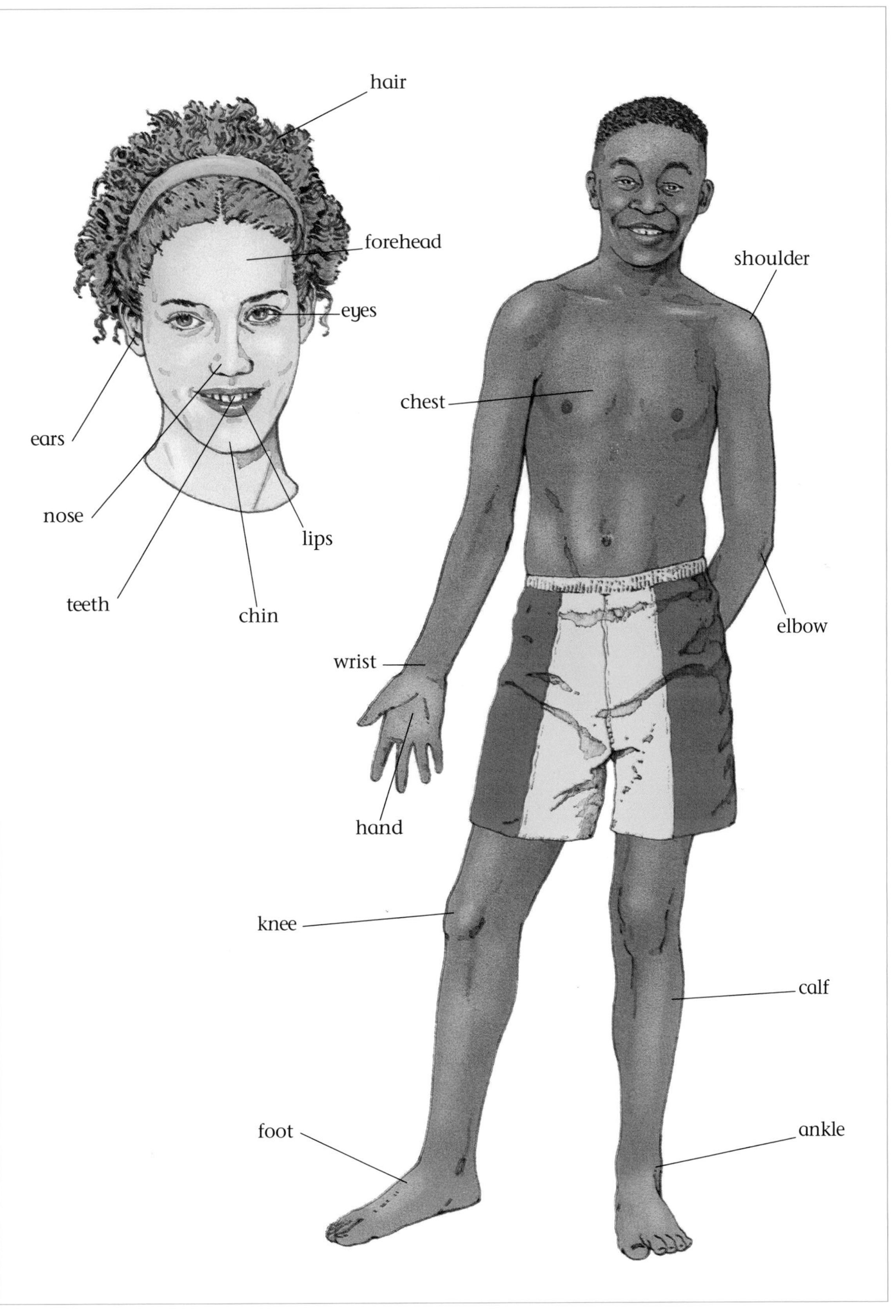
hair
forehead
eyes
ears
nose
lips
teeth
chin
shoulder
chest
elbow
wrist
hand
knee
calf
foot
ankle

a b c d e f g h i j k l m n o p q r s t u v w x y z

boot *noun*
For other things you wear on your feet, see **shoe**

bore *verb*
to bore a hole through something.
OTHER VERBS YOU MIGHT USE ARE **to drill** **to pierce**

boring *adjective*
a boring television programme.
OTHER WORDS YOU MIGHT USE ARE **dreary** **dry** **dull** **monotonous** **tedious** **tiresome** **uninteresting** **wearisome**
The opposite is **interesting**

borrow *verb*
If someone lets you use something for a time, you borrow it.
If you give something to someone to use, you lend it.

boss *noun*
For other words, see **chief**

bother *verb*
Is the loud music bothering you?
OTHER VERBS YOU MIGHT USE ARE **to annoy** **to disturb** **to irritate** **to pester** **to trouble** **to upset** **to worry**

bottle *noun*
For other kinds of container, see **container**

bottom *noun*
1 the bottom of a wall.
OTHER WORDS YOU MIGHT USE ARE **base** **foot** **foundation**
The opposite is **top**
2 the bottom of the sea.
ANOTHER WORD IS **bed**
The opposite is **surface**
3 the bottom that you sit on.
OTHER WORDS ARE **backside** **behind** **buttocks**

boulder *noun*
There were some huge boulders on the beach.
OTHER WORDS ARE **rock** **stone**

bounce *verb*
The ball bounced off the wall.
ANOTHER VERB IS **to rebound**

bound *verb*
The dog bounded over the gate.
OTHER VERBS YOU MIGHT USE ARE **to jump** **to leap** **to spring**

bound *adjective*
bound to It's bound to rain if we go out.
PHRASES ARE **certain to** **sure to**
bound for The rocket is bound for the moon.
PHRASES YOU MIGHT USE ARE **aimed at** **going towards**

boundary *noun*
OTHER WORDS YOU MIGHT USE ARE **border** **edge** **frontier** **limit**

bouquet *noun*
a bouquet of flowers.
OTHER WORDS YOU MIGHT USE ARE
bunch **posy** **spray**

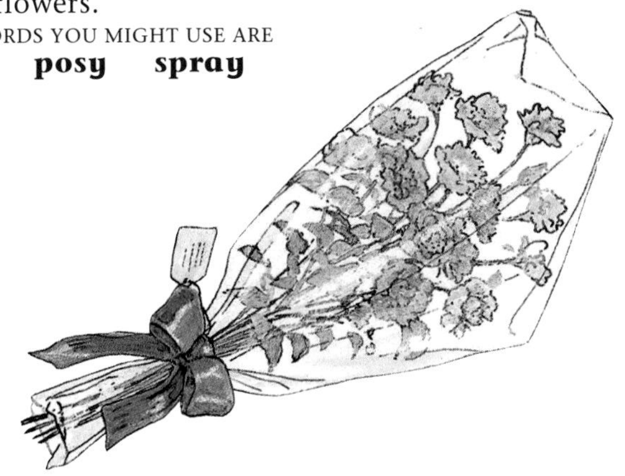

bowl *noun*
OTHER WORDS YOU MIGHT USE ARE **basin** **dish** **tureen**

box *noun*
OTHER WORDS YOU MIGHT USE ARE **carton** **case** **chest** **crate**

brains *noun*
Use your brains!
OTHER WORDS YOU MIGHT USE ARE **intelligence** **mind** **reason** **understanding**

branch *noun*
a branch of a tree.
OTHER WORDS YOU MIGHT USE ARE **bough** **limb**

brand *noun*
Which brand of butter do you buy?
OTHER WORDS YOU MIGHT USE ARE **kind** **make**

brave *adjective*
OTHER WORDS YOU MIGHT USE ARE **bold** **courageous** **daring** **fearless** **heroic** **plucky**
The opposite is **cowardly**

bravery *noun*
OTHER WORDS YOU MIGHT USE ARE **courage** **daring** **heroism** **valour**

bread *noun*
DIFFERENT FORMS IN WHICH YOU BUY BREAD ARE
baguette **French stick** **loaf** **roll** **sliced bread**
For different kinds of bread, see **food**

break *noun*
1 a break in a pipe. a break in the fence.
OTHER WORDS YOU MIGHT USE ARE **crack** **cut** **gap** **hole** **leak** **opening** **slit** **split** **tear**
2 a break in a game.
OTHER WORDS ARE **half time** **interval** **lull** **pause** **rest**

a b c d e f g h i j k l m n o p q r s t u v w x y z

break *verb*
DIFFERENT WAYS THINGS BREAK ARE
to chip **to collapse** **to crack** **to crumble** **to decay** **to fall apart** **to fracture** **to shatter** **to snap** **to splinter** **to split**

DIFFERENT WAYS YOU CAN BREAK THINGS ARE
to crush **to demolish** **to destroy** **to drop** **to smash** **to squash** **to wreck**

breed *noun*
What breed of dog is that?
OTHER WORDS YOU MIGHT USE ARE **kind** **species** **variety**

breed *verb*
Most birds breed in the spring.
OTHER VERBS YOU MIGHT USE ARE **to produce young ones** **to reproduce**

bridge *noun*
KINDS OF BRIDGE ARE **flyover** **viaduct**

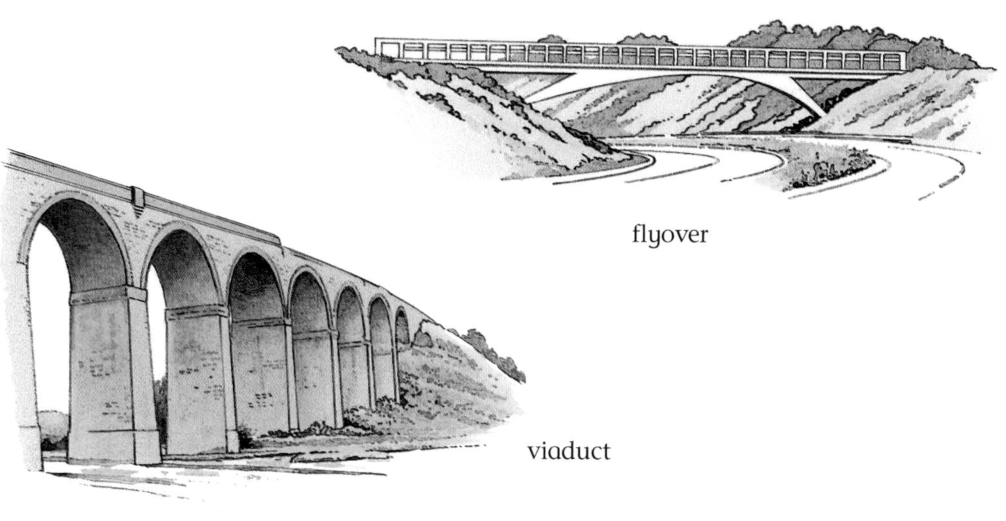
flyover
viaduct

brief *adjective*
OTHER WORDS YOU MIGHT USE ARE **concise** **little** **short**
The opposite is **long**

bright *adjective*
1 bright lights.
OTHER WORDS YOU MIGHT USE ARE **brilliant** **colourful** **dazzling** **flashing** **gleaming** **glittering** **shining** **shiny** **sparkling**
2 a bright boy.
OTHER WORDS ARE **brainy** **clever** **intelligent** **quick** **smart**
3 a bright smile.
OTHER WORDS ARE **cheerful** **happy** **radiant**
The opposite is **dull**

brilliant *adjective*
For other words, see **bright**

brim *noun*
My cup was full to the brim.
OTHER WORDS YOU MIGHT USE ARE **brink** **edge** **rim** **top**

bring *verb*
1 I helped to bring the shopping home.
OTHER VERBS YOU MIGHT USE ARE **to carry** **to fetch** **to take**
2 The captain brought her team onto the field.
OTHER VERBS ARE **to guide** **to lead**

brisk *adjective*
We set off at a brisk walk.
OTHER WORDS YOU MIGHT USE ARE **fast** **lively** **quick** **rapid**

brittle *adjective*
The shell of an egg is brittle.
OTHER WORDS YOU MIGHT USE ARE **fragile** **weak**
The opposite is **strong**

broad *adjective*
a broad area of sand.
OTHER WORDS YOU MIGHT USE ARE **extensive** **large** **wide**
The opposite is **narrow**

brook *noun*
ANOTHER WORD IS **stream**

brother *noun*
For other members of a family, see **family**

brush *noun*
A brush with a long handle is a **broom**

bubbles *noun*
OTHER WORDS YOU MIGHT USE ARE **foam** **froth** **lather** **suds**

bubbly *adjective*
OTHER WORDS YOU MIGHT USE ARE **boiling** **effervescent** **fizzy** **foaming** **sparkling**

build *verb*
OTHER VERBS YOU MIGHT USE ARE **to construct** **to erect** **to put up**

building *noun*, see next page

bully *verb*
I was angry with the big girl who bullied the small ones.
OTHER VERBS YOU MIGHT USE ARE **to frighten** **to persecute** **to threaten** **to torment**

bump *noun*
Jo has a nasty bump on the head.
OTHER WORDS YOU MIGHT USE ARE **bulge** **hump** **lump** **swelling**

bump *verb*
For other words, see **hit**

building *noun*

VARIOUS BUILDINGS ARE

abbey **barn** **bungalow** **cabin**
castle **cathedral** **chapel** **church**
cinema **cottage** **factory** **farmhouse**
flats **garage** **hotel** **house**
inn **lighthouse** **mansion** **monastery**
mosque **museum** **pagoda** **palace**
police station **post office** **power station** **prison**
pub **restaurant** **shop** **skyscraper**
stable **synagogue** **temple** **theatre**
tower **warehouse** **windmill**

PARTS OF BUILDINGS ARE

balcony **doors** **floors** **foyer**
lobby **passage** **porch** **rooms**
staircase **veranda** **walls** **windows**

TOP PARTS OF A BUILDING ARE

ceilings **chimney** **dome** **eaves**
gable **gutters** **rafters** **roof**
spire **steeple** **tower** **turret**

UNDERGROUND PARTS OF A BUILDING ARE

basement **cellar** **crypt** **foundations**

For various rooms in a house, see **home**

church

lighthouse

pagoda

windmill

bunch *noun*
1 a bunch of carrots.
OTHER WORDS YOU MIGHT USE ARE **clump** **cluster**
2 a bunch of flowers.
OTHER WORDS ARE **bouquet** **posy** **spray**
3 a bunch of friends.
OTHER WORDS ARE **crowd** **gathering** **group** **set**

bundle *noun*
a bundle of papers.
OTHER WORDS YOU MIGHT USE ARE **pack** **package** **parcel** **sheaf**

burden *noun*
a heavy burden.
OTHER WORDS YOU MIGHT USE ARE **load** **weight**

burglar *noun*
OTHER WORDS YOU MIGHT USE ARE **intruder** **robber** **thief**
For other words, see **steal**

burn *verb*
OTHER VERBS YOU MIGHT USE ARE **blaze** **flame** **flare** **smoulder**
WAYS YOU CAN DAMAGE THINGS BY HEAT ARE **to char** **to scald** **to scorch** **to singe**
To burn a dead person's body is **to cremate** it.
For other useful words, see **fire**

burrow *noun*
Rabbits live in a burrow.
OTHER WORDS YOU MIGHT USE ARE **hole** **tunnel**
A place where rabbits make a lot of burrows is a **warren**.

burst *verb*
1 He burst open the door.
OTHER VERBS YOU MIGHT USE ARE **to break** **to force open**
2 The balloon burst.
OTHER VERBS ARE **to explode** **to pop**

bush *noun*
ANOTHER WORD IS **shrub**

business *noun*
1 Dad's business is selling cars.
OTHER WORDS YOU MIGHT USE ARE **job** **occupation** **trade** **work**
2 I work for a computer business.
OTHER WORDS ARE **company** **firm** **industry** **organization** **shop**
3 Don't be nosey—it's none of your business!
OTHER WORDS ARE **affair** **concern**

busy *adjective*
1 Our teacher is always busy.
OTHER WORDS YOU MIGHT USE ARE **active** **doing things** **occupied**
(*informal*) **on the go**
The opposite is **idle**
2 The shops are busy during the sales.
OTHER WORDS ARE **bustling** **lively**

buy *verb*
I bought my bike for £30.
OTHER VERBS YOU MIGHT USE ARE **to get** **to obtain** **to purchase**

Cc

a b c d e f g h i j k l m n o p q r s t u v w x y z

cable *noun*
1 electric cables.
OTHER WORDS YOU MIGHT USE ARE **flex** **lead** **wire**
2 cables for tying up a ship.
OTHER WORDS ARE **cord** **line** **rope**

café *noun*
We went into a café for a snack.

OTHER PLACES WHERE YOU MIGHT GET THINGS TO EAT ARE
bar **bistro** **buffet** **cafeteria** **canteen**
fish and chip shop **restaurant** **snack bar** **takeaway**

cage *noun*
OTHER WORDS FOR PLACES TO KEEP ANIMALS IN ARE
an **aviary** for birds
a **coop** for chickens
an **enclosure** for zoo animals
a **hutch** for rabbits
a **kennel** for a dog
a **pen** for sheep

cake *noun*
For kinds of cake, see **food**

call *verb*
1 I heard someone call.
OTHER VERBS YOU MIGHT USE ARE **to cry out** **to exclaim** **to shout** **to yell**
2 They called the baby Robert.
ANOTHER VERB IS **to name**
3 Mum called us in for dinner.
OTHER VERBS ARE **to send for** **to summon**
4 I didn't call because the phone wasn't working.
OTHER VERBS ARE **to phone** **to ring** **to telephone**

calm *adjective*
1 a calm sea.
OTHER WORDS YOU MIGHT USE ARE **even** **flat** **peaceful** **smooth** **still**
The opposite is **stormy**
2 Don't panic—keep calm!
OTHER WORDS ARE **cool** **patient** **quiet** **sensible**

camera *noun*, see opposite page

cancel *verb*
They cancelled the game because of the snow.
OTHER VERBS YOU MIGHT USE ARE **to abandon** **to give up** **to postpone**

cap *noun*
For things you wear on your head, see **hat**

camera *noun*

DIFFERENT KINDS OF CAMERA ARE
camcorder **cine-camera** **Polaroid**

PARTS OF A CAMERA ARE
flash **focus** **lens** **light meter**
shutter **viewfinder** **zoom lens**

capacity *noun*
What is the capacity of this kettle?
OTHER WORDS YOU MIGHT USE ARE **size** **volume**

captain *noun*
the captain of a team.
For words for people in charge, see **chief**

captive *noun*
The captives were locked in a dungeon.
OTHER WORDS YOU MIGHT USE ARE **hostage** **prisoner**

capture *verb*
Did they capture the thief?
OTHER VERBS YOU MIGHT USE ARE **to arrest** **to catch** **to seize**

car *noun*
VARIOUS KINDS OF CAR ARE
estate **hatchback** **racing car** **saloon** **taxi**
For other things you ride in, see **travel**

card *noun*

1 CARDS YOU CAN SEND TO PEOPLE ARE
birthday card **Christmas card** **get-well card** **invitation**
postcard **Valentine**

2 IN CARD GAMES, THE SUITS ARE
clubs **diamonds**
hearts **spades**

THE CARDS WITH PICTURES ON ARE
Jack **Joker**
King **Queen**

a b **c** d e f g h i j k l m n o p q r s t u v w x y z

care *noun*

1 He hasn't a care in the world!
OTHER WORDS YOU MIGHT USE ARE **trouble** **worry**

2 Mum drives with great care.
OTHER WORDS ARE **attention** **caution**

to take care Take care when you cross the road.
VERBS YOU MIGHT USE ARE **to be careful** **to look out**

to take care of I took care of Jo's money while she went swimming.
PHRASES YOU MIGHT USE ARE **to keep something safe** **to look after something**

care *verb*

He doesn't care who wins.
ANOTHER VERB IS **to mind**

to care for

1 We care for our pets.
OTHER VERBS ARE **to look after** **to protect** **to take care of**

2 You send a Valentine card to show that you care for someone.
For other words, see **love**

careful *adjective*

1 Mum is a careful driver.
OTHER WORDS YOU MIGHT USE ARE **alert** **attentive** **cautious**

2 Jo's work is always careful.
OTHER WORDS ARE **neat** **orderly** **organized** **thorough**

The opposite is **careless**

careless *adjective*

1 careless driving.
OTHER WORDS YOU MIGHT USE ARE **negligent** **reckless** **thoughtless**

2 careless work.
OTHER WORDS ARE **disorganized** **hasty** **messy** **untidy**

The opposite is **careful**

cargo *noun*

The ship unloaded its cargo at the docks.
OTHER WORDS YOU MIGHT USE ARE **freight** **goods**

carnival *noun*

OTHER WORDS YOU MIGHT USE ARE **fair** **festival** **fête** **gala** **show**

carry *verb*

1 Sam carried the food into the dining room.
OTHER VERBS YOU MIGHT USE ARE **to bring** **to lift** **to move** **to take** **to transfer**

2 Trains can carry a lot of passengers.
OTHER VERBS ARE **to convey** **to transport**

cart *noun*

OTHER WORDS YOU MIGHT USE ARE **barrow** **wagon** **wheelbarrow**

carve *verb*

For ways to cut things, see **cut**

castle *noun*

OTHER WORDS YOU MIGHT USE ARE
fort **fortress**

PARTS OF A CASTLE ARE
battlements **courtyard** **drawbridge** **dungeon** **keep**
moat **parapet** **portcullis** **tower** **turret**

cat *noun*, see next page

catalogue *noun*

1 a shopping catalogue.
ANOTHER WORD IS **brochure**

2 a catalogue of books in the library.
OTHER WORDS FOR A LIST OF NAMES OR THINGS YOU MIGHT WANT TO LOOK UP ARE **directory** **index** **register**

catch *verb*

1 to catch a ball.
OTHER VERBS YOU MIGHT USE ARE **to grasp** **to hold** **to seize** **to take hold of**

The opposite is **miss**

2 to catch a thief.
OTHER VERBS ARE **to arrest** **to capture** **to stop**

3 to catch fish.
OTHER VERBS ARE **to hook** **to net**

4 to catch an animal.
OTHER VERBS ARE **to snare** **to trap**

5 to catch a bus.
ANOTHER VERB IS **to get**

catching *adjective*

I hope your cold isn't catching.
ANOTHER WORD IS **infectious**

cat *noun*

INFORMAL WORDS ARE
moggy **pussy** **pussy cat**
A young cat is a **kitten**.
A male cat is a **tomcat**.

KINDS OF CAT ARE
Manx **marmalade cat**
Persian **Siamese** **tabby**
For other pets, see **pet**

Siamese

'BIG CATS' OR WILD ANIMALS RELATED TO CATS ARE
cheetah **jaguar** **leopard**
lion **lynx** **panther**
puma **tiger** **wildcat**

lynx

Persian

cattle *noun*

ANIMALS THAT FARMERS KEEP AS CATTLE ARE
bull **bullock** **cow** **ox**
Young cattle are called **calves**.

cause *verb*
The storm caused terrible floods.
PHRASES YOU MIGHT USE ARE **to bring about** **to lead to** **to result in**

cautious *adjective*
For other words, see **careful**

cave *noun*
OTHER WORDS YOU MIGHT USE ARE **cavern** **grotto** **pothole**

cease *verb*
Cease work!
OTHER VERBS YOU MIGHT USE ARE **to break off** **to end** **to finish** **to stop**

cellar *noun*
OTHER UNDERGROUND PARTS OF BUILDINGS ARE **basement** **crypt** **vault**

cemetery *noun*
ANOTHER WORD IS **graveyard**
A graveyard round a church is a **churchyard**.

centre *noun*
the centre of the earth.
OTHER WORDS YOU MIGHT USE ARE **core** **heart** **middle**
The centre of a wheel is the **hub**.

cereal *noun*
OTHER WORDS ARE
corn **grain**
1 KINDS OF CEREAL FARMERS GROW ARE
barley **maize** or **sweet corn** **oats** **rice** **rye** **wheat**
2 KINDS OF BREAKFAST CEREAL ARE
bran **cornflakes** **muesli** **porridge**

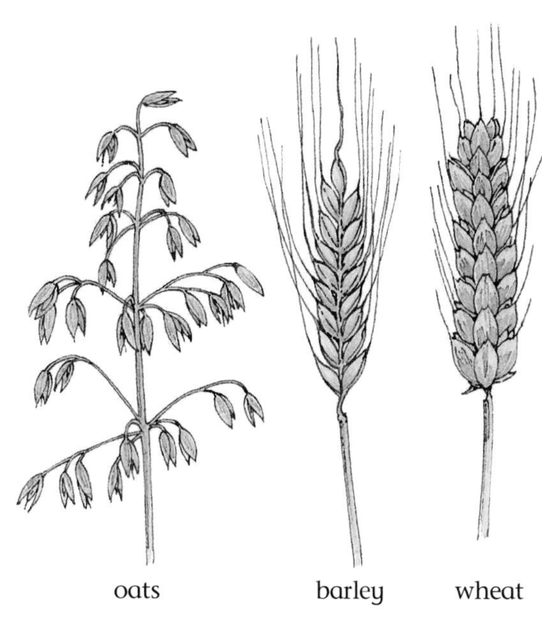
oats barley wheat

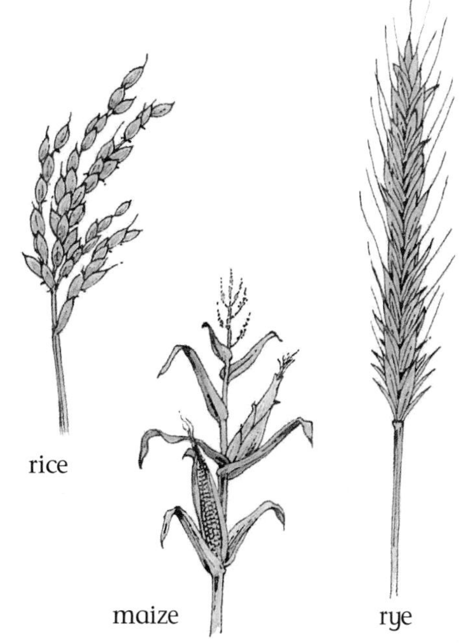
rice maize rye

certain *adjective*
Are you certain it will rain?
OTHER WORDS YOU MIGHT USE ARE **confident** **definite** **positive** **sure**

chair *noun*
For things to sit on, see **seat**

champion *noun*
OTHER WORDS YOU MIGHT USE ARE **hero** **winner** **victor**

chance *noun*
1 This is your last chance.
ANOTHER WORD IS **opportunity**
2 I met him by chance.
OTHER WORDS ARE **accident** **coincidence**
3 There's a chance of rain.
OTHER WORDS ARE **danger** **possibility** **risk**

change *noun*
I need some change to pay for the bus.
OTHER WORDS YOU MIGHT USE ARE **cash** **coins**

change *verb*

1 I changed the end of my story.
OTHER VERBS YOU MIGHT USE ARE **to adjust** **to alter** **to make different** **to revise** **to transform**

2 I want to change this apple for an orange.
OTHER VERBS YOU MIGHT USE ARE **to exchange** **to substitute** **to switch** (*informal*) **to swap**

3 Tadpoles change into frogs.
OTHER VERBS YOU MIGHT USE ARE **to become** **to develop into** **to turn into**

channel *noun*

1 a channel to take water away.
OTHER WORDS YOU MIGHT USE ARE **canal** **ditch** **gutter**

2 a TV channel.
ANOTHER WORD IS **station**

chaos *noun*

There was chaos when the lights went out.
OTHER WORDS YOU MIGHT USE ARE **confusion** **a mix-up**

character *noun*

1 My favourite character in the pantomime was Cinderella.
OTHER WORDS YOU MIGHT USE ARE **part** **role**

2 Granny has a kind character.
OTHER WORDS ARE **manner** **nature** **personality**

3 Who is that character at the bus stop?
OTHER WORDS ARE **individual** **person**

charge *verb*

1 They charge £1 for an ice cream.
PHRASES YOU MIGHT USE ARE **to ask** **to make you pay**

2 The soldiers charged the enemy.
OTHER VERBS ARE **to attack** **to rush at**

charm *verb*

He charmed us with his music.
OTHER VERBS ARE **to bewitch** **to enchant** **to fascinate**

charming *adjective*

OTHER WORDS YOU MIGHT USE ARE **attractive** **pretty**
For other words, see **beautiful**

chart *noun*

OTHER WORDS YOU MIGHT USE ARE **diagram** **graph** **map** **plan**

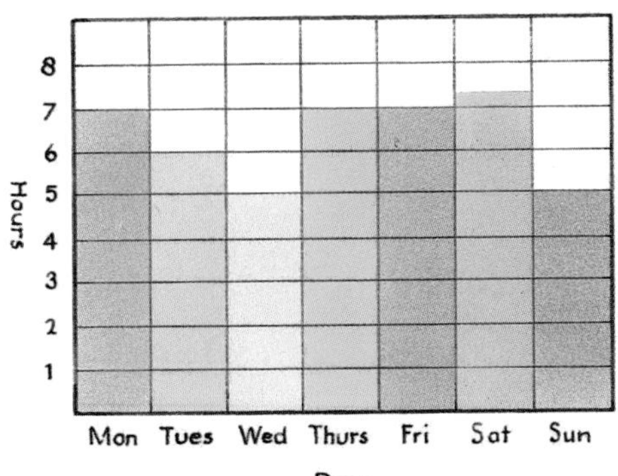

chase *verb*
The dog chased the hare for miles.
OTHER VERBS YOU MIGHT USE ARE **to follow** **to hunt** **to pursue** **to tail** **to track** **to trail**

chat, chatter *verbs*
For other verbs, see **talk**

cheap *adjective*
Jo bought a cheap coat in a sale.
OTHER WORDS YOU MIGHT USE ARE **cut-price** **inexpensive** **reasonable**
The opposite is **expensive**

cheat *verb*
He cheated us by keeping all the money for himself.
OTHER VERBS YOU MIGHT USE ARE **to deceive** **to fool** **to swindle** **to trick**

check *verb*
1 Mum always checks the car before we go on a journey.
OTHER VERBS YOU MIGHT USE ARE **to examine** **to look over** **to test**
2 A traffic jam checked our progress.
OTHER VERBS YOU MIGHT USE ARE **to halt** **to hold up** **to prevent** **to slow down** **to stop**

cheeky *adjective*
My teacher hates cheeky behaviour.
OTHER WORDS YOU MIGHT USE ARE **bold** **impertinent** **impolite** **impudent** **insolent** **rude**
The opposite is **polite**

cheer *verb*
The audience cheered.
ANOTHER VERB IS **to applaud**
to cheer someone up
OTHER VERBS YOU MIGHT USE ARE **to comfort** **to encourage**

cheerful *adjective*
OTHER WORDS YOU MIGHT USE ARE **bright** **happy** **jolly** **laughing** **light-hearted** **lively** **merry** **pleased**
The opposite is **gloomy**

chest *noun*
a chest full of treasure.
OTHER WORDS YOU MIGHT USE ARE **box** **case** **crate**
For other words, see **container**

chew *verb*
For other verbs, see **eat**

chief *adjective*
We learned the chief spelling rules.

OTHER WORDS YOU MIGHT USE ARE
basic **essential** **important** **main** **major** **principal**

a
b
c
d
e
f
g
h
i
j
k
l
m
n
o
p
q
r
s
t
u
v
w
x
y
z

chief *noun*
WORDS FOR PEOPLE IN CHARGE OF VARIOUS THINGS ARE
boss **captain** **commander** **director** **employer** **governor** **head** **leader** **manager** **president** **principal** **ruler**

child *noun*
OTHER WORDS ARE **baby** **boy** **girl** **infant** (*informal*) **kid** (*informal*) **toddler** (*informal*) **youngster**

china *noun*
When you wash up, make sure you don't chip the china.

OTHER WORDS YOU MIGHT USE ARE
crockery **porcelain** **pots** **pottery**

THINGS MADE OF CHINA ARE
bowl **cup** **dish** **jug** **plate** **saucer** **teapot**

chip *noun*
OTHER WORDS FOR A SMALL PIECE BROKEN OFF SOMETHING ARE **flake** **fragment** **splinter**

choke *verb*
This collar is choking me.
OTHER VERBS YOU MIGHT USE ARE **to stifle** **to strangle** **to suffocate**

choose *verb*
We chose Jo as captain.
OTHER VERBS YOU MIGHT USE ARE **to decide on** **to elect** **to name** **to pick** **to select** **to settle on** **to vote for**

chunk *noun*
a chunk of cheese.
OTHER WORDS YOU MIGHT USE ARE **block** **hunk** **lump** **piece** **slab**

church *noun*
For places where people worship, see **religion**

cinema *noun*
OTHER WORDS ARE **the pictures** **the movies**

circle *noun*
OTHER WORDS YOU MIGHT USE ARE **disc** **hoop** **ring**
For other shapes, see **shape**

circus *noun*
PEOPLE WHO PERFORM IN A CIRCUS ARE
acrobat **clown** **juggler** **lion-tamer** **ringmaster** **trapeze artist**

citizen *noun*
the citizens of a town.
OTHER WORDS YOU MIGHT USE ARE **inhabitant** **resident**

claim *verb*
Jo claimed her lost property.
OTHER VERBS YOU MIGHT USE ARE **to ask for** **to demand** **to request**

clap *verb*
We clapped at the end of the play.
ANOTHER VERB IS **to applaud**

class *noun*
Which class are you in?
OTHER WORDS YOU MIGHT USE ARE **form** **group** **set**

clean *adjective*
1 clean clothes.
ANOTHER WORD IS **spotless**
2 clean water.
OTHER WORDS YOU MIGHT USE ARE **clear** **fresh** **pure**
3 a clean sheet of paper.
OTHER WORDS ARE **blank** **unmarked** **unused**
The opposite is **dirty**

clean *verb*
Sam cleaned the floor while Jo was cleaning the car.

WAYS TO CLEAN THINGS ARE
to brush **to dust** **to hoover** **to mop up**
to rinse **to scrub** **to shampoo** **to sponge down**
to sweep out **to swill** **to vacuum** **to wash**
to wipe

clear *adjective*
THIS WORD HAS MANY USES. HERE ARE SOME OF THE WAYS YOU CAN USE IT, AND SOME OTHER WORDS YOU COULD CHOOSE
1 clear water.
clean **colourless** **pure**
2 a clear sky.
blue **bright** **cloudless** **starlit** **sunny**
3 clear plastic.
transparent
4 a clear photograph.
focused **sharp** **well defined**
5 a clear voice.
audible **distinct**
6 a clear space.
empty **free** **open**
7 a clear case of cheating.
obvious
8 a clear explanation.
plain **simple** **understandable**

a b c d e f g h i j k l m n o p q r s t u v w x y z

clear *verb*

1 We cleared a space to play in.
OTHER VERBS YOU MIGHT USE ARE **to empty** **to free**

2 Please clear the dishes.
OTHER VERBS ARE **to carry away** **to move** **to remove** **to take away**

3 The fog cleared.
OTHER VERBS ARE **to disappear** **to melt away** **to vanish**

clever *adjective*

1 a clever pupil.
OTHER WORDS YOU MIGHT USE ARE (*informal*) **brainy** **bright** **brilliant** **intelligent** **quick** **sharp** **talented** **wise**

2 clever with your hands.
OTHER WORDS ARE **expert** **handy** **skilful**

3 a clever trick.
OTHER WORDS ARE **crafty** **cunning**

The opposite is **stupid**

cliff *noun*

ANOTHER WORD IS **precipice**

climb *verb*

Take care when you climb the ladder.
OTHER VERBS YOU MIGHT USE ARE **to ascend** **to go up** **to mount**

cling *verb*

1 The ivy clings to the wall.
ANOTHER VERB IS **to stick**

2 The baby clung to her mother.
OTHER VERBS YOU MIGHT USE ARE **to hold on on** **to grasp** **to hug**

clock *noun*

THINGS WHICH TELL THE TIME ARE
alarm clock **digital clock** **grandfather clock** **hourglass** **sundial** **watch**

clog *verb*

The leaves clogged up the drain.
OTHER VERBS YOU MIGHT USE ARE **to block** (*informal*) **to bung up**

close (rhymes with *dose*) *adjective*

1 Our house is close to the park.
ANOTHER WORD IS **near**

2 Mum took a close look at the cut on Jo's hand.
OTHER WORDS YOU MIGHT USE ARE **careful** **thorough**

close (rhymes with *doze*) *verb*

1 Please close the door.
OTHER VERBS YOU MIGHT USE ARE **to fasten** **to lock** **to shut**

2 We closed the concert with some songs.
OTHER VERBS ARE **to conclude** **to end** **to finish**

The opposite is **open**

cloth *noun*

OTHER WORDS YOU MIGHT USE ARE
fabric **material** **textiles**

DIFFERENT KINDS OF CLOTH ARE

canvas	**corduroy**	**cotton**	**denim**	**felt**	**flannel**
lace	**linen**	**muslin**	**nylon**	**polyester**	**satin**
silk	**tartan**	**tweed**	**velvet**	**viscose**	**wool**

clothes, clothing *noun*, see next page

cloudy *adjective*

1 a cloudy sky.
OTHER WORDS YOU MIGHT USE ARE **dull** **grey** **overcast**

2 cloudy water.
OTHER WORDS ARE **milky** **murky**

3 a cloudy atmosphere.
OTHER WORDS ARE **misty** **steamy**

The opposite is **clear**

club *noun*

1 a football club. a chess club.
OTHER WORDS YOU MIGHT USE ARE **association** **group** **league** **organization** **society**

2 The intruder tried to hit me with a club.
OTHER WORDS ARE **baton** **cudgel** **stick** **truncheon**

clue *noun*

Give me a clue about what we are having for dinner.
OTHER WORDS YOU MIGHT USE ARE **hint** **indication** **sign** **suggestion**

clumsy *adjective*

She's clumsy and keeps dropping things.
OTHER WORDS YOU MIGHT USE ARE **awkward** **blundering**

clutch *verb*

I clutched the rope to stop myself from falling.
OTHER VERBS YOU MIGHT USE ARE **to cling to** **to grab** **to grasp** **to grip** **to hold on to** **to seize** **to snatch**

clothes, clothing *nouns*

OTHER WORDS YOU MIGHT USE ARE

costume **dress** **garments**

DIFFERENT THINGS YOU WEAR ARE

belt **blazer** **blouse** **braces** **cardigan**
coat **dress** **frock** **jacket** **jeans**
jersey **jumper** **kilt** **leotard** **miniskirt**
pullover **rompers** **sari** **shawl** **shorts**
skirt **socks** **stockings** **suit** **sweater**
sweatshirt **tie** **trousers** **t-shirt** **tunic**
waistcoat

THINGS YOU WEAR TO KEEP CLEAN ARE

apron **bib** **dungarees** **overalls** **pinafore**

CLOTHES YOU WEAR WHEN YOU GO OUT ARE

anorak **cagoule** **cloak** **duffle coat** **gloves**
(*informal*) **mac** or **mack** **mackintosh** **mittens** **muffler**
overcoat **raincoat** **scarf**

CLOTHES YOU USE AT NIGHT ARE

dressing gown **nightdress** **nightie** **pyjamas**

UNDERCLOTHES ARE

bra **knickers** **panties** **pants** **petticoat**
slip **tights** **underpants** **vest**

THINGS YOU WEAR WHEN YOU GO SWIMMING ARE

bikini **swimming costume** **swimsuit** **trunks**

For things you wear on your head, see **hat**
For things you wear on your feet, see **shoe**

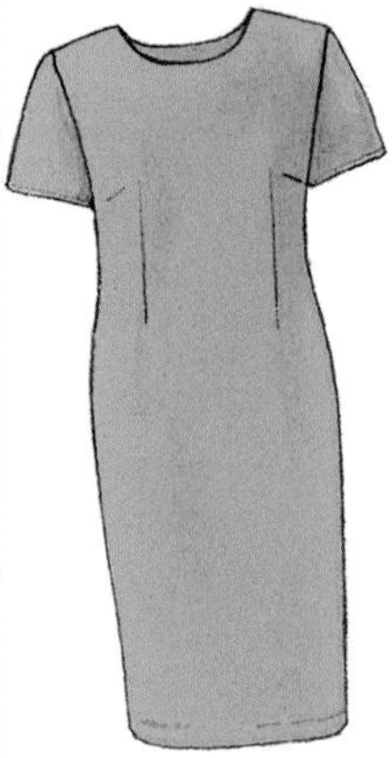

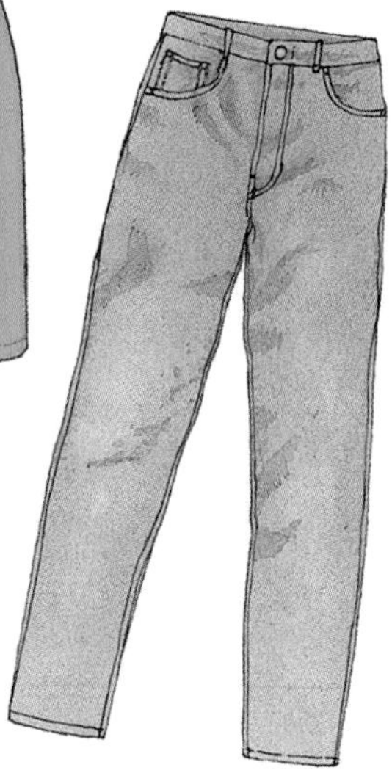

coach *noun*
1 We went to the seaside by coach.
For other things you travel in, see **travel**
2 Our team has got a new coach.
ANOTHER WORD IS **trainer**

coarse *adjective*
The coarse cloth tickled my skin.
OTHER WORDS YOU MIGHT USE ARE **hairy** **rough** **scratchy**
The opposite is **smooth**

coat *noun*
For things we wear, see **clothes**

coil *verb*
The snake coiled round a branch.
OTHER VERBS YOU MIGHT USE ARE **to curl** **to entwine** **to loop** **to twist** **to wind**

cold *adjective*
1 cold weather.
OTHER WORDS YOU MIGHT USE ARE **Arctic** **bitter** **chilly** **cool** **freezing** **fresh** **frosty** **icy** (*informal*) **nippy** **wintry**
2 I feel cold.
OTHER WORDS ARE **chilled** **frozen** **shivery**
The opposite is **hot**

collapse *verb*
1 The shed collapsed in the storm.
PHRASES YOU MIGHT USE ARE (*informal*) **to cave in** **to fall down** **to tumble down**
2 People collapsed because it was so hot.
ANOTHER VERB IS **to faint**

collect *verb*
1 A crowd collected to watch the fire.
OTHER VERBS YOU MIGHT USE ARE **to assemble** **to gather**
2 We collected all the litter.
OTHER VERBS ARE **to accumulate** **to gather together** **to heap up** **to pile up**
3 Mum collected Jo from school.
OTHER VERBS ARE **to bring** **to fetch** **to pick up**

collection *noun*
Jo has a collection of toys.
OTHER WORDS YOU MIGHT USE ARE **assortment** **gathering** **hoard** **pile** **set** **stack**
For other words, see **group**

collide *verb*
The car collided with a van.
OTHER PHRASES YOU MIGHT USE ARE **to bump into** **to crash into** **to run into**
For other words, see **hit**

collision *noun*
OTHER WORDS YOU MIGHT USE ARE **accident** **bump** **crash** **smash**

colour *noun*

We admired the lovely colours of the sunset.

OTHER WORDS YOU MIGHT USE ARE

hue **shade** **tint**

DIFFERENT COLOURS ARE

amber	**black**	**blue**	**bronze**	**brown**
cream	**crimson**	**fawn**	**gold**	**green**
grey	**ivory**	**jet-black**	**khaki**	**maroon**
mauve	**navy blue**	**orange**	**pink**	**purple**
red	**rosy**	**scarlet**	**tan**	**turquoise**
vermilion	**violet**	**white**	**yellow**	

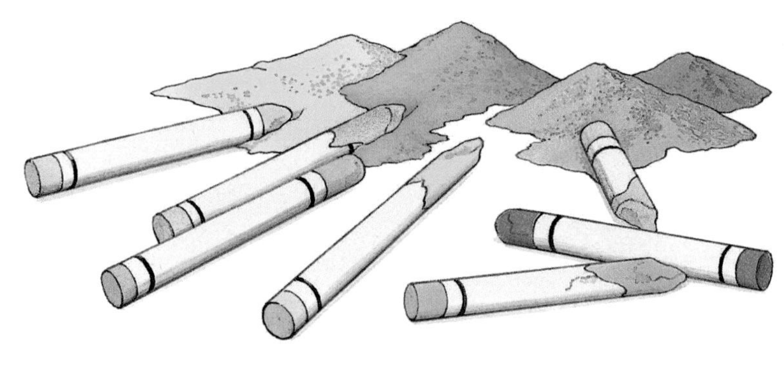

colour *verb*

OTHER VERBS YOU MIGHT USE ARE

to dye **to paint** **to stain** **to tinge** **to tint**

colourful *adjective*

1 colourful flowers.

OTHER WORDS YOU MIGHT USE ARE **bright** **brilliant** **flashy** **gaudy** **showy**

2 a colourful description.

OTHER WORDS ARE **lively** **interesting** **vivid**

The opposite is **dull**

column *noun*
The palace had stone columns in front of the door.
OTHER WORDS YOU MIGHT USE ARE **pillar** **pole** **post** **shaft** **support**

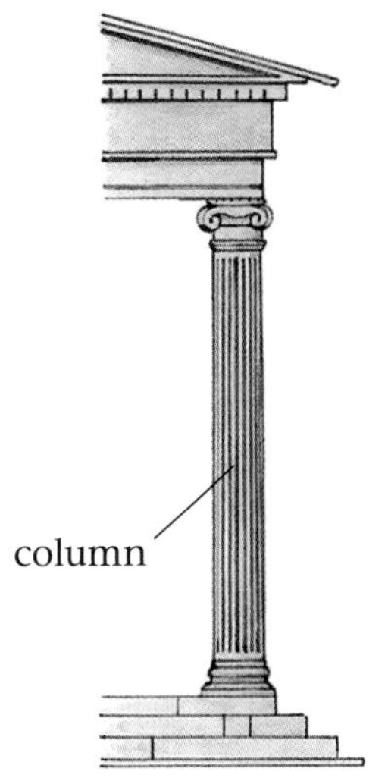

combine *verb*
1 Our class combined with Jo's class to put on a play.
OTHER VERBS YOU MIGHT USE ARE **to come together** **to join** **to merge** **to unite**
2 I combined the cake ingredients in a big bowl.
OTHER VERBS ARE **to add together** **to blend** **to mix** **to put together**

come *verb*
1 Some dark clouds are coming.
OTHER VERBS YOU MIGHT USE ARE **to advance** **to approach** **to draw near**
2 Our visitors have come.
OTHER VERBS ARE **to appear** **to arrive** **to turn up**
The opposite is **go**

comfort *verb*
Jo comforts the baby when he cries.
OTHER VERBS YOU MIGHT USE ARE **to calm** **to reassure** **to soothe**

comfortable *adjective*
a comfortable chair.
OTHER WORDS YOU MIGHT USE ARE **cosy** **luxurious** **relaxing** **snug** **soft**

comic *adjective*
We laughed at his comic remarks.
OTHER WORDS YOU MIGHT USE ARE **amusing** **comical** **funny** **humorous** **laughable** **witty**
The opposite is **serious**

command *verb*
1 The general commanded that the fighting must stop.
OTHER VERBS YOU MIGHT USE ARE **to instruct** **to order**
2 The captain commands the ship.
OTHER VERBS ARE **to be in charge of** **to control** **to govern** **to manage** **to supervise** **to take over**

comment *noun*
The teacher asked for our comments.
OTHER WORDS YOU MIGHT USE ARE **opinion** **remark**

commit *verb*
to commit a crime.
OTHER VERBS YOU MIGHT USE ARE **to be guilty of** **to carry out**

a b c d e f g h i j k l m n o p q r s t u v w x y z

common *adjective*

1 It's common for people to go to the seaside for a holiday.
OTHER WORDS YOU MIGHT USE ARE **customary** **normal** **ordinary** **usual**

2 Colds are common in winter.
OTHER WORDS ARE **frequent** **widespread**

3 'Too many cooks spoil the broth' is a common saying.
ANOTHER WORD IS **well known**

The opposite is **rare**

communications *noun*

DIFFERENT WAYS TO COMMUNICATE ARE
computer network **letter** **newspaper** **magazine** **radar** **radio** **satellite** **telephone** **television**

compact *adjective*

1 a compact set of instructions.
OTHER WORDS YOU MIGHT USE ARE **brief** **concise** **short**

2 a compact typewriter.
OTHER WORDS ARE **neat** **portable** **small**

company *noun*

We enjoy the company of other people.
OTHER WORDS YOU MIGHT USE ARE **companionship** **friendship**

For other words, see **crowd**

compare *verb*

Compare your answers with your neighbour's.
OTHER VERBS YOU MIGHT USE ARE **to check** **to contrast**

compartment *noun*

The box has separate compartments for knives, forks, and spoons.
OTHER WORDS YOU MIGHT USE ARE **division** **section** **space**

compel *verb*

You can't compel me to go swimming in this weather!
OTHER VERBS YOU MIGHT USE ARE **to force** **to order**

competition *noun*

1 a sports competition.
OTHER WORDS YOU MIGHT USE ARE **championship** **contest** **game** **match** **tournament**

2 There was fierce competition between the two teams.
ANOTHER WORD IS **rivalry**

complain *verb*

We complained about the bad food.
OTHER VERBS YOU MIGHT USE ARE **to grumble** **to object** **to protest**

complete *adjective*

1 Did he tell you the complete story?
OTHER WORDS YOU MIGHT USE ARE **entire** **full** **whole**

2 He was talking complete rubbish.
OTHER WORDS ARE **absolute** **pure** **total** **utter**

complete *verb*

Can I go out when I've completed my homework?
OTHER VERBS YOU MIGHT USE ARE **to carry out** **to end** **to finish**

complicated *adjective*
The instructions were too complicated for me to understand.
OTHER WORDS YOU MIGHT USE ARE **complex** **difficult** **involved**
The opposite is **simple**

computer *noun*, see next page

conceal *verb*
1 The bird concealed its nest.
OTHER VERBS YOU MIGHT USE ARE **to camouflage** **to disguise** **to hide**
2 He tried to conceal the truth.
PHRASES ARE **to cover up** **to keep quiet about**
The opposite is **show**

conceited *adjective*
There's no need to be conceited just because you got a prize.
OTHER WORDS YOU MIGHT USE ARE **boastful** (*informal*) **cocky** **proud**
The opposite is **modest**

concentrate *verb*
Concentrate on your work.
PHRASES YOU MIGHT USE ARE **to attend to** **to think about**

concern *verb*
Road safety concerns all of us.
OTHER VERBS YOU MIGHT USE ARE **to affect** **to be important to** **to involve** **to matter to**

concerned *adjective*
Dad is concerned about Jo's cough.
OTHER WORDS YOU MIGHT USE ARE **anxious** **bothered** **worried**

conclude *verb*
1 We concluded the concert with a song.
OTHER VERBS YOU MIGHT USE ARE **to close** **to end** **to finish** **to round off**
2 After waiting 15 minutes, I concluded that I'd missed the bus.
OTHER VERBS ARE **to decide** **to reach a conclusion**

condemn *verb*
1 The head condemned the vandals who broke the window.
OTHER VERBS YOU MIGHT USE ARE **to blame** **to criticize**
2 The judge condemned the thief to spend a year in prison.
OTHER VERBS ARE **to convict** **to punish** **to sentence**

condition *noun*
1 Is your bike in good condition?
ANOTHER WORD IS **order**
2 Is your dog in good condition?
ANOTHER WORD IS **health**

confess *verb*
Jo confessed that she had lost her gloves.
OTHER VERBS YOU MIGHT USE ARE **to admit** **to own up**

a b **c** d e f g h i j k l m n o p q r s t u v w x y z

computer *noun*

WORDS TO DO WITH COMPUTING ARE

cursor **data** **disk drive** **floppy disk** **hard disk** **hardware** **interface** **joystick** **keyboard** **microchip** **microcomputer** **microprocessor** **monitor** **mouse** **PC** **printer** **printout** **program** **screen** **software** **terminal** **VDU** **word processor**

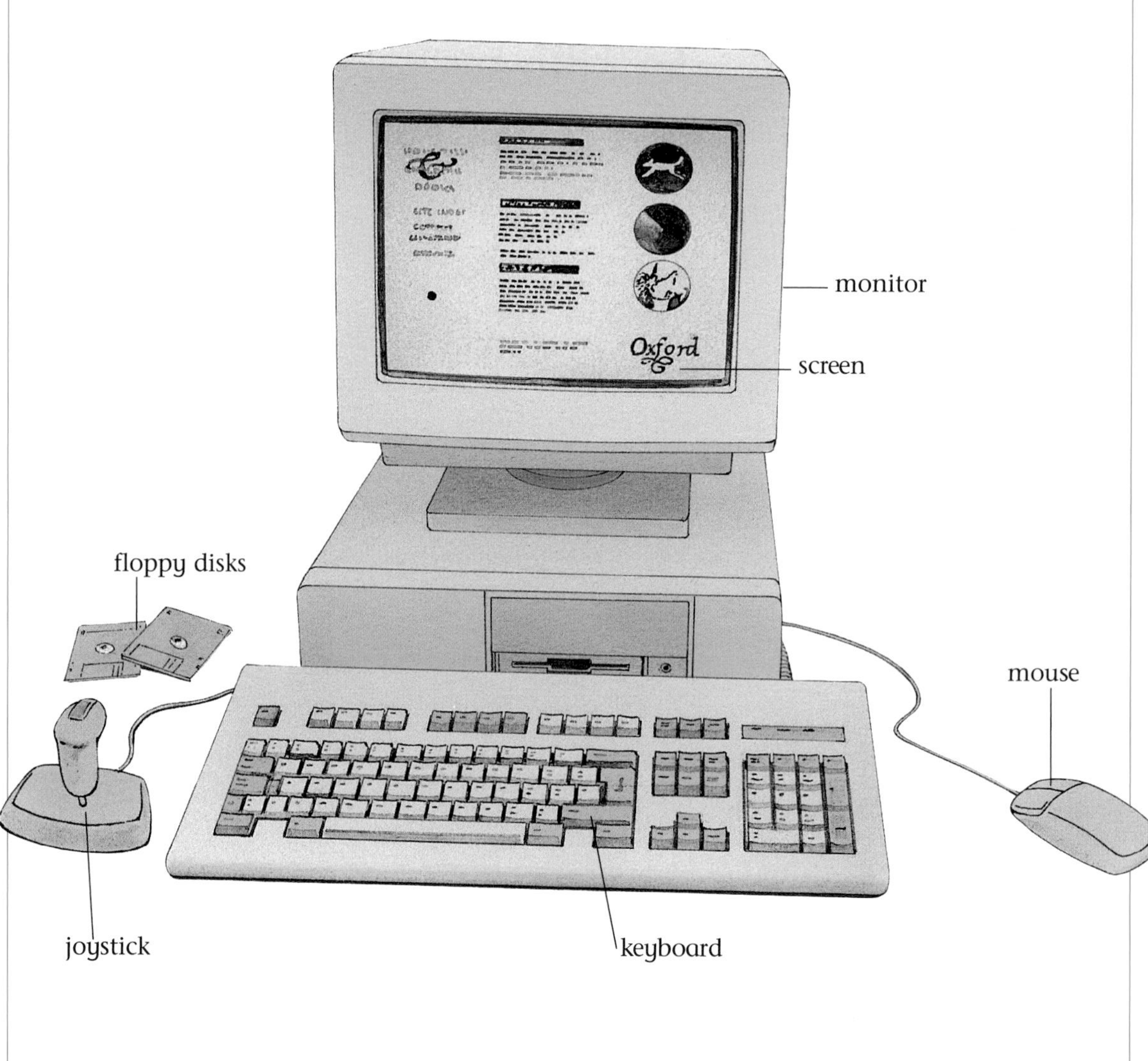

confident *adjective*

1 Sam is a confident swimmer.

OTHER WORDS YOU MIGHT USE ARE **bold** **fearless**

The opposite is **nervous**

2 Jo was confident that she knew the answer.

OTHER WORDS ARE **certain** **definite** **positive** **sure**

The opposite is **doubtful**

confuse *verb*

1 Complicated sums confuse me.
OTHER VERBS YOU MIGHT USE ARE **to bewilder** **to puzzle**

2 I always confuse the names of the twins.
OTHER VERBS ARE **to mix up** **to muddle**

congratulate *verb*

We congratulated Sam when he won.
OTHER VERBS YOU MIGHT USE ARE **to compliment** **to praise**

connect *verb*

Dad connected a loudspeaker to the TV set.
OTHER VERBS YOU MIGHT USE ARE **to attach** **to join** **to link**

conquer *verb*

We easily conquered the opposition.
OTHER VERBS YOU MIGHT USE ARE **to beat** **to defeat** **to overcome** (*informal*) **to thrash** **to win against**

conscious *adjective*

In spite of the knock on the head, he remained conscious.
OTHER WORDS YOU MIGHT USE ARE **alert** **awake**
The opposite is **unconscious**

consent *verb*

We can go on the trip if Mum and Dad consent.
OTHER VERBS YOU MIGHT USE ARE **to agree** **to allow it** **to approve** **to permit it**

consider *verb*

We considered the problem.
OTHER VERBS YOU MIGHT USE ARE **to study** **to think about**

considerate *adjective*

It was considerate of you to lend me your umbrella.
OTHER WORDS YOU MIGHT USE ARE **friendly** **helpful** **kind** **thoughtful** **unselfish**
The opposite is **selfish**

construct *verb*

We constructed a model aeroplane.
OTHER VERBS YOU MIGHT USE ARE **to assemble** **to build** **to make** **to put together**

contain *verb*

1 What does this box contain?
ANOTHER VERB IS **to hold**

2 What does this stew contain?
A PHRASE IS **to consist of**

container *noun*, see next page

contented *adjective*

The cat looks very contented.
OTHER WORDS YOU MIGHT USE ARE **happy** **relaxed** **satisfied**

contest *noun*

For other words, see **competition** or **fight**

container *noun*

THINGS THAT CONTAIN WATER OR LIQUID ARE
barrel basin bath bin bottle bucket can cask casserole cauldron churn cup dish flask glass goblet jar jug kettle mug pail pan pot saucepan tank teapot tub tumbler vase watering can

CONTAINERS FOR OTHER THINGS ARE
bag basket box carton case casket chest dustbin envelope handbag haversack holdall knapsack money box pouch purse rucksack sack satchel suitcase tin trunk wallet

continent *noun*

THE SEVEN CONTINENTS ARE
Africa Antarctica Asia Oceania Europe North America South America

continual *adjective*

Continual chatter annoys the teacher.
OTHER WORDS YOU MIGHT USE ARE **ceaseless constant continuous endless everlasting incessant non-stop persistent repeated unending**

continue *verb*

1 How long will this rain continue?
OTHER VERBS YOU MIGHT USE ARE **to go on to keep on to last to persist**
2 Please continue with your work.
OTHER VERBS ARE **to carry on to keep going to persevere**

continuous *adjective*

For other words, see **continual**

contribute *verb*

I contributed £1 to the collection.
OTHER VERBS YOU MIGHT USE ARE **to donate to give**

control *verb*

She couldn't control the horse.
OTHER VERBS YOU MIGHT USE ARE **to command to deal with to handle to manage to restrain**

convenient *adjective*

1 There's a convenient shop just round the corner.
OTHER WORDS YOU MIGHT USE ARE **handy useful**
2 It isn't convenient for Granny to visit us today.
OTHER WORDS ARE **appropriate easy suitable**
The opposite is **inconvenient**

conversation *noun*

Jo and Sam had a long conversation about their holiday.
OTHER WORDS ARE (*informal*) **chat discussion talk**

cook *noun*

The chief cook in a big restaurant or hotel is the **chef**.

cook *verb*
WAYS TO COOK THINGS ARE
to bake **to barbecue** **to boil** **to fry** **to grill** **to poach** **to roast** **to steam** **to stew** **to toast**

cool *adjective*
1 a cool wind.
OTHER WORDS YOU MIGHT USE ARE **chilly** **cold**
The opposite is **warm**
2 Don't panic–keep cool!
ANOTHER WORD IS **calm**

copy *noun*
The painting was not genuine: it was a copy.
OTHER WORDS YOU MIGHT USE ARE **counterfeit** **fake** **forgery**

copy *verb*
1 The budgie copies Jo's voice.
OTHER VERBS YOU MIGHT USE ARE **to imitate** **to impersonate**
2 Our teacher copied our poems so that everyone could read them.
OTHER VERBS ARE **to duplicate** **to photocopy** **to reproduce**

corn *noun*
ANOTHER WORD IS **cereal**
KINDS OF CORN ARE **barley** **maize** or **sweet corn** **oats** **rye** **wheat**

corner *noun*
1 a corner between two walls.
ANOTHER WORD IS **angle**
2 the corner of the road.
OTHER WORDS ARE **bend** **crossroads** **junction**

correct *adjective*
Is that the correct time?
OTHER WORDS YOU MIGHT USE ARE **accurate** **exact** **precise** **right** **true**
The opposite is **wrong**

corridor *noun*
ANOTHER WORD IS **passage**

costly *adjective*
costly jewels.
OTHER WORDS YOU MIGHT USE ARE **expensive** **precious** **valuable**
The opposite is **cheap**

costume *noun*
costumes for a play.
OTHER WORDS YOU MIGHT USE ARE **clothes** **clothing** **disguise** **fancy dress**

cosy *adjective*
For other words, see **comfortable**

council *noun*
GROUPS OF PEOPLE WHO DISCUSS THINGS AND MAKE DECISIONS ARE
assembly **committee** **conference** **parliament**

count *verb*
Jo counted her pocket money.
OTHER VERBS YOU MIGHT USE ARE **to add up** **to calculate** **to total** **to work out**

country *noun*
1 I like to visit other countries.
OTHER WORDS YOU MIGHT USE ARE **land** **nation** **state**
2 There's some lovely country near here.
OTHER WORDS ARE **countryside** **landscape** **scenery**

courage *noun*
The firemen showed great courage.
OTHER WORDS ARE **bravery** **daring** **heroism**

cover *noun*
DIFFERENT KINDS OF COVER ARE
cap **coat** **covering** **envelope** **folder** **hat** **lid** **roof** **top** **wrapper**

cover *verb*
DIFFERENT WAYS TO COVER THINGS ARE
to bury **to camouflage** **to clothe** **to conceal** **to hide** **to mask** **to screen**

crack *noun*
a crack in the wall.
OTHER WORDS YOU MIGHT USE ARE **break** **crevice** **gap** **opening** **split**

crafty *adjective*
People say that the fox is a crafty animal.
OTHER WORDS YOU MIGHT USE ARE **clever** **cunning** **sly** **wily**

crash *noun*
1 a crash on the motorway.
OTHER WORDS YOU MIGHT USE ARE **accident** **collision**
For other words, see **hit**
2 There was a loud crash when Sam dropped the plates.
For other words, see **sound**

crazy *adjective*
1 The poor dog went crazy when she was stung by a wasp.
OTHER WORDS YOU MIGHT USE ARE **berserk** **frantic** **wild**
2 It was a crazy idea to go for a walk in the rain.
OTHER WORDS ARE **absurd** **mad** **ridiculous** **silly** **stupid**
The opposite is **sensible**

crease *verb*
Don't crease the paper.
OTHER VERBS YOU MIGHT USE ARE **to crumple** **to fold** **to wrinkle**

create *verb*
Mum created a new kind of cake.
OTHER VERBS YOU MIGHT USE ARE **to invent** **to make** **to produce** **to think up**
For other words, see **make**

creator *noun*
ANOTHER WORD IS **maker**
The creator of a new way to do something is an **inventor**.
The creator of a book is an **author** or **poet** or **writer**.
The creator of a piece of music is a **composer**.
The creator of a painting or a statue is an **artist**.

creature *noun*
For names of different creatures, see **animal** and **bird**

creep *verb*
For other ways to move, see **move**

crime *noun*
OTHER WORDS YOU MIGHT USE ARE
dishonesty **offence** **wrongdoing**

SOME CRIMES ARE
arson **blackmail** **burglary** **forgery** **hijacking** **joyriding** **kidnapping** **manslaughter** **murder** **poaching** **robbery** **shoplifting** **smuggling** **stealing**

criminal *noun*
OTHER WORDS YOU MIGHT USE ARE
(*informal*) **crook** **culprit** **delinquent** **offender** **wrongdoer**

DIFFERENT KINDS OF CRIMINAL ARE
blackmailer **burglar** **gangster** **hijacker** **kidnapper** **mugger** **murderer** **poacher** **robber** **shoplifter** **smuggler** **terrorist** **vandal**

crippled *adjective*
She has been crippled since her road accident.
OTHER WORDS YOU MIGHT USE ARE **disabled** **handicapped** **lame**

crisp *adjective*
I like biscuits if they are crisp.
OTHER WORDS TO DESCRIBE THINGS WHICH BREAK EASILY ARE **brittle** **crackly** **fragile**
The opposite is **soft**

crooked *adjective*
a crooked path.
OTHER WORDS YOU MIGHT USE ARE **bent** **twisting** **winding** **zigzag**
The opposite is **straight**

cross *adjective*
For other words, see **angry**

cross *verb*
Take care when you cross the road.
A PHRASE YOU MIGHT USE IS **to go across**
to cross something out
OTHER VERBS ARE **to cancel** **to delete** **to erase**

a b c d e f g h i j k l m n o p q r s t u v w x y z

crossroads *noun*
OTHER WORDS ARE **intersection** **junction**

crouch *verb*
We had to crouch to go through the small opening.
OTHER VERBS YOU MIGHT USE ARE **to bend** **to stoop**

crowd *noun*
a crowd of people.
OTHER WORDS YOU MIGHT USE ARE **company** **group** **horde**
A noisy, violent crowd is a **mob**.
Another word for the crowd at a football match is **spectators**.
For other words, see **group**

cruel *adjective*
I think it's cruel to hunt foxes.
OTHER WORDS YOU MIGHT USE ARE **bloodthirsty** **brutal** **cold-hearted** **heartless** **merciless** **pitiless** **ruthless** **unkind** **vicious**
The opposite is **kind**

crumb *noun*
a crumb of bread.
OTHER WORDS YOU MIGHT USE ARE **bit** **fragment** **scrap**

crumple *verb*
Don't crumple the clothes I've just ironed!
OTHER VERBS YOU MIGHT USE ARE **to crease** **to crush** **to fold** **to wrinkle**

crush *verb*
I crushed my finger in the door.
OTHER VERBS YOU MIGHT USE ARE **to smash** **to squash** **to squeeze**

cry *verb*
The baby cries when she's tired.
OTHER VERBS YOU MIGHT USE ARE **to grizzle** **to shed tears** **to sob** **to wail** **to weep**

to cry out
OTHER VERBS ARE **to call** **to shout** **to yell**

cuddle *verb*
Sam loves to cuddle the baby.
OTHER VERBS YOU MIGHT USE ARE **to embrace** **to hug**

cunning *adjective*
We had a cunning plan to trick our friends.
OTHER WORDS YOU MIGHT USE ARE **clever** **crafty** **ingenious** **skilful** **sly** **wily**

cup *noun*
THINGS YOU CAN DRINK FROM ARE
beaker **glass** **goblet** **mug** **tumbler**

cure *noun*
Have you got a cure for a cold?
OTHER WORDS YOU MIGHT USE ARE **medicine** **remedy** **treatment**

cure *verb*
Will this medicine cure me?
ANOTHER VERB IS **to heal**

curious *adjective*

1 Jo is curious about what she will get for Christmas.
OTHER WORDS YOU MIGHT USE ARE **inquisitive** **interested**

2 Sam thought there was a curious smell in the pantry.
OTHER WORDS ARE **funny** **odd** **peculiar** **queer** **strange** **unusual**

curl *verb*

I curl my hair round my fingers.
OTHER VERBS YOU MIGHT USE ARE **to bend** **to coil** **to loop** **to twist** **to wind**

curse *verb*

He cursed when he hit his finger with the hammer.
ANOTHER VERB IS **to swear**

curtain *noun*

OTHER WORDS YOU MIGHT USE ARE **blind** **drape** **screen**

curve *noun*

The driver slowed down as she approached the curve in the road.

OTHER WORDS YOU MIGHT USE ARE
bend **turn** **twist**

THINGS THAT MAKE THE SHAPE OF A CURVE ARE
arch **bow** **curl** **hook** **horseshoe** **loop** **rainbow** **semicircle** **wave**

curved *adjective*

OTHER WORDS YOU MIGHT USE ARE
arched **bent** **bowed** **concave** **convex** **crescent-shaped** **curled** **rounded** **twisted**

custom *noun*

It's a custom to give presents on a person's birthday.
OTHER WORDS YOU MIGHT USE ARE **convention** **habit** **tradition**

cut *noun*, see next page

cutlery *noun*

ITEMS OF CUTLERY ARE
breadknife **carving knife** **dessertspoon** **fork** **knife** **spoon** **tablespoon** **teaspoon**

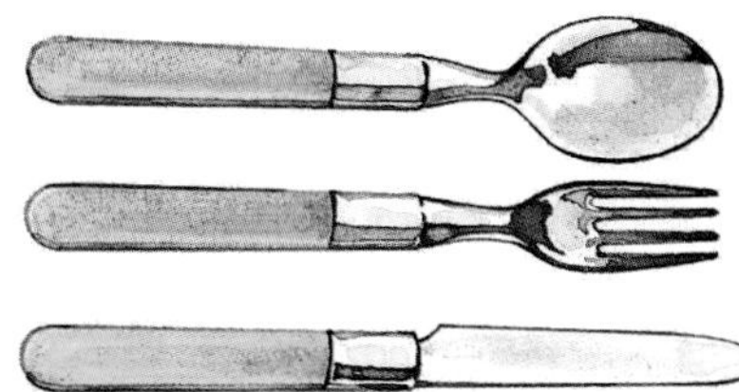

a b c d e f g h i j k l m n o p q r s t u v w x y z

cut *noun*

a cut on your finger.

OTHER WORDS ARE

gash **injury** **nick** **wound**

cut *verb*

There are a lot of verbs which mean 'to cut'.
You **carve** meat, or an artist can **carve** a statue.
You can **chisel** wood.
You **chop** things with an axe.
You **clip** the hedge with shears.
You **mince** meat into tiny pieces.
You **mow** the lawn.
You can **prune** branches off a tree.
You **saw** wood.
You **shave** with a razor.
You **slice** bread with a breadknife.
You can **slit** open an envelope.
You **snip** things with scissors.
You **stab** with a dagger.
You **trim** your hair to make it tidy.
To **cut** prices is to lower or reduce them.

cycle *noun*

A cycle with two wheels is a **bicycle** or **bike**.
A cycle with three wheels is a **tricycle**.
A cycle with an engine is a **moped** or **motorbike**.

Dd

damage *noun*

The storm caused a lot of damage.

OTHER WORDS YOU MIGHT USE ARE **destruction** **havoc**

damage *verb*
OTHER VERBS YOU MIGHT USE ARE **to harm** **to hurt** **to injure** **to spoil**
WAYS YOU CAN DAMAGE THINGS ARE **to break** **to chip** **to dent** **to scratch** **to smash** **to wound**

damp *adjective*
Don't sit on the damp grass.
OTHER WORDS YOU MIGHT USE ARE **moist** **rather wet**
The opposite is **dry**

dance *noun*
Sam and Jo went to a dance on St Valentine's Day.
A very formal dance is a **ball**.
A dance where music is played on records is a **disco**.
A dance you see in a theatre or on TV which tells a story is a **ballet**.

dance *verb*
OTHER VERBS YOU MIGHT USE ARE **to jump about** **to leap about** **to prance** **to skip**

danger *noun*
1 The rocks are a danger to ships.
ANOTHER WORD IS **peril**
2 In summer there's a danger of getting sunburnt.
OTHER WORDS YOU MIGHT USE ARE **chance** **possibility** **risk** **threat**

dangerous *adjective*
1 a dangerous adventure.
OTHER WORDS YOU MIGHT USE ARE **hazardous** **perilous** **risky** **unsafe**
2 a dangerous criminal.
OTHER WORDS ARE **desperate** **treacherous** **violent**
3 a dangerous poison.
OTHER WORDS ARE **deadly** **harmful** **lethal**
The opposite is **safe**

daring *adjective*
Sam thought Jo was very daring to climb up the big rock.
OTHER WORDS YOU MIGHT USE ARE **adventurous** **bold** **brave** **fearless**
The opposite is **cowardly**

dark *adjective*
1 a dark night.
OTHER WORDS YOU MIGHT USE ARE **black** **starless**
2 a dark place.
OTHER WORDS YOU MIGHT USE ARE **gloomy** **shadowy** **shady** **sunless** **unlit**
The opposite is **bright**

darling *noun*
OTHER WORDS YOU MIGHT USE ARE **beloved** **dear** **love** **sweetheart**

dawdle *verb*
Don't dawdle: we're late!
OTHER VERBS YOU MIGHT USE ARE **to be slow** **to hang about** **to linger**
The opposite is **hurry**

a b c **d** e f g h i j k l m n o p q r s t u v w x y z

day *noun*
THE DAYS OF THE WEEK ARE
Monday **Tuesday** **Wednesday** **Thursday** **Friday** **Saturday** **Sunday**
For times of the day and special days of the year, see **time**

dead *adjective*
OTHER WORDS YOU MIGHT USE ARE **deceased** **killed** **lifeless**
The opposite is **alive**

deal *verb*
I dealt the cards.
OTHER VERBS YOU MIGHT USE ARE **to distribute** **to give out** **to share out**
to deal with
Jo can deal with the problem.
OTHER VERBS ARE **to attend to** **to handle** **to manage** **to sort out**

dear *adjective*
1 a dear friend.
OTHER WORDS YOU MIGHT USE ARE **beloved** **loved** **precious**
2 Mum didn't buy any shoes because they were too dear.
OTHER WORDS ARE **costly** **expensive** (*informal*) **pricey**

decay *verb*
Meat smells nasty when it decays.
OTHER VERBS YOU MIGHT USE ARE **to decompose** **to go bad** **to rot**

deceitful *adjective*
We knew he was often deceitful, so we didn't believe him.
OTHER WORDS YOU MIGHT USE ARE **dishonest** **insincere** **lying** **untrustworthy**
The opposite is **honest**

deceive *verb*
He tried to deceive us, but we discovered the truth.
OTHER VERBS YOU MIGHT USE ARE **to cheat** **to mislead** **to swindle** **to trick**

decorate *verb*
1 I decorated the room with flowers.
ANOTHER VERB YOU MIGHT USE IS **to adorn**
2 Dad decorated Sam's bedroom.
OTHER VERBS ARE **to paint** **to paper**

decrease *verb*
1 They decreased my pocket money!
OTHER VERBS YOU MIGHT USE ARE **to cut** **to reduce**
2 The number of children in Jo's class decreased this term.
OTHER VERBS ARE **to get smaller** **to go down** **to lessen**
The opposite is **increase**

deep *adjective*
deep water. a deep hole.
The opposite is **shallow**

defeat *verb*
Our team defeated them 8–0.
OTHER VERBS YOU MIGHT USE ARE **to beat** **to conquer** (*informal*) **to thrash**

defend *verb*
The mother bird defended her babies.
OTHER VERBS YOU MIGHT USE ARE **to guard** **to keep safe** **to protect**
The opposite is **attack**

definite *adjective*
1 Is it definite that I can go?
OTHER WORDS YOU MIGHT USE ARE **certain** **positive** **settled**
2 He gave a definite signal.
OTHER WORDS ARE **clear** **noticeable** **obvious** **sure**
The opposite is **vague**

delay *verb*
1 A traffic jam delayed us.
OTHER VERBS YOU MIGHT USE ARE **to hinder** **to hold up** **to slow down**
2 They had to delay the start of the match.
OTHER VERBS ARE **to postpone** **to put off**
3 Don't delay—do it now!
OTHER VERBS ARE **to hang about** **to hesitate** **to wait**

deliberate *adjective*
a deliberate mistake.
OTHER WORDS YOU MIGHT USE ARE **intentional** **planned**
The opposite is **accidental**

delicate *adjective*
1 delicate material.
OTHER WORDS YOU MIGHT USE ARE **dainty** **fine** **flimsy** **fragile** **soft**
2 a delicate child.
OTHER WORDS ARE **sickly** **unhealthy** **weak**
The opposite is **strong**

delicious *adjective*
a delicious dinner.
OTHER WORDS YOU MIGHT USE ARE **appetizing** **tasty**
For other words, see **taste**

delighted *adjective*
I was delighted with your gift.
ANOTHER WORD IS **pleased**
For other words, see **happy**

deliver *verb*
The postman delivers letters.
PHRASES YOU MIGHT USE ARE **to hand over** **to take round**

demand *verb*
When the new TV didn't work, Mum demanded to have her money back.
OTHER VERBS YOU MIGHT USE ARE **to ask** **to beg** **to request**

demolish *verb*
They had to demolish some houses when they built the new road.
OTHER VERBS YOU MIGHT USE ARE **to destroy** **to dismantle** **to knock down**

demonstration *noun*
1 We gave a PE demonstration.
OTHER WORDS YOU MIGHT USE ARE **display** **exhibition** **show**
2 There was a big demonstration against the new motorway.
OTHER WORDS YOU MIGHT USE ARE (*informal*) **demo** **march** **protest**

a b c d e f g h i j k l m n o p q r s t u v w x y z

dense *adjective*
1 dense fog. a dense crowd.
ANOTHER WORD IS **thick**
2 a dense pupil.
For other words, see **stupid**

deny *verb*
He denied that he had cheated.
PHRASES YOU MIGHT USE ARE **to refuse** **to agree** **to reject the idea**

depart *verb*
She departed without saying where she was going.
OTHER VERBS YOU MIGHT USE ARE **to go away** **to go out** **to leave** **to set off** **to set out**

depend *verb*
We can depend on Jo to do her best.
OTHER VERBS YOU MIGHT USE ARE **to count on** **to rely on** **to trust**

depress *verb*
His dog's death depressed him.
OTHER VERBS YOU MIGHT USE ARE **to sadden** **to upset**
depressed, **depressing** *adjectives*, see **sad**

describe *verb*
Can you describe what happened?
OTHER VERBS YOU MIGHT USE ARE **to explain** **to tell**

deserted *adjective*
a deserted house.
OTHER WORDS YOU MIGHT USE ARE **abandoned** **empty** **forsaken**

design *verb*
When we moved into our new house, we helped Mum design the garden.
OTHER VERBS YOU MIGHT USE ARE **to draw** **to plan** **to sketch**

desire *verb*
The fairy promised he could have what he desired.
OTHER VERBS YOU MIGHT USE ARE **to fancy** **to long for** **to want** **to wish for**

desperate *adjective*
The situation was desperate.
OTHER WORDS YOU MIGHT USE ARE **hopeless** **serious**

destroy *verb*
1 The explosion destroyed the building.
OTHER VERBS YOU MIGHT USE ARE **to demolish** **to knock down** **to ruin** **to wreck**
2 Dad used a special powder to destroy the ants in the garden.
OTHER VERBS YOU MIGHT USE ARE **to exterminate** (*informal*) **to finish off** **to kill** **to wipe out**

detest *verb*
Jo detests the smell of onions.
OTHER VERBS YOU MIGHT USE ARE **to dislike** **to hate** **to loathe**
The opposite is **love**

develop *verb*
1 Jo's swimming is developing.
OTHER VERBS YOU MIGHT USE ARE **to get better** **to improve** **to progress**
2 You must water plants if you want them to develop.
OTHER VERBS YOU MIGHT USE ARE **to get bigger** **to grow**

device *noun*
Our new tin-opener is a clever device.
OTHER WORDS YOU MIGHT USE ARE **contraption** **gadget** **implement** **instrument** **tool**

diagram *noun*
We drew a diagram to show how the machine worked.
OTHER WORDS YOU MIGHT USE ARE **chart** **graph** **plan** **sketch**

die *verb*
OTHER VERBS YOU MIGHT USE ARE **to pass away** **to perish**

difference *noun*
1 Will it make any difference to our plans if it rains?
OTHER WORDS YOU MIGHT USE ARE **alteration** **change**
2 Can you see any difference between these two colours?
OTHER WORDS YOU MIGHT USE ARE **contrast** **distinction**

different *adjective*
1 The sweets are different flavours.
OTHER WORDS YOU MIGHT USE ARE **assorted** **mixed** **various**
2 Jo and Sam often have different ideas about things.
OTHER WORDS YOU MIGHT USE ARE **contradictory** **contrasting** **dissimilar** **opposite**
The opposite is **the same**

difficult *adjective*
a difficult problem.
OTHER WORDS YOU MIGHT USE ARE **complex** **complicated** **hard** **tough** (*informal*) **tricky**
The opposite is **easy**

difficulty *noun*
The explorers met many difficulties before they reached home.
OTHER WORDS YOU MIGHT USE ARE **complication** **hardship** **obstacle** **problem** **snag** **trouble**

dig *verb*
OTHER VERBS ARE **to burrow** **to excavate** **to hollow out** **to scoop** **to tunnel**

dignified *adjective*
Please behave in a dignified way.
OTHER WORDS YOU MIGHT USE ARE **calm** **formal** **proper** **serious** **sober** **solemn** **stately**

dilute *verb*
You dilute squash with water.
PHRASES YOU MIGHT USE ARE **to make weaker** **to water down**

dim *adjective*
We saw a dim outline in the mist.
OTHER WORDS YOU MIGHT USE ARE **dark** **faint** **gloomy** **indistinct** **shadowy**
The opposite is **clear**

a b c d e f g h i j k l m n o p q r s t u v w x y z

din *noun*
OTHER WORDS YOU MIGHT USE ARE **noise** (*informal*) **racket** (*informal*) **row** **uproar**
For other words, see **sound**

direct *verb*
1 Please direct me to the bus stop.
OTHER VERBS YOU MIGHT USE ARE **to guide** **to point** **to show**
2 The officer directed the soldiers to stand in a line.
OTHER VERBS YOU MIGHT USE ARE **to command** **to instruct** **to order** **to tell**

dirt *noun*
OTHER WORDS YOU MIGHT USE ARE **dust** **filth** **grime** **muck** **mud** **pollution**

dirty *adjective*
OTHER WORDS YOU MIGHT USE ARE **dusty** **filthy** **foul** **grimy** **grubby** **mucky** **muddy** **polluted** **soiled** **stained**
The opposite is **clean**

disagree *verb*
OTHER VERBS YOU MIGHT USE ARE **to argue** **to differ** **to quarrel**
The opposite is **agree**

disappear *verb*
OTHER VERBS YOU MIGHT USE ARE **to fade** **to melt away** **to vanish**
The opposite is **appear**

disapprove *verb*
We disapprove of cruelty to pets.
OTHER VERBS YOU MIGHT USE ARE **to condemn** **to criticize** **to dislike**

disaster *noun*
Many people died in the disaster.
OTHER WORDS YOU MIGHT USE ARE **accident** **calamity** **catastrophe**

discipline *noun*
Our teacher likes to have discipline in the classroom.
OTHER WORDS YOU MIGHT USE ARE **control** **obedience** **order**

discover *verb*
1 I discovered a lot about dinosaurs in the library.
OTHER VERBS YOU MIGHT USE ARE **to find** **to learn** **to research** **to track down**
2 Dad discovered an old coin in the garden.
OTHER VERBS YOU MIGHT USE ARE **to come across** **to uncover** **to unearth**
The opposite is **hide**

discuss *verb*
Let's discuss the problem.
OTHER VERBS YOU MIGHT USE ARE **to argue about** **to consider** **to talk about**

disease *noun*
OTHER WORDS YOU MIGHT USE ARE **ailment** **illness** **sickness**
For other words, see **health**

disguise *verb*
1 Dad disguised himself as Father Christmas.
PHRASES ARE **to dress up as** **to pretend to be**
2 We disguised our hiding place.
OTHER VERBS ARE **to camouflage** **to conceal** **to cover up** **to hide**

disgust *verb*
The dirty kitchen disgusted us.
OTHER VERBS YOU MIGHT USE ARE **to offend** **to revolt** **to sicken**
disgusting *adjective*, see **nasty**

dishonest *adjective*
1 It is dishonest to tell lies.
OTHER WORDS YOU MIGHT USE ARE **deceitful** **insincere**
2 It is dishonest to steal.
OTHER WORDS YOU MIGHT USE ARE **cheating** **criminal** **unfair**
The opposite is **honest**

dislike *verb*
OTHER VERBS YOU MIGHT USE ARE **to detest** **to loathe** **to hate**
The opposite is **like**

dismiss *verb*
1 The teacher dismissed the class.
OTHER VERBS YOU MIGHT USE ARE **to let go** **to release** **to send away**
2 The boss dismissed her from her job.
OTHER VERBS ARE **to fire** **to sack**

disorder *noun*
Jo and Sam cleared up the disorder after the party.
OTHER WORDS YOU MIGHT USE ARE **chaos** **confusion** **muddle**

display *noun*
We put up a display of our work.
OTHER WORDS YOU MIGHT USE ARE **exhibition** **presentation** **show**

display *verb*
We display our work when parents come to school.
OTHER VERBS YOU MIGHT USE ARE **to exhibit** **to present** **to show**

distance *noun*
What's the distance between the goal posts?
OTHER WORDS YOU MIGHT USE ARE **gap** **space**
For more words, see **measurement**

distant *adjective*
distant places.
OTHER WORDS YOU MIGHT USE ARE **faraway** **remote**
The opposite is **near**

distinct *adjective*
1 I heard a distinct echo.
OTHER WORDS YOU MIGHT USE ARE **audible** **clear**
2 The footprints in the mud were quite distinct.
OTHER WORDS ARE **definite** **obvious** **plain** **visible**
3 The twins wear distinct colours.
OTHER WORDS ARE **contrasting** **different**

distressed *adjective*
The mother blackbird was very distressed when she saw the cat.
OTHER WORDS YOU MIGHT USE ARE **anxious** **frightened** **upset** **worried**

distribute *verb*
Jo distributed the pencils and paper.
OTHER VERBS YOU MIGHT USE ARE **to deal out** **to give out** **to hand out** **to share out**

a b c d e f g h i j k l m n o p q r s t u v w x y z

district *noun*
We live in a hilly district.
OTHER WORDS YOU MIGHT USE ARE **area** **locality** **region** **zone**

disturb *verb*
1 Don't disturb me while I'm working.
OTHER VERBS YOU MIGHT USE ARE **to bother** **to interrupt** **to trouble** **to worry**
2 A fox disturbed the chickens.
OTHER VERBS ARE **to alarm** **to excite** **to frighten** **to upset**

dive *verb*
We watched the sea birds diving into the water.
OTHER VERBS YOU MIGHT USE ARE **to drop** **to plunge** **to swoop**

divide *verb*
1 Divide the sweets between you.
OTHER VERBS YOU MIGHT USE ARE **to deal out** **to distribute** **to share**
2 At the next junction the road divides.
OTHER VERBS YOU MIGHT USE ARE **to branch** **to fork** **to separate** **to split**

dizzy *adjective*
I feel dizzy if I stand up quickly.
OTHER WORDS YOU MIGHT USE ARE **faint** **giddy** **unsteady**

do *verb*
THIS VERB HAS MANY USES. HERE ARE SOME OF THE WAYS YOU CAN USE IT, AND SOME OTHER VERBS YOU COULD CHOOSE.
1 I have done my work.
to carry out **to complete** **to finish** **to perform**
2 Sam is going to do the dinner.
to attend to **to deal with** **to handle** **to make** **to manage** **to prepare**
3 Will four big potatoes do?
to be enough **to be sufficient** **to be suitable**

doctor *noun*
For other people who look after our health, see **health**

dog *noun*, see opposite page

dot *noun*
OTHER WORDS YOU MIGHT USE ARE **mark** **point** **speck** **spot**

doubt *noun*
There's some doubt about whether Sam is well enough to play.
OTHER WORDS YOU MIGHT USE ARE **anxiety** **hesitation** **question** **uncertainty** **worry**

doubtful *adjective*
The rain made us doubtful about our picnic.
OTHER WORDS YOU MIGHT USE ARE **uncertain** **unsure** **worried**
The opposite is **certain**

drag *verb*
The tractor was dragging a load of logs.
OTHER VERBS YOU MIGHT USE ARE **to draw** **to haul** **to pull** **to tow** **to tug**

dog *noun*

A female dog is a **bitch**.
A young dog is a **pup** or **puppy**.
VARIOUS BREEDS OF DOG ARE
Alsatian **bloodhound** **bulldog** **collie** **dachshund** **Dalmatian** **greyhound** **Labrador** **Pekinese** **poodle** **retriever** **Rottweiler** **sheepdog** **spaniel** **terrier** **whippet**
A dog of mixed breed is a **mongrel**.

drama *noun*

1 Drama is one of Sam's favourite lessons.
OTHER WORDS YOU MIGHT USE ARE **acting** **improvisation** **plays**

2 We had some drama today when the fire engines came.
ANOTHER WORD IS **excitement**

draw *verb*

1 Jo drew a picture with a pencil.
ANOTHER VERB IS **to sketch**

2 The pony was drawing a cart.
OTHER VERBS YOU MIGHT USE ARE **to haul** **to pull** **to tow**

3 The match drew a large crowd.
OTHER VERBS ARE **to attract** **to bring in** **to pull in**

4 We drew 1–1 on Saturday.
OTHER VERBS ARE **to be equal** **to tie**

dreadful *adjective*

a dreadful storm.
OTHER WORDS YOU MIGHT USE ARE **alarming** **awful** **fearful** **frightening** **horrifying** **terrible**
The opposite is **wonderful**

dream *noun*

A nasty dream is a **nightmare**.
SOMETHING LIKE A DREAM WHICH YOU HAVE WHILE YOU ARE AWAKE IS A
daydream **fantasy** **illusion** **vision**

dream *verb*
OTHER VERBS YOU MIGHT USE ARE **to fancy** **to imagine**

dress *noun*
A DRESS FOR A SPECIAL OCCASION IS **evening dress** **gown** **party dress**
For things you wear, see **clothes**

dribble *verb*
When I cut my knee, blood dribbled down my leg.
OTHER VERBS YOU MIGHT USE ARE **to drip** **to flow** **to ooze** **to run** **to trickle**

drink *verb*

To drink greedily is **to gulp** or **to guzzle** or **to swig**.
To drink a tiny bit at a time is **to sip**.
To drink with your tongue like a cat is **to lap**.

DIFFERENT COLD DRINKS ARE
juice **lemonade** **milk** **mineral water** **orangeade** **squash** **water**

SOME ALCOHOLIC DRINKS ARE
beer **champagne** **cider** **lager** **whisky** **wine**

SOME HOT DRINKS ARE
cocoa **coffee** **tea**

drip *verb*
Don't let paint drip on to the carpet!
OTHER VERBS YOU MIGHT USE ARE **to dribble** **to drop** **to leak** **to trickle**

drive *verb*
1 Is it easy to drive a car?
OTHER VERBS YOU MIGHT USE ARE **to control** **to steer**
2 I drove the cow into the field.
OTHER VERBS ARE **to force** **to push** **to urge**

droop *verb*
The weather was so dry that the flowers began to droop.
OTHER VERBS YOU MIGHT USE ARE **to flop** **to go limp** **to sag** **to wilt**

drop *noun*
drops of water.
OTHER WORDS YOU MIGHT USE ARE **bead** **drip** **tear**

drop *verb*

1 A lorry dropped its load on the motorway.
OTHER VERBS YOU MIGHT USE ARE **to dump** **to shed**

2 The waterfall drops from a high cliff.
OTHER VERBS ARE **to cascade** **to fall** **to plunge**

3 The temperature drops at night.
OTHER VERBS ARE **to decrease** **to fall** **to go down**

dry *adjective*

1 Is the washing dry?
The opposite is **wet**

2 I feel dry: can I have a drink?
OTHER WORDS YOU MIGHT USE ARE **parched** **thirsty**

duck *noun*

A male duck is a **drake**.
A young duck is a **duckling**.

dull *adjective*

1 dull colours.
OTHER WORDS YOU MIGHT USE ARE **dingy** **drab** **gloomy**

2 a dull day.
OTHER WORDS ARE **cloudy** **grey** **overcast**

3 a dull pupil.
OTHER WORDS ARE **dim** **slow** **stupid**
The opposite is **bright**

4 a dull film.
OTHER WORDS ARE **boring** **uninteresting**
The opposite is **interesting**

dumb *adjective*

She was dumb with amazement.
OTHER WORDS YOU MIGHT USE ARE **mute** **silent** **speechless**

dump *verb*

1 I hate people who dump rubbish by the side of the road.
OTHER VERBS YOU MIGHT USE ARE **to abandon** **to discard** **to throw away**

2 I dumped my things on the table.
OTHER VERBS ARE **to drop** **to leave** **to unload**

duty *noun*

1 If you see a crime, it's your duty to tell the police.
ANOTHER WORD IS **responsibility**

2 We can go to play when we've finished our duties.
OTHER WORDS ARE **job** **task**

Ee

eager *adjective*
We were eager to start the game.
OTHER WORDS YOU MIGHT USE ARE **enthusiastic** **impatient** **keen**

earn *verb*
How much does Sam earn when he washes the car?
OTHER VERBS YOU MIGHT USE ARE **to deserve** **to get** **to make**

earth *noun*
1 We live on the planet Earth.
OTHER WORDS YOU MIGHT USE ARE **the globe** **the world**
2 Plants grow in the earth.
OTHER WORDS ARE **ground** **land** **soil**

easy *adjective*
1 Jo finished her work quickly because the sums were easy.
OTHER WORDS YOU MIGHT USE ARE **simple** **straightforward** **uncomplicated**
The opposite is **difficult**
2 The cat has an easy life.
OTHER WORDS ARE **carefree** **comfortable** **relaxing** **restful**

eat *verb*
The dog ate our dinner!
OTHER VERBS YOU MIGHT USE ARE
to consume **to feed on** **to swallow** **to tuck into**

DIFFERENT WAYS TO EAT THINGS ARE
to bite **to chew** **to munch**

IF YOU EAT FOOD GREEDILY, OTHER VERBS ARE
to bolt **to devour** **to gobble** **to gulp** **to guzzle**

If you eat a tiny bit at a time, you **nibble**.
A cow **grazes** on grass.
A chicken **pecks** at its food.
A dog will **gnaw** at a bone.

edge *noun*
THIS WORD HAS MANY USES. HERE ARE SOME OF THE WAYS YOU CAN USE IT, AND SOME OTHER WORDS YOU CAN CHOOSE
1 The edge of a picture.
border **frame**
2 The edge of a cricket field.
boundary **perimeter**
3 The edge of the road.
side **verge**
4 The edge of a curtain.
frill **fringe** **hem**
5 The edge of a cup.
brim **rim**
6 The edge of a circle.
circumference

The space down the edge of a piece of paper you have written on is the **margin**.

educate *verb*
Our parents and teachers educate us.

OTHER VERBS YOU MIGHT USE ARE
to bring up **to instruct** **to teach** **to train**

PLACES WHERE PEOPLE GO TO BE EDUCATED ARE
college **playgroup** **school** **university**

DIFFERENT KINDS OF SCHOOL ARE
boarding school **comprehensive school** **infant school**
junior school **kindergarten** **nursery school**
playgroup **primary school** **secondary school**

effort *noun*
1 You deserve a rest after all that effort.
OTHER WORDS YOU MIGHT USE ARE **labour** **toil** **trouble** **work**
2 I made an effort to be good.
OTHER WORDS ARE **attempt** **try**

elect *verb*
We elected Jo as captain of the rounders team.
OTHER VERBS YOU MIGHT USE ARE **to choose** **to pick** **to select** **to vote for**

election *noun*
We had an election to choose the captain of the team.
OTHER WORDS YOU MIGHT USE ARE **ballot** **vote**

embarrassed *adjective*
1 Jo was embarrassed when she forgot her words in the play.
OTHER WORDS YOU MIGHT USE ARE **ashamed** **upset**
2 He was too embarrassed to ask for a second helping.
ANOTHER WORD IS **shy**

emergency *noun*
We knew there was an emergency when we heard the fire engine.
ANOTHER WORD IS **crisis**

empty *adjective*
1 an empty cup.
ANOTHER WORD IS **unfilled**
The opposite is **full**
2 an empty space.
ANOTHER WORD IS **hollow**
The opposite is **solid**
3 an empty house.
OTHER WORDS YOU MIGHT USE ARE **deserted** **uninhabited** **unoccupied** **vacant**
The opposite is **occupied**

encourage *verb*
We shouted to encourage our team.
OTHER VERBS YOU MIGHT USE ARE **to support** **to urge on**

a b c d e f g h i j k l m n o p q r s t u v w x y z

end *noun*

1 We didn't stay for the end of the film.
OTHER WORDS YOU MIGHT USE ARE **conclusion** **ending** **finish**

2 We walked to the end of the train.
OTHER WORDS ARE **back** **rear** **tail**

3 He poked me with the end of a stick.
OTHER WORDS ARE **point** **tip**

end *verb*

1 We waited for the storm to end.
OTHER VERBS YOU MIGHT USE ARE **to cease** **to finish** **to stop**
The opposite is **begin**

2 It would be wonderful if we could end all wars.
ANOTHER VERB IS **to abolish**

enemy *noun*

OTHER WORDS YOU MIGHT USE ARE **attacker** **foe** **opponent**
Opposites are **ally**, **friend**

energetic *adjective*

Mum says that we are so energetic that she can't keep up with us.
OTHER WORDS YOU MIGHT USE ARE **active** **enthusiastic** **lively** **vigorous**
The opposite is **lazy**

energy *noun*

You use up a lot of energy playing rounders.
OTHER WORDS YOU MIGHT USE ARE **power** **strength**

engine *noun*

Cars, ships, and aeroplanes have engines to keep them going.

DIFFERENT KINDS OF ENGINE ARE
diesel engine **electric motor** **jet engine** **petrol engine** **steam engine**
A railway engine is a **locomotive**.

enjoy *verb*

The things Jo enjoys most are ice-skating and reading.
OTHER VERBS YOU MIGHT USE ARE **to appreciate** **to like** **to love**
The opposite is **dislike**

enough *adjective*

Have you had enough food?
OTHER WORDS YOU MIGHT USE ARE **adequate** **sufficient**

enter *verb*

Don't enter the classroom until the teacher tells you to.
PHRASES YOU MIGHT USE ARE **to come in** **to go in**

entertain *verb*

A conjuror entertained us at Jo's party.
ANOTHER VERB IS **to amuse**

entertainment *noun*

OTHER WORDS YOU MIGHT USE ARE
amusement **enjoyment** **fun**

ENTERTAINMENTS YOU GO OUT TO ENJOY INCLUDE
ballet **cinema** **circus** **concert** **dance** **disco** **drama** **fair** **opera** **pantomime** **play** **waxworks** **zoo**

ENTERTAINMENTS YOU ENJOY AT HOME INCLUDE
computer games **music** **radio** **television** **video**

PEOPLE WHO ENTERTAIN US IN THE THEATRE OR ON RADIO AND TV ARE
actor **actress** **broadcaster** **comedian** **comic** **conjuror** **dancer** **DJ** **magician** **musician** **singer** **ventriloquist**

PEOPLE WHO ENTERTAIN US IN A CIRCUS ARE
acrobat **clown** **juggler** **lion tamer** **trapeze artist**

enthusiastic *adjective*
Sam is an enthusiastic member of the football team.
OTHER WORDS YOU MIGHT USE ARE **eager** **interested** **keen**

entrance *noun*
Pay your money at the entrance.
OTHER WORDS YOU MIGHT USE ARE **door** **entry** **way in**
The opposite is **exit**

envious *adjective*
Jo was a bit envious when she saw what Sam got for his birthday.
ANOTHER WORD IS **jealous**

equal *adjective*
At half time the scores were equal.
OTHER WORDS YOU MIGHT USE ARE **even** **identical** **level** **the same**
The opposite is **different**

equipment *noun*
We keep the games equipment in a shed in the playground.
OTHER WORDS YOU MIGHT USE ARE **apparatus** (*informal*) **gear** **tackle**

error *noun*
Our teacher corrects the errors in our work.
OTHER WORDS YOU MIGHT USE ARE **fault** **mistake** (*informal*) **slip**

escape *verb*
The cat chased the mouse, but it escaped.
PHRASES YOU MIGHT USE ARE **to get away** **to run away**

essential *adjective*
It's essential to start early if you want to avoid traffic jams.
OTHER WORDS YOU MIGHT USE ARE **important** **necessary** **vital**
The opposite is **unnecessary**

estimate *verb*
Jo estimated how many sandwiches everyone would eat at her party.
OTHER VERBS YOU MIGHT USE ARE **to calculate** **to guess** **to work out**

even *adjective*
1 You need an even field for playing rounders.
OTHER WORDS ARE **flat** **level** **smooth**
The opposite is **bumpy**
2 At half time the scores were even.
OTHER WORDS YOU MIGHT USE ARE **equal** **level** **the same**
The opposite is **different**
3 Even numbers are numbers you can divide by two, such as 2, 8, 20.
The opposite is **odd**

evening *noun*
VARIOUS TIMES OF THE EVENING ARE **dusk** **sunset** **twilight**

event *noun*
The fathers' sack race was the funniest event on sports day.
OTHER WORDS YOU MIGHT USE ARE **happening** **incident** **occasion**

evidence *noun*
The police had evidence that he was guilty.
OTHER WORDS YOU MIGHT USE ARE **information** **proof**

evil *adjective*
Murder is an evil thing.
OTHER WORDS YOU MIGHT USE ARE **hateful** **immoral** **sinful** **wicked** **wrong**
The opposite is **good**

exact *adjective*
Have you got the exact time?
OTHER WORDS YOU MIGHT USE ARE **accurate** **correct** **precise** **right** **true**

examination *noun*
1 Sam had a music examination at the end of term.
OTHER WORDS YOU MIGHT USE ARE (*informal*) **exam** **test**
2 When I was ill, I went to the doctor's for an examination.
ANOTHER WORD IS (*informal*) **check-up**

examine *verb*
1 We examined the strange insect carefully.
OTHER VERBS YOU MIGHT USE ARE **to inspect** **to study**
2 The police examined the suspect.
OTHER VERBS ARE **to interrogate** **to question**

example *noun*
When the parents come to school, we display examples of our work.
OTHER WORDS YOU MIGHT USE ARE **sample** **specimen**

excellent *adjective*
OTHER WORDS YOU MIGHT USE ARE (*informal*) **brilliant** (*informal*) **fantastic** **marvellous** **outstanding** (*informal*) **tremendous** **wonderful**
For other words, see **good**

exchange *verb*
Sam exchanged his old bike for some roller skates.
OTHER VERBS YOU MIGHT USE ARE **to substitute** (*informal*) **to swop** **to trade in**

excite *verb*
The amazing goal excited the crowd.
OTHER VERBS YOU MIGHT USE ARE **to arouse** **to provoke** **to rouse** **to stimulate** **to stir up** **to thrill**

excited *adjective*
We were excited on the morning before we had the party.
OTHER WORDS YOU MIGHT USE ARE **boisterous** **lively** **worked up**

excitement *noun*
The game was full of excitement.
OTHER WORDS YOU MIGHT USE ARE **action** **drama** **suspense** **thrills**

exclaim *verb*
OTHER VERBS YOU MIGHT USE ARE **to call out** **to shout** **to yell**

excuse *verb*
1 Please excuse our dog's bad behaviour.
OTHER VERBS YOU MIGHT USE ARE **to forgive** **to overlook** **to pardon**
2 I was excused from swimming because I had a cold.
A PHRASE IS **to let off**

exhausted *adjective*
I was exhausted after my long walk.
OTHER WORDS YOU MIGHT USE ARE **tired** **weary** **worn out**

exhibition *noun*
We had an exhibition of our work.
OTHER WORDS YOU MIGHT USE ARE **display** **show**

exist *verb*
Plants can't exist without water.
OTHER VERBS YOU MIGHT USE ARE **to keep going** **to live** **to survive**

exit *noun*
OTHER WORDS YOU MIGHT USE ARE **door** **way out**
The opposite is **entrance**

expect *verb*
I expect it will rain later.
ANOTHER VERB IS **to forecast**

expedition *noun*
On Saturday, Mum and Jo went on an expedition to the shops.
OTHER WORDS YOU MIGHT USE ARE **journey** **outing** **trip**

expel *verb*
The dog was expelled from the shop because he was a nuisance.
OTHER VERBS YOU MIGHT USE ARE (*informal*) **to kick out** **to throw out**
TO EXPEL SOMEONE FROM A COUNTRY **to banish** **to deport** **to exile**
TO EXPEL SOMEONE FROM THEIR HOME **to evict**

expensive *adjective*
Mum didn't buy me any new jeans because they were too expensive.
OTHER WORDS YOU MIGHT USE ARE **costly** **dear** (*informal*) **pricey**
The opposite is **cheap**

explain *verb*
Mum explained how computers work.
OTHER VERBS YOU MIGHT USE ARE **to make clear** **to show**

explode *verb*
The firework exploded.
OTHER VERBS YOU MIGHT USE ARE **to blow up** **to burst** **to go off**

a b c d e f g h i j k l m n o p q r s t u v w x y z

explore *verb*
Sam went off with his friends to explore the caves.
OTHER VERBS YOU MIGHT USE ARE **to investigate** **to look round**

expression *noun*
I noticed Jo's unhappy expression.

OTHER WORDS YOU MIGHT USE ARE
face **look**

DIFFERENT EXPRESSIONS YOU SEE ON PEOPLE'S FACES ARE
frown **glare** **grin** **laugh** **scowl** **smile** **sneer** **yawn**

extra *adjective*
Do you want some extra milk in your tea?
OTHER WORDS YOU MIGHT USE ARE **additional** **more**

extraordinary *adjective*
I didn't believe his extraordinary story about a space ship.
OTHER WORDS YOU MIGHT USE ARE **amazing** **incredible** **odd** **peculiar** **queer** **remarkable** **strange** **unbelievable** **uncommon** **unusual**
The opposite is **ordinary**

extravagant *adjective*
Mum says it's extravagant to cook more food than you can eat.
OTHER WORDS YOU MIGHT USE ARE **expensive** **wasteful**

extreme *adjective*
1 extreme cold.
OTHER WORDS YOU MIGHT USE ARE **exceptional** **great** **intense** **severe**
2 the extreme corner of the playground.
OTHER WORDS ARE **farthest** **furthest**

Ff

face *noun*
1 He made a funny face.
For other words, see **expression**
2 Each face of a dice has a different number of dots.
OTHER WORDS YOU MIGHT USE ARE **side** **surface**

facts *noun*
You find lots of facts in an encyclopedia.
OTHER WORDS YOU MIGHT USE ARE **data** **evidence** **information**

fade *verb*
1 The sun faded the curtains.
OTHER VERBS YOU MIGHT USE ARE **to bleach** **to discolour** **to whiten**
2 In the evening, the light fades and the stars begin to shine.
OTHER VERBS ARE **to disappear** **to dwindle** **to melt away**

fail *verb*

1 He failed to stop at the red light.
OTHER VERBS YOU MIGHT USE ARE **to neglect** **to omit**

2 He failed his driving test.
A PHRASE IS **to be unsuccessful**

The opposite is **pass**

faint *adjective*

1 I saw a faint shape in the mist.
OTHER WORDS YOU MIGHT USE ARE **blurred** **dim** **hazy** **misty** **pale** **unclear**

The opposite is **clear**

2 We heard faint cries for help.
OTHER WORDS ARE **distant** **low** **muffled** **weak**

The opposite is **loud**

3 Sam felt faint because he stood up too quickly.
OTHER WORDS ARE **dizzy** **giddy** **unsteady**

faint *verb*

It was so hot that he fainted.
OTHER VERBS ARE **to become unconscious** **to collapse**

fair *adjective*

1 fair hair.
OTHER WORDS YOU MIGHT USE ARE **blond** **light** **pale**

The opposite is **dark**

2 It's not fair if she gets more than me.
OTHER WORDS ARE **just** **proper** **right**

The opposite is **unfair**

3 Was the referee fair?
OTHER WORDS YOU MIGHT USE ARE **honest** **unbiased**

The opposite is **biased**

4 I had a fair chance of winning.
OTHER WORDS ARE **moderate** **reasonable**

faithful *adjective*

The dog is his faithful companion.
OTHER WORDS YOU MIGHT USE ARE **devoted** **loyal** **reliable** **trustworthy**

The opposite is **treacherous**

fall *verb*

1 The dog was so excited that he fell in the river.
OTHER VERBS YOU MIGHT USE ARE **to drop** **to plunge** **to slip** **to topple** **to tumble**

2 The burning tower fell to the ground.
OTHER VERBS YOU MIGHT USE ARE **to collapse** **to crash**

3 The temperature falls at night.
OTHER VERBS ARE **to decrease** **to go down**

The opposite is **rise**

false *adjective*

1 He gave us false information.
OTHER WORDS YOU MIGHT USE ARE **inaccurate** **incorrect** **made-up** **misleading** **wrong**

The opposite is **correct**

2 Father Christmas wore a false beard.
OTHER WORDS ARE **artificial** **fake** **imitation**

The opposite is **real**

a b c d e **f** g h i j k l m n o p q r s t u v w x y z

familiar *adjective*
I like to be back in my familiar surroundings after a holiday.
OTHER WORDS YOU MIGHT USE ARE **normal** **regular** **usual** **well-known**
The opposite is **strange**

family *noun*

The members of your family are your **relations** or **relatives**.

MEMBERS OF YOUR IMMEDIATE FAMILY ARE
brother **daughter** **father** **husband** **mother** **sister** **son** **stepfather** **stepmother** **wife**

OTHER RELATIONS YOU MIGHT HAVE ARE
aunt **cousins** **grandfather** **grandmother** **nephew** **niece** **uncle**

Members of your family who lived in the past are your **ancestors**.

famous *adjective*
a famous TV actor.
ANOTHER WORD IS **well-known**

fan *noun*
Sam is a fan of our football team.
OTHER WORDS YOU MIGHT USE ARE **admirer** **follower** **supporter**

fancy *verb*
1 What do you fancy to eat?
OTHER VERBS YOU MIGHT USE ARE **to feel like** **to long for** **to want** **to wish for**
2 I fancied I saw a ghost.
OTHER VERBS ARE **to dream** **to imagine** **to think**

fantastic *adjective*
1 We heard a fantastic story about dragons and wizards.
OTHER WORDS YOU MIGHT USE ARE **amazing** **extraordinary** **incredible** **strange** **weird**
2 (*informal*) We had a fantastic time at the party.
For other words, see **good**

farm *noun*, see next page

fashion *noun*
Sam knows about the latest fashion in music.
OTHER WORDS YOU MIGHT USE ARE **craze** **style** **trend**

fast *adjective*
1 We started off at a fast pace.
OTHER WORDS YOU MIGHT USE ARE **brisk** **hurried** **quick** **rapid** **smart** **speedy** **swift**
2 Granny caught a fast train to London.
OTHER WORDS ARE **express** **high-speed**
The opposite is **slow**

fat *adjective*
1 a fat person.
OTHER WORDS YOU MIGHT USE ARE **chubby** **overweight** **plump** (*informal*) **podgy** **stout** (*informal*) **tubby**
2 a fat book.
ANOTHER WORD IS **thick**
The opposite is **thin**

fat *noun*
KINDS OF FAT YOU MIGHT EAT OR USE IN COOKING ARE
butter **cooking oil** **dripping** **lard** **margarine** **suet**

fault *noun*
The teacher pointed out the faults in my work.
OTHER WORDS YOU MIGHT USE ARE **error** **flaw** **mistake** (*informal*) **slip** **weakness**

favour *noun*
She did me a favour and lent me her umbrella.
OTHER WORDS YOU MIGHT USE ARE **good deed** **kindness**

fear *noun*
Fear spread through the town when the earthquake started.
OTHER WORDS YOU MIGHT USE ARE **alarm** **dread** **fright** **horror** **panic** **terror**

feeble *adjective*
I felt feeble after I was ill.
OTHER WORDS YOU MIGHT USE ARE **delicate** **frail** **weak**
The opposite is **strong**

feel *verb*
1 Feel the cat's soft fur.
OTHER VERBS YOU MIGHT USE ARE **to finger** **to stroke** **to touch**
2 Granny feels the cold more than I do.
OTHER VERBS YOU MIGHT USE ARE **to notice** **to suffer from**

feeling *noun*
My feeling is that it will be fine tomorrow.
OTHER WORDS YOU MIGHT USE ARE **guess** **instinct** **intuition** **opinion**
feelings
1 When you are very sad, it's hard not to show your feelings.
ANOTHER WORD IS **emotions**
2 Vegetarians often have strong feelings about killing animals.
OTHER WORDS ARE **beliefs** **opinions**

female *noun*
THERE ARE SPECIAL WORDS FOR MALE AND FEMALE HUMAN BEINGS AND SOME ANIMALS.
A female human being is a **girl** or **woman**.
A female dog is a **bitch.**
A female deer or rabbit is a **doe.**
A female sheep is a **ewe**.
A female bird is a **hen**.
A female lion is a **lioness**.
A female horse is a **mare.**
A female goat is a **nanny goat**.
A female pig is a **sow**.
A female fox is a **vixen**.

farm *noun*

Another word for a small farm is **smallholding**.
A word for a small farm in Scotland is a **croft**.
A word for a cattle farm in North America is a **ranch**.

BUILDINGS YOU SEE ON A FARM ARE

barn **cowshed** **farmhouse**
granary **pigsty** **stable**

MACHINES AND EQUIPMENT YOU SEE ON A FARM ARE

combine harvester **cultivator** **drill**
harrow **milking machine** **mower**
plough **tractor** **wagon**

OTHER THINGS YOU MIGHT SEE ON A FARM ARE

battery **cages** **farmyard**
hayrick or **haystack** **silo**

Farmers grow various crops.

KINDS OF CORN OR CEREALS ARE

barley **maize** or **sweetcorn** **oats**
rye **wheat**

OTHER CROPS ARE

potatoes **sugar beet** **vegetables**

ANIMALS THAT FARMERS KEEP ARE

bull **calf** **cow**
goat **horse** **lamb**
pig **sheep**

Bulls and cows are called **cattle**.

BIRDS THAT YOU SEE ON A FARM ARE

chicken **duck** **goose**
hen **turkey**

These birds are called **poultry**.

chicken horse goose

barn

tractor

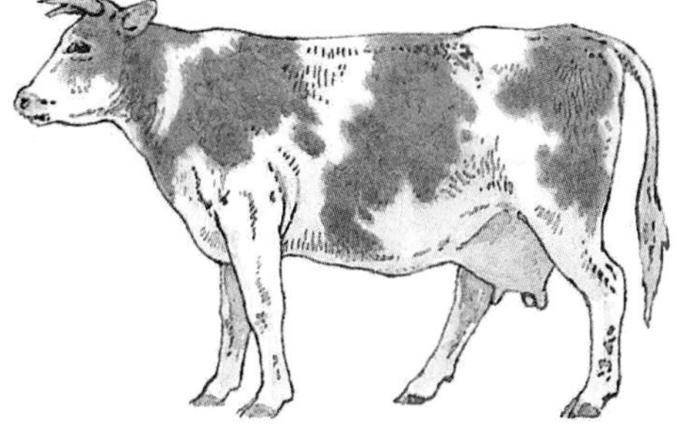
cow

goat

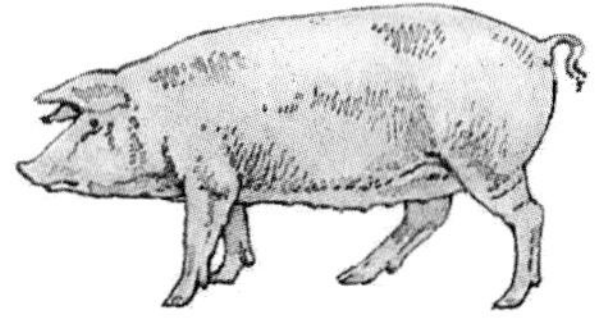
pig

sugar beet

cabbage

a b c d e **f** g h i j k l m n o p q r s t u v w x y z

fence *noun*
OTHER THINGS USED TO MARK THE EDGE OF A PIECE OF LAND ARE **barrier** **hedge** **railings** **wall**

fetch *verb*
Jo's dog fetched the newspaper.
OTHER VERBS YOU MIGHT USE ARE **to bring** **to carry** **to collect** **to get**

fidget *verb*
Please don't fidget!
OTHER VERBS YOU MIGHT USE ARE **to be restless** **to fiddle**

field *noun*
OTHER WORDS YOU MIGHT USE ARE
a field of grass: **meadow** **pasture**
a small field for horses: **paddock**

fierce *adjective*
a fierce dog.
OTHER WORDS YOU MIGHT USE ARE **ferocious** **savage** **vicious**
The opposite is **gentle**

fight *noun*
OTHER WORDS YOU MIGHT USE ARE
combat **conflict** **contest** **quarrel** (*informal*) **row**

WORDS FOR DIFFERENT KINDS OF FIGHTING ARE
a fight between armies
battle **war**
a fight between two people
duel
a fight between two families or gangs
feud
a fight in the street
brawl **riot** **scuffle**
a fight to entertain people
bout **boxing match** **wrestling match**
a fight between knights in old times
joust
a friendly or unimportant fight
(*informal*) **scrap** **squabble** **tussle**

WORDS FOR FIGHTER ARE
soldier **warrior**
An archer used to fight with a **bow** and **arrow**.
A boxer fights with **fists**.
A gladiator used to fight to **entertain** people.
A gunman fights with **guns**.
Knights used to fight on **horses**.
A wrestler fights with **hands** and **arms**.
For other words, see **soldier**

figure *noun*
1 Jo added up the figures.
OTHER WORDS YOU MIGHT USE ARE **digit** **number**
2 Sam has a slim figure.
ANOTHER WORD IS **shape**

file *noun*
We lined up in a single file.
OTHER WORDS YOU MIGHT USE ARE **column** **line** **queue** **row**

fill *verb*
I filled the box with sweets.
OTHER VERBS YOU MIGHT USE ARE **to cram** **to load** **to pack**

film *noun*
I watched a good film on TV.
ANOTHER WORD IS
movie

DIFFERENT KINDS OF FILM ARE
adventure **cartoon** **comedy** **documentary** **horror** **science fiction** **western**

filthy *adjective*
Put those filthy jeans in the washing machine!
OTHER WORDS YOU MIGHT USE ARE **dirty** **foul** (*informal*) **grubby** **messy** (*informal*) **mucky** **muddy**
The opposite is **clean**

final *adjective*
They scored in the final moments of the game.
OTHER WORDS YOU MIGHT USE ARE **closing** **concluding** **last**
The opposite is **first**

find *verb*
1 Did you find the money you lost?
OTHER VERBS YOU MIGHT USE ARE **to come across** **to discover** **to get back** **to recover**
The opposite is **lose**
2 Did the police find the thief?
OTHER VERBS ARE **to trace** **to track down**
3 I found the information I need.
ANOTHER VERB IS **to discover**

fine *adjective*
1 fine thread.
OTHER WORDS YOU MIGHT USE ARE **slender** **thin**
The opposite is **thick**
2 fine sand.
ANOTHER WORD IS **powdery**
The opposite is **coarse**
3 fine weather.
OTHER WORDS ARE **bright** **dry** **sunny**
The opposite is **wet**
4 a fine piece of work.
OTHER WORDS ARE **good** **great** **excellent**
The opposite is **bad**

a b c d e f g h i j k l m n o p q r s t u v w x y z

finish *verb*

1 Finish your work now.
OTHER VERBS YOU MIGHT USE ARE **to complete** **to round off** **to stop**

2 The film finished with an exciting car chase.
OTHER VERBS ARE **to conclude** **to end**

3 Did you finish those sweets?
OTHER WORDS ARE **to consume** **to use up**

The opposite is **start**

fire *noun*
We watched the firemen put out the fire.

OTHER WORDS YOU MIGHT USE ARE
blaze **flames** **inferno**

FIRES USED FOR HEAT OR COOKING ARE
barbecue **boiler** **camp fire** **central heating** **coal fire** **electric fire** **furnace** **gas fire** **gas ring** **grill** **hot plate** **immersion heater** **oven** **stove**

FIRES WHICH BURN THINGS WE DON'T WANT ARE
bonfire **incinerator**

fire *verb*
to fire a gun.
OTHER VERBS YOU MIGHT USE ARE **to let off** **to shoot**

firm *adjective*

1 Make sure the rock is firm before you step on it.
OTHER WORDS YOU MIGHT USE ARE **fixed** **secure** **steady**

2 Mum whisked the cream until it was firm.
OTHER WORDS ARE **set** **solid** **stiff**

first *adjective*

1 Jo was the first to arrive at the party.
OTHER WORDS YOU MIGHT USE ARE **earliest** **soonest**

2 Who was the first man in space?
ANOTHER WORD IS **original**

The opposite is **last**

fish *noun*, see opposite page

fisherman *noun*
A person who fishes with a rod is an **angler**.
A person who goes to sea in a boat to catch fish is a **trawlerman**.

fit *adjective*

1 You have to be fit to play football.
OTHER WORDS YOU MIGHT USE ARE **healthy** **strong** **well**

2 Is the old house fit to live in?
ANOTHER WORD IS **suitable**

fit *verb*
Jo helped Sam fit the pieces of his model aeroplane together.
OTHER VERBS YOU MIGHT USE ARE **to assemble** **to put together**

fish *noun*

SOME DIFFERENT KINDS OF FISH ARE

carp **cod** **eel** **goldfish** **haddock** **herring** **mackerel** **minnow** **perch** **pike** **pilchard** **plaice** **salmon** **sardine** **shark** **sole** **stickleback** **trout**

ANIMALS WHICH LIVE IN WATER BUT ARE NOT REAL FISH ARE

dolphin **jellyfish** **octopus** **porpoise** **whale**

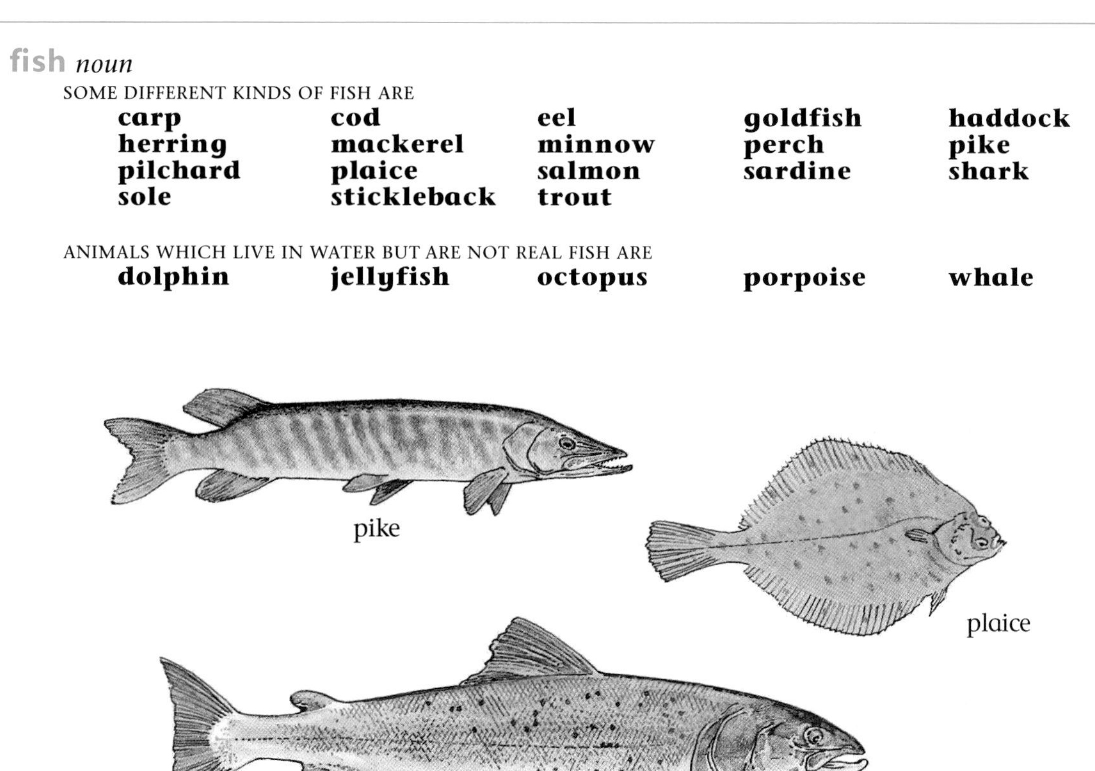

fix *verb*

Dad fixed a shelf to the wall.

OTHER VERBS YOU MIGHT USE ARE **to attach** **to secure**

For other verbs, see **fasten**

fizzy *adjective*

fizzy drinks.

OTHER WORDS YOU MIGHT USE ARE **bubbly** **effervescent** **sparkling**

flap *verb*

The flags flapped in the wind.

OTHER VERBS YOU MIGHT USE ARE **to flutter** **to wave**

flat *adjective*

A games field must be flat.

OTHER WORDS YOU MIGHT USE ARE **even** **level** **smooth**

flavour *noun*

I like the flavour of this drink.

ANOTHER WORD IS **taste**

fling *verb*

I flung a pebble into the water.

OTHER VERBS YOU MIGHT USE ARE (*informal*) **to chuck** **to throw** **to toss**

a b c d e **f** g h i j k l m n o p q r s t u v w x y z

float *verb*

1 Will this toy boat float?

A PHRASE IS **to stay up**

The opposite is **sink**

2 The smoke from the bonfire floated in the air.

OTHER VERBS YOU MIGHT USE ARE **to drift** **to hover**

flock *noun*

For other words, see **group**

flow *verb*

Water flowed from the broken pipe.

OTHER VERBS YOU MIGHT USE ARE

to flow fast **to gush** **to pour** **to run** **to spurt** **to squirt** **to stream**

to flow slowly **to dribble** **to drip** **to leak** **to ooze** **to trickle**

to flow over the edge **to overflow** **to spill**

flower *noun*

OTHER WORDS YOU MIGHT USE ARE

bloom **blossom**

WORDS FOR A BUNCH OF FLOWERS ARE

arrangement **bouquet** **posy**

FLOWERS YOU SEE IN GARDENS ARE

carnation **chrysanthemum** **crocus** **daffodil**
daisy **forget-me-not** **geranium** **hollyhock**
hyacinth **lily** **marigold** **pansy** **rose**
snowdrop **sunflower** **tulip** **wallflower** **lupin**

FLOWERS THAT OFTEN GROW WILD ARE

bluebell **buttercup**
dandelion **foxglove**
poppy **primrose**
violet

daisy

tulip

sunflower

rose

fluffy *adjective*

OTHER WORDS YOU MIGHT USE ARE **feathery** **furry** **soft** **woolly**

fly *verb*

Birds, bats, and aeroplanes fly.

OTHER VERBS YOU MIGHT USE ARE **to glide** **to hover** **to rise** **to soar** **to swoop**

fog *noun*

I couldn't see because of the fog.

OTHER WORDS YOU MIGHT USE ARE **haze** **mist**

fold *verb*
The paper will go in the envelope if you fold it.
OTHER VERBS YOU MIGHT USE ARE **to bend over** **to crease** **to double over**

follow *verb*
1 A dog followed me.
OTHER VERBS YOU MIGHT USE ARE **to chase** **to come after** **to pursue** **to tail** **to track**
2 Follow this road.
OTHER VERBS ARE **to go along** **to take**
3 Did you follow what she said?
ANOTHER VERB IS **to understand**

food *noun*, see next page

foolish *adjective*
It's foolish to run across the main road.
OTHER WORDS YOU MIGHT USE ARE (*informal*) **daft** **idiotic** **mad** **silly** **stupid** **unwise**
The opposite is **sensible**

foot *noun*
An animal's foot is a **hoof** or **paw**.
A bird has **toes** or **claws**.
For other parts of the body, see **body**

forbid *verb*
The head forbids eating in class.
OTHER VERBS YOU MIGHT USE ARE **to ban** **to prohibit**
The opposite is **allow**

force *noun*
We had to use force to open the door.
OTHER WORDS YOU MIGHT USE ARE **might** **power** **strength** **violence**

force *verb*
They can't force me to play.
OTHER VERBS YOU MIGHT USE ARE **to compel** **to make** **to order**

forest *noun*
Don't get lost in the forest!
OTHER WORDS YOU MIGHT USE ARE **jungle** **wood**

forgery *noun*
The shopkeeper checked to see if the £10 note was a forgery.
OTHER WORDS YOU MIGHT USE ARE **copy** **fake** **imitation**

forget *verb*
I forgot my money.
OTHER VERBS YOU MIGHT USE ARE **to leave behind** **to overlook**
The opposite is **remember**

forgetful *adjective*
He was so forgetful that he left his money behind.
OTHER WORDS YOU MIGHT USE ARE **absent-minded** **careless** **scatterbrained** **thoughtless**

forgive *verb*
Sam forgave Jo for forgetting his birthday.
OTHER VERBS YOU MIGHT USE ARE **to excuse** **to pardon**

food *noun*

OTHER WORDS YOU MIGHT USE ARE

diet **nourishment** **provisions** **refreshments**

Food for farm animals is **fodder**.

BASIC INGREDIENTS OF FOOD ARE

carbohydrate **fat** **fibre** **protein** **starch** **vitamins**

CEREALS ARE

barley **maize** or **sweetcorn** **oats** **rice** **rye** **wheat**

FOOD MADE FROM CEREALS:

bran **cornflakes** **cornflour** **flour** **muesli** **oatmeal** **porridge**

KINDS OF BREAD:

bagel **brown bread** **chapatti** **crusty bread** **French bread** **nan** **rye bread** **white bread** **wholemeal bread**

OTHER FOODS MADE FROM FLOUR:

biscuits **cake** **dumplings** **noodles** **pasta** **pastry** **pizza**

SOME KINDS OF CAKE ARE

bun **doughnut** or **donut** **flan** **fruit cake** **gingerbread** **meringue** **muffin** **scone** **shortbread** **sponge cake** **tart**

KINDS OF PASTA:

lasagne **macaroni** **spaghetti**

THINGS MADE WITH PASTRY:

pasty **pie** **mince pies** **quiche** **sausage rolls**

FOOD MADE WITH MILK:

blancmange **butter** **cheese** **cream** **custard** **milk pudding** **yogurt**

KINDS OF MEAT ARE

bacon **beef** **chicken** **ham** **lamb** **pork** **turkey** **veal** **venison**

FOOD USUALLY MADE WITH MEAT:

burgers **chop suey** **curry** **fritters** **goulash** **hash** **hotpot** **meat pie** **mince** **paté** **rissole** **sausage** **stew**

Food which doesn't contain any meat is **vegetarian** food.

FOOD MADE WITH EGGS:

omelette pancakes soufflé

FISH WHICH PEOPLE EAT ARE

cod haddock herring kipper mackerel pilchard plaice salmon sardine scampi shellfish sole trout tuna

A mixture of fish and shellfish is **seafood**.
Caviare is a very expensive food from a fish called **sturgeon**.

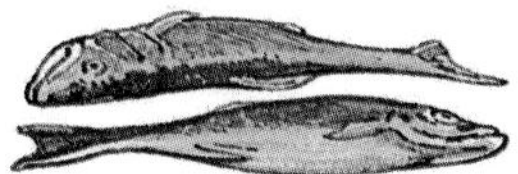

FRUIT WHICH YOU CAN EAT ARE

apple apricot banana blackberry blackcurrant cherry coconut damson date fig gooseberry grape grapefruit kiwi fruit lemon lime melon orange peach pear pineapple plum raspberry strawberry tangerine tomato

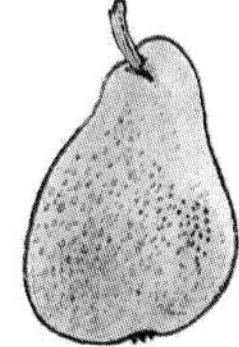

VEGETABLES PEOPLE EAT INCLUDE

asparagus beans Brussels sprouts cabbage carrot cauliflower greens leek marrow nuts onion parsnip pea potato pumpkin spinach swede turnip

VEGETABLES WE EAT IN SALAD ARE

beetroot celery cress cucumber lettuce mustard & cress onion potato radish tomato watercress

SOME SWEET FOODS:

honey ice cream icing jam jelly marmalade mousse pudding syrup tart treacle trifle

THINGS USED TO ADD FLAVOUR TO FOOD

chutney dressing garlic gravy herbs ketchup mayonnaise mustard pepper pickle salt sauce seasoning spice sugar vanilla vinegar

a b c d e f g h i j k l m n o p q r s t u v w x y z

form *noun*
The wizard could change his form.
OTHER WORDS YOU MIGHT USE ARE **appearance** **shape**

fortunate *adjective*
It's fortunate that it didn't rain.
ANOTHER WORD IS **lucky**
The opposite is **unlucky**

foul *adjective*
foul slime. foul weather.
OTHER WORDS YOU MIGHT USE ARE **dirty** **disgusting** **filthy** **horrible** **nasty** **revolting**
The opposite is **nice**

fragile *adjective*
Take care with the best china because it is fragile.
OTHER WORDS YOU MIGHT USE ARE **brittle** **delicate** **thin**
The opposite is **strong**

fragment *noun*
When Jo broke the teapot, Mum made her sweep up the fragments.
OTHER WORDS YOU MIGHT USE ARE **bit** **chip** **piece** **scrap**

frail *adjective*
I felt frail after my illness.
OTHER WORDS YOU MIGHT USE ARE **delicate** **feeble** **weak**
The opposite is **strong**

free *adjective*
1 The cat is free to wander about.
A PHRASE YOU MIGHT USE IS **at liberty**
2 Is the bathroom free?
OTHER WORDS ARE **available** **unoccupied** **vacant**

free *verb*
The prisoner asked the guards when they were going to free him.
OTHER VERBS YOU MIGHT USE ARE **to let out** **to liberate** **to release**
The opposite is **capture**

frequent *adjective*
Our picnic was spoiled by frequent showers.
OTHER WORDS YOU MIGHT USE ARE **many** **numerous** **repeated**

fresh *adjective*
1 fresh bread.
ANOTHER WORD IS **new**
The opposite is **stale**
2 fresh air.
OTHER WORDS YOU MIGHT USE ARE **clean** **cool** **pure**
3 fresh after a rest.
OTHER WORDS ARE **lively** **rested**
4 a fresh page.
OTHER WORDS ARE **different** **new** **unused**

friend *noun*
An informal word is **mate**.
A friend who fights on your side is an **ally**
A friend who works with you is a **partner**.
Someone you don't know very well is an **acquaintance**.
The opposite is **enemy**

friendly *adjective*
a friendly smile.
OTHER WORDS YOU MIGHT USE ARE **affectionate** **kind** **loving**
The opposite is **unfriendly**

frighten *verb*
Don't frighten the animals.
OTHER VERBS YOU MIGHT USE ARE **to alarm** **to scare** **to startle** **to terrify**
frightened *adjective*, see **afraid**
frightening *adjective*, see **terrible**

froth *noun*
The soap leaves froth in the bowl.
OTHER WORDS YOU MIGHT USE ARE **bubbles** **foam** **lather** **scum**

frown *verb*
Dad frowns when he is angry.
OTHER VERBS YOU MIGHT USE ARE **to look stern** **to scowl**

fruit *noun*
For fruit you can eat, see **food**

fuel *noun*
THINGS WE USE AS FUEL ARE
coal **electricity** **gas** **oil** **petrol** **wood**

full *adjective*
1 The bus was full.
OTHER WORDS YOU MIGHT USE ARE **crowded** **jammed** **packed**
2 My cup is full.
ANOTHER WORD IS **overflowing**
The opposite is **empty**

fun *noun*
We had lots of fun at Jo's party.
OTHER WORDS YOU MIGHT USE ARE **amusement** **enjoyment** **games** **jokes** **laughing** **pleasure**

funeral *noun*
KINDS OF FUNERAL ARE **burial** **cremation**

funny *adjective*
1 funny jokes.
OTHER WORDS YOU MIGHT USE ARE **amusing** **comic** **comical** **humorous** **laughable** **ridiculous** **witty**
The opposite is **serious**
2 The ice cream has a funny taste.
For other words, see **peculiar**

furious *adjective*
For other words, see **angry**

a
b
c
d
e
f
g
h
i
j
k
l
m
n
o
p
q
r
s
t
u
v
w
x
y
z

furniture *noun*

KINDS OF FURNITURE YOU PUT THINGS IN OR ON ARE
bookcase **bureau** **cabinet** **chest of drawers** **coffee table** **cupboard** **desk** **dresser** **sideboard** **table** **wardrobe**

KINDS OF FURNITURE YOU SIT ON ARE
armchair **chair** **pouffe** **rocking chair** **settee** **sofa** **stool**

KINDS OF FURNITURE YOU CAN SLEEP ON ARE
bed **cot** **couch** **divan**

furry *adjective*
furry animals.
OTHER WORDS YOU MIGHT USE ARE **fluffy** **hairy** **woolly**

fuss *noun*
There was a lot of fuss when a lion escaped from the zoo.
OTHER WORDS YOU MIGHT USE ARE **bother** **commotion** **excitement** **trouble** **uproar**

fussy *adjective*
Our cat is fussy about her food.
OTHER WORDS YOU MIGHT USE ARE **choosy** **particular**

Gg

gain *verb*
Sam gained first prize for swimming.
OTHER VERBS YOU MIGHT USE ARE **to earn** **to get** **to obtain** **to receive** **to win**

game *noun*
1 What's your favourite game?
OTHER WORDS YOU MIGHT USE ARE
amusement **entertainment** **pastime** **sport**
2 Let's have a game of chess.
OTHER WORDS ARE
competition **match** **tournament**
VARIOUS GAMES ARE
bingo **cards** **charades** **chess** **darts** **dominoes** **draughts** **hide-and-seek** **hopscotch** **ludo** **marbles** **skittles** **snooker** **table tennis** **tiddlywinks**
For other games, see **sport**

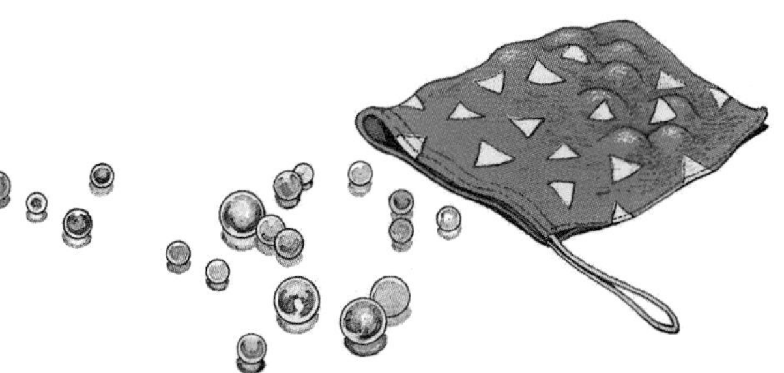
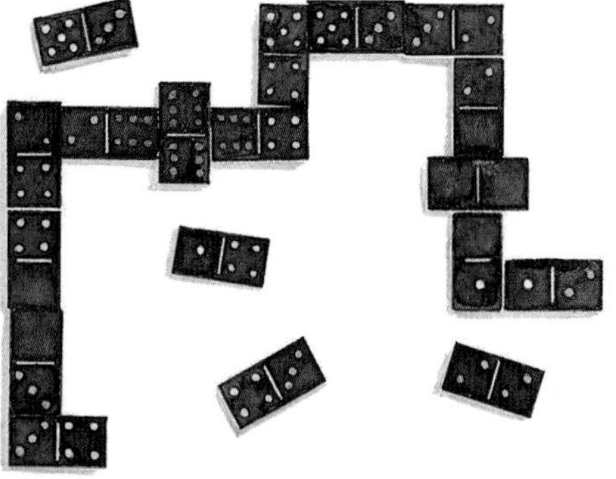

a b c d e f g h i j k l m n o p q r s t u v w x y z

gang *noun*
For other words, see **group**

gaol *noun*
Some people spell this word as 'jail'
OTHER WORDS ARE **dungeon** **prison**

gap *noun*
1 a gap in the fence.
OTHER WORDS YOU MIGHT USE ARE **break** **hole** **space**
2 a gap between lessons.
OTHER WORDS ARE **break** **interval** **pause** **rest**

garden *noun*, see opposite page

garment *noun*
For other words, see **clothes**

gasp *verb*
The smoke made us gasp.
OTHER VERBS YOU MIGHT USE ARE **to choke** **to pant** **to puff** **to wheeze**

gather *verb*
1 People gathered to watch the fire.
OTHER VERBS YOU MIGHT USE ARE **to assemble** **to crowd round** **to meet**
2 We gathered information for our project.
OTHER VERBS ARE **to collect** **to put together**

general *adjective*
1 The general opinion is that our team is the best.
OTHER WORDS YOU MIGHT USE ARE **common** **usual** **widespread**
2 He only gave us a general idea of what he wanted.
OTHER WORDS ARE **broad** **vague**

generous *adjective*
1 It was generous of Jo to share her sweets.
OTHER WORDS YOU MIGHT USE ARE **kind** **unselfish**
The opposite is **mean**
2 Mum gave us generous helpings of pudding.
OTHER WORDS ARE **big** **large** **sizeable**
The opposite is **small**

gentle *adjective*
1 a gentle kiss.
OTHER WORDS YOU MIGHT USE ARE **kind** **soft-hearted** **tender**
2 a gentle breeze.
OTHER WORDS ARE **pleasant** **slight**
The opposite is **rough**
3 gentle music.
OTHER WORDS ARE **quiet** **relaxing** **restful** **soft**
The opposite is **noisy**

genuine *adjective*
genuine gold.
ANOTHER WORD IS **real**
The opposite is **false**

garden *noun*

THINGS YOU GROW IN A GARDEN ARE

flowers **fruit** **shrubs** **trees** **vegetables**

PARTS OF A GARDEN ARE

border **compost heap** **flower bed** **greenhouse** **hedge** **lawn** **orchard** **path** **patio** **pond** **rockery** **shed** **shrubbery**

TOOLS YOU USE IN THE GARDEN ARE

broom **fork** **hoe** **lawnmower** **rake** **shears** **spade** **trowel** **watering can**

OTHER THINGS YOU USE IN THE GARDEN ARE

compost **fertilizer** **manure** **peat** **weedkiller**

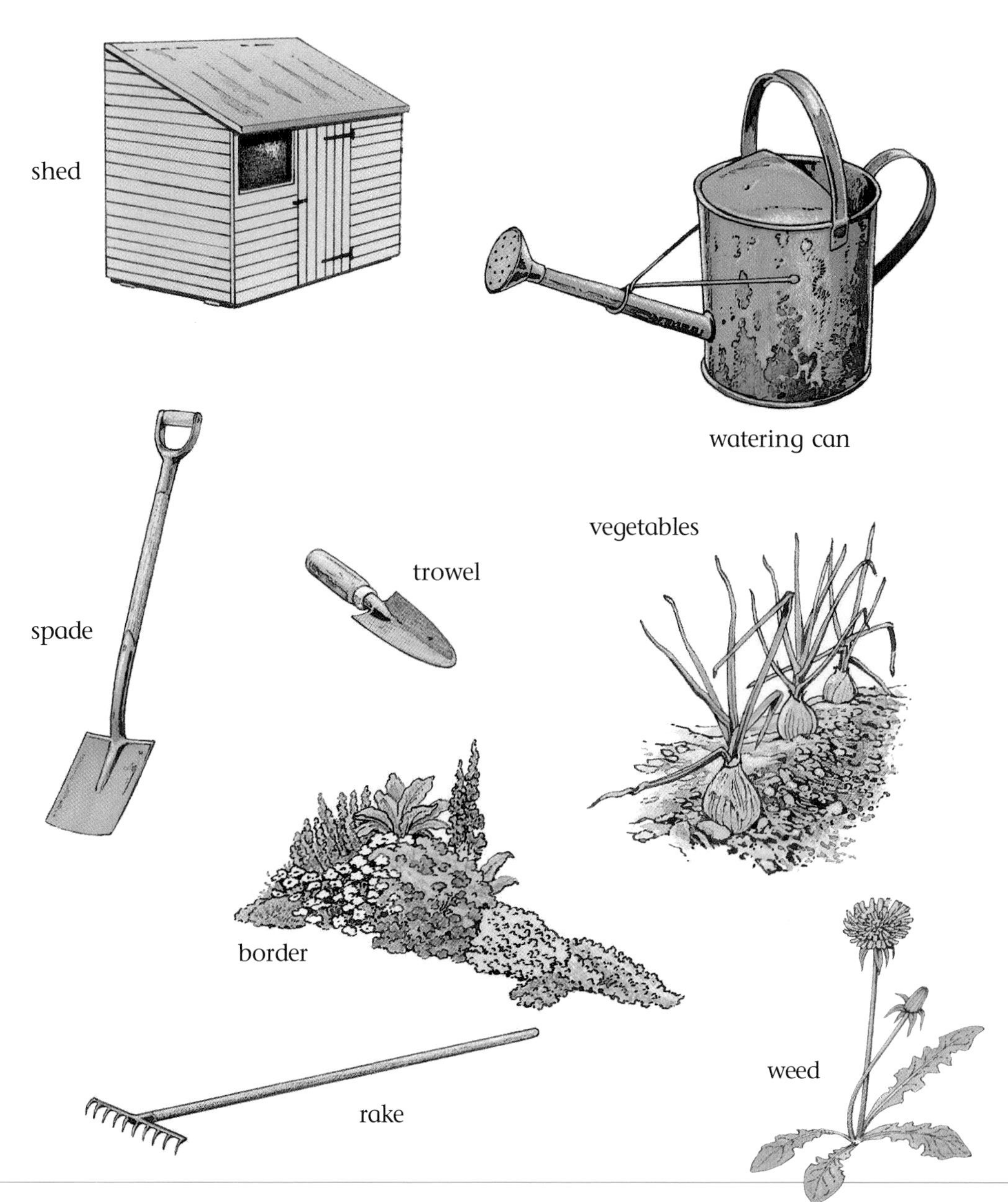

a b c d e f **g** h i j k l m n o p q r s t u v w x y z

get *verb*

THIS WORD HAS MANY USES. HERE ARE SOME OF THE WAYS YOU CAN USE IT, AND SOME OTHER WORDS YOU COULD CHOOSE

1 What did you get at the shop?
to buy **to obtain** **to purchase**

2 Sam got a nice present from Jo.
to be given **to receive**

3 Jo got first prize for swimming.
to earn **to win**

4 Did the thief get anything valuable?
to steal **to take**

5 Tell the dog to get the ball.
to bring **to fetch** **to retrieve**

6 I got cold waiting for the bus.
to become **to grow** **to turn**

ghost *noun*
Sam doesn't believe in ghosts.
OTHER WORDS YOU MIGHT USE ARE **phantom** **spectre** **spirit** (*informal*) **spook**

gift *noun*
1 a birthday gift.
ANOTHER WORD IS **present**
2 a gift to charity.
OTHER WORDS YOU MIGHT USE ARE **contribution** **donation** **offering**

give *verb*
1 I gave some sweets to Sam.
OTHER VERBS YOU MIGHT USE ARE **to hand over** **to offer** **to pass** **to present**
2 Dad gives money to charity.
OTHER VERBS ARE **to contribute** **to donate**
3 Our teacher gave us pencils to write with.
OTHER VERBS ARE **to provide with** **to supply with**
4 Jo gave out the books.
OTHER VERBS ARE **to deal out** **to distribute** **to hand out**

glass *noun*
A sheet of glass in a window is a **pane**.
A glass you drink out of is a **tumbler**.
Glasses you wear to help you see better are **spectacles**.
GLASSES YOU LOOK THROUGH TO MAKE DISTANT OBJECTS SEEM NEARER ARE
binoculars **field glasses**

gloomy *adjective*
1 a gloomy room.
OTHER WORDS YOU MIGHT USE ARE **cheerless** **dark** **depressing** **dismal**
2 a gloomy face.
OTHER WORDS ARE **depressed** **glum** **miserable** **sad** **unhappy**
The opposite is **cheerful**

glow *verb*
The ashes of the bonfire glowed in the dark.
OTHER VERBS YOU MIGHT USE ARE **to gleam** **to shine**

glue *noun*
OTHER SUBSTANCES YOU STICK THINGS WITH ARE **adhesive** **cement** **gum** **paste**

go *verb*
1 Jo has gone to the shops.
OTHER VERBS YOU MIGHT USE ARE **to travel** **to walk**
For more verbs, see **move**
2 What time does the train go?
OTHER VERBS ARE **to depart** **to leave** **to set out** **to start**
3 This road goes into the town.
OTHER VERBS ARE **to continue** **to lead**
4 My watch doesn't go.
OTHER VERBS ARE **to function** **to operate** **to work**
5 She went quiet when she heard the bad news.
OTHER VERBS ARE **to become** **to grow** **to turn**

good *adjective*
SOME WORDS WHICH MEAN GOOD IN A GENERAL WAY ARE
lovely **marvellous** **nice** **wonderful**

SOME INFORMAL WORDS ARE
brilliant **fabulous** **great**

THESE ARE SOME PARTICULAR WAYS WE USE THE WORD, AND SOME OF THE OTHER WORDS YOU MIGHT USE
1 good work.
correct **faultless** **perfect** **thorough**
2 a good friend.
caring **considerate** **faithful** **generous** **helpful** **honest** **kind** **loving** **loyal** **reliable** **thoughtful** **true**
3 a good dog.
obedient **well-behaved**
4 a good footballer.
clever **skilful** **skilled** **talented**
5 a good film.
entertaining **exciting** **interesting**
The opposite is **bad**

govern *verb*
At election time, we choose people to govern the country.
OTHER VERBS YOU MIGHT USE ARE **to be in charge of** **to control** **to look after** **to manage** **to rule** **to run**

government *noun*
The person in charge of the government is the **prime minister**.
The people who help the prime minister run the government are the **cabinet**.
Decisions about how to govern the country are discussed in **parliament**.

grab *verb*
For other verbs, see **seize**

graceful *adjective*
graceful movements.
OTHER WORDS YOU MIGHT USE ARE **attractive** **elegant** **flowing**
The opposite is **clumsy**

a b c d e f **g** h i j k l m n o p q r s t u v w x y z

gradual *adjective*
There was a gradual improvement in the weather.
OTHER WORDS YOU MIGHT USE ARE **slow** **steady**
The opposite is **sudden**

grand *adjective*
The wedding was a grand occasion.
For other words, see **great**

grant *verb*
The fairy granted Cinderella what she wanted.
OTHER VERBS YOU MIGHT USE ARE **to allow** **to give**

grass *noun*
An area of grass in a garden is a **lawn**.
An area of grass on a farm is a **field** or **meadow** or **pasture.**
An area of grass in a village is a **green**.
A large area of grass in North America is a **prairie**.
A large area of grass in South Africa is **veld** or **veldt**.

grateful *adjective*
I was grateful for her help.
OTHER WORDS YOU MIGHT USE ARE **appreciative** **thankful**
The opposite is **ungrateful**

grave *adjective*
Mum looked grave when she heard the bad news.
OTHER WORDS YOU MIGHT USE ARE **gloomy** **serious** **solemn** **thoughtful**
The opposite is **cheerful**

greasy *adjective*
I don't like greasy chips.
OTHER WORDS YOU MIGHT USE ARE **fatty** **oily**

great *adjective*
1 a great storm.
OTHER WORDS YOU MIGHT USE ARE **huge** **tremendous**
For more words, see **big**
2 a great occasion.
OTHER WORDS ARE **grand** **important** **impressive** **magnificent** **spectacular** **splendid**
3 a great piece of music.
OTHER WORDS ARE **classic** **famous** **well-known**
4 We had a great time.
OTHER WORDS ARE **excellent** **marvellous** **wonderful**
For more words, see **good**

greedy *adjective*
It was greedy to eat all the cake.
OTHER WORDS YOU MIGHT USE ARE (*informal*) **piggish** **selfish**

greet *verb*
I greeted our guests at the door.
ANOTHER VERB IS **to welcome**

grief *noun*
I sympathized with Jo's grief when the dog died.
OTHER WORDS YOU MIGHT USE ARE **misery** **sadness** **sorrow** **unhappiness**

grim *adjective*
a grim look on someone's face.
OTHER WORDS YOU MIGHT USE ARE **bad-tempered** **gloomy** **serious** **severe** **stern** **unfriendly**
The opposite is **happy**

groan *verb*
The injured man groaned because of the pain.
OTHER VERBS YOU MIGHT USE ARE **to moan** **to wail**

grope *verb*
I groped about to find the light switch.
OTHER VERBS YOU MIGHT USE ARE **to feel** **to fumble**

ground *noun*
1 Potatoes grow in the ground.
OTHER WORDS YOU MIGHT USE ARE
earth **soil**
2 We play football on a piece of ground behind the school.
ANOTHER WORD IS
land

PLACES WHERE YOU CAN PLAY GAMES ARE
playground **playing field** **pitch** **recreation ground** **stadium**

Ground where you build something is a **plot** or **site**.
A big area of ground owned by one person or used for a special purpose is an **estate**.
The grounds of a big school or college are called a **campus**.

group *noun*, see next page

grow *verb*
1 Jo grows flowers in the garden.
OTHER VERBS YOU MIGHT USE ARE **to cultivate** **to plant** **to raise**
2 The seeds only grow when the weather is warm.
OTHER VERBS ARE **to germinate** **to spring up** **to sprout**
3 Jo looks to see how much her vegetables have grown.
OTHER VERBS ARE **to develop** **to fill out** **to get bigger** **to get taller** **to increase**

grown-up *adjective*
OTHER WORDS YOU MIGHT USE ARE **adult** **mature**

gruesome *adjective*
I didn't like the gruesome picture of the accident.
OTHER WORDS YOU MIGHT USE ARE **disgusting** **gory** **horrible** **nasty** **sickening**

gruff *adjective*
a gruff voice.
OTHER WORDS YOU MIGHT USE ARE **deep** **harsh** **hoarse** **rough**

grumble *verb*
Mum doesn't like it when Sam grumbles about the food.
OTHER VERBS YOU MIGHT USE ARE **to complain** (*informal*) **to moan**

a b c d e f **g** h i j k l m n o p q r s t u v w x y z

group *noun*
OTHER WORDS YOU MIGHT USE ARE
a group of things:
assortment **collection** **set**
a group of people:
assembly **company** **crowd** **gang** **gathering** **mob** **throng**
an organized group of people:
alliance **army** **association** **club** **force** **society** **team**
a group of musicians:
band **choir** **chorus** **orchestra**
OTHER GROUPS ARE:
An **army** of ants.
A **brood** of chicks.
A **bunch** of flowers.
A **class** of children.
A **clump** of trees.
A **clutch** of eggs.
A **colony** of ants.
A **congregation** in church.
A **constellation** or **galaxy** of stars.
A **convoy** or **fleet** of ships.
A **covey** of partridges.
A **crew** of sailors.
A **flock** of birds.
A **flock** of sheep.
A **gaggle** of geese.
A **gang** of robbers.
A **herd** of cows.
A **herd** of elephants.
A **leap** of leopards.
A **litter** of puppies.
A **pack** of wolves.
A **pride** of lions.
A **school** of whales.
A **shoal** of fish.
A **swarm** of bees.
A **troop** of soldiers.

guard *verb*
The farmer's dog guards the sheep.
OTHER VERBS YOU MIGHT USE ARE **to care for** **to defend** **to look after** **to protect** **to shield** **to tend** **to watch over**

guess *verb*
1 I guess you are hungry.
OTHER VERBS YOU MIGHT USE ARE **to assume** **to suppose**
2 Jo tried to guess how many sweets there were in the jar.
ANOTHER VERB IS **to estimate**

guide *verb*
I wish someone would guide us out of this maze!
OTHER VERBS YOU MIGHT USE ARE **to direct** **to escort** **to lead** **to steer**

guilty *adjective*
He was guilty of stealing.
The opposite is **innocent**

gun *noun*
KINDS OF GUN ARE
airgun **cannon** **machine-gun** **pistol** **revolver** **rifle** **shotgun**

Hh

habit *noun*
1 It's our habit to send people a card when they have a birthday.
OTHER WORDS YOU MIGHT USE ARE **custom** **practice** **tradition**
2 Smoking is a bad habit.
ANOTHER WORD IS **addiction**

hair *noun*
DIFFERENT WAYS PEOPLE DO THEIR HAIR ARE
in curls **with a fringe** **permed** **in a pigtail** **in plaits** **in a ponytail**

WORDS TO DESCRIBE THE COLOUR OF PEOPLE'S HAIR ARE
auburn **black** **blond** **brown** **fair** **ginger** **grey** **red** **silver** **white**

WORDS FOR HAIR ON AN ANIMAL ARE
bristles **fur**

hairy *adjective*
OTHER WORDS YOU MIGHT USE ARE **bristly** **furry** **fuzzy** **shaggy** **woolly**

halt *verb*
You must halt if the light is red.
OTHER VERBS YOU MIGHT USE ARE **to draw up** **to pull up** **to stop**

hand *noun*
For other parts of the body, see **body**

handicap *noun*
When you run for the bus, it's a handicap to have lots of shopping.

OTHER WORDS YOU MIGHT USE ARE
disadvantage **drawback** **hindrance** **inconvenience**

handicapped *adjective*
It's hard for you to do some things if you are handicapped.

WAYS YOU CAN BE HANDICAPPED ARE
blind **deaf** **disabled** **dumb** **lame** **limbless** **paralysed**

handle *verb*

1 Handle the kittens carefully.
OTHER VERBS YOU MIGHT USE ARE **to feel** **to stroke** **to touch**

2 The rider handled the frightened horse well.
OTHER VERBS ARE **to control** **to deal with** **to look after** **to manage**

handsome *adjective*

a handsome man.
OTHER WORDS YOU MIGHT USE ARE **attractive** **good-looking**
The opposite is **ugly**

hang *verb*

to hang on to something Hang on to the rope!
OTHER VERBS YOU MIGHT USE ARE **to cling on to** **to grasp** **to hold** **to seize**
to hang about Don't hang about after school.
OTHER VERBS ARE **to be slow** **to dawdle** **to delay** **to loiter**

happen *verb*

Did anything interesting happen?
OTHER VERBS YOU MIGHT USE ARE **to occur** **to take place**

happy *adjective*

Jo is happy when the sun shines.
OTHER WORDS YOU MIGHT USE ARE **cheerful** **contented** **delighted** **glad** **good-humoured** **joyful** **light-hearted** **merry** **pleased**
The opposite is **sad**

harbour *noun*

PLACES WHERE SHIPS UNLOAD GOODS ARE
docks **port**
A place where you see lots of **pleasure boats** is a **marina**.

PLACES WHERE SHIPS TIE UP ARE
jetty **landing stage** **mooring** **pier** **quay** **wharf**

hard *adjective*

1 hard concrete.
OTHER WORDS YOU MIGHT USE ARE **firm** **rigid** **solid**
The opposite is **soft**

2 hard work.
OTHER WORDS ARE **exhausting** **tiring** **tough**
The opposite is **easy**

3 a hard problem.
OTHER WORDS ARE **complex** **complicated** **difficult** **puzzling**
The opposite is **simple**

4 a hard punishment.
OTHER WORDS ARE **cruel** **harsh** **merciless** **severe**
The opposite is **merciful**

hardly *adverb*

I'm so tired I can hardly walk.
OTHER WORDS YOU MIGHT USE ARE **barely** **only just** **scarcely**

harm *verb*

1 Jo would never harm an animal.
OTHER VERBS YOU MIGHT USE ARE **to hurt** **to injure** **to wound**

2 Did the accident harm the car?
OTHER VERBS ARE **to damage** **to spoil**

harmful *adjective*

It can be harmful to take too much medicine.

OTHER WORDS YOU MIGHT USE ARE **bad** **damaging** **dangerous**

harsh *adjective*

1 The teacher's harsh voice showed that she was angry.

OTHER WORDS YOU MIGHT USE ARE **grating** **rough** **shrill**

2 We blinked in the harsh light.

OTHER WORDS ARE **brilliant** **dazzling** **glaring**

3 We thought the decision to send the player off was harsh.

OTHER WORDS ARE **cruel** **hard** **merciless** **severe**

The opposite is **gentle**

hasty *adjective*

The teacher said we were too hasty doing our work.

OTHER WORDS YOU MIGHT USE ARE **careless** **hurried** **impetuous** **quick** (*informal*) **slapdash** **thoughtless**

hat *noun*

DIFFERENT THINGS PEOPLE WEAR ON THEIR HEADS ARE

beret **bonnet** **cap** **crash helmet** **crown** **helmet** **hood** **turban**

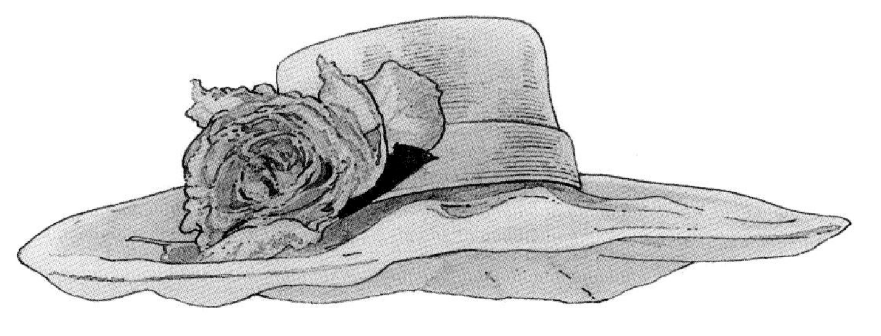

hate *verb*

Sam can't understand why some people hate cabbage.

OTHER VERBS YOU MIGHT USE ARE **to detest** **to dislike** **to loathe**

The opposite is **like**

a b c d e f g **h** i j k l m n o p q r s t u v w x y z

haul *verb*
We hauled our sledge to the top of the hill.
OTHER VERBS YOU MIGHT USE ARE **to drag** **to draw** **to pull** **to tow** **to tug**

have *verb*
THIS VERB HAS MANY USES. HERE ARE SOME OF THE WAYS YOU CAN USE IT, AND SOME OTHER VERBS YOU COULD CHOOSE.
1 Jo has a new kitten.
to own **to possess**
2 Jo's class has thirty pupils.
to consist of **to contain** **to include**
3 I was having a good time, but Sam had a cold.
to enjoy **to experience** **to suffer**
4 I had some nice presents on my birthday.
to be given **to get** **to obtain** **to receive**

hazy *adjective*
The view from the top of the hill was hazy.
OTHER WORDS YOU MIGHT USE ARE **blurred** **foggy** **misty**
The opposite is **clear**

head *noun*
For other parts of your body, see **body**

heal *verb*
The ointment helps to heal spots.
OTHER VERBS YOU MIGHT USE ARE **to cure** **to make better** **to remedy**

health *noun*, see opposite page

healthy *adjective*
We all want to be healthy.
OTHER WORDS YOU MIGHT USE ARE **fit** **sound** **strong** **well**
The opposite is **ill**

heap *noun*
Sam left his clothes in a heap.
OTHER WORDS ARE **mound** **pile** **stack**

hear *verb*
Did you hear the weather forecast?
ANOTHER VERB IS **to listen to**

heart *noun*
The explorers were lost in the heart of the jungle.
OTHER WORDS YOU MIGHT USE ARE **centre** **core** **middle**

heat *noun*
The cat loves the heat from the fire.
OTHER WORDS YOU MIGHT USE ARE **glow** **warmth**

heat *verb*
VARIOUS WAYS TO HEAT THINGS ARE **to boil** **to burn** **to melt** **to scald** **to scorch**
For other verbs, see **cook**

health *noun*
We all want to have good health.

OTHER WORDS YOU MIGHT USE ARE
fitness **strength**

PEOPLE WHO LOOK AFTER OUR HEALTH ARE
doctor **health visitor** **nurse**
A **paediatrician** is a specialist in children's health.
A **midwife** helps to deliver babies.
A **surgeon** does operations.
A **dentist** looks after your teeth.
An **optician** looks at your eyes.
A **physiotherapist** helps people recover from injuries.
A **pharmacist** makes up medicines.
A person who looks after the health of animals is a **vet** or **veterinary surgeon**.

PLACES WHERE WE CAN GET HELP WITH OUR HEALTH ARE
clinic **health centre** **hospital** **nursing home** **surgery**
We can get medicines at a **chemist's** or a **pharmacy**.
OTHER WORDS FOR MEDICINE ARE
cure **remedy** **treatment**
Medicine you get with a note from the doctor is a **prescription**.
SOME MEDICINES YOU MIGHT TAKE ARE
antibiotic **aspirin** **capsule** **drug** **gargle** **linctus** **lotion** **ointment** **pill** **tablet** **tonic**

ILLNESSES PEOPLE CAN HAVE ARE
allergy **appendicitis** **arthritis** **asthma**
bilious attack **bronchitis** **cancer** **catarrh**
chickenpox **chill** **cholera** **cold**
constipation **cough** **diabetes** **diarrhoea**
diphtheria **dysentery** **earache** **epilepsy**
fever **flu** **hay fever** **headache**
indigestion **influenza** **jaundice** **leprosy**
leukaemia **malaria** **measles** **migraine**
mumps **paralysis** **plague** **pneumonia**
polio **rabies** **rheumatism** **scarlet fever**
seasickness **smallpox** **spina bifida** **stroke**
sunstroke **tonsillitis** **toothache** **tuberculosis**
typhoid **typhus** **whooping cough**

COMPLAINTS YOU CAN GET ON YOUR SKIN ARE
abscess **blister** **boil** **chilblains**
corns **dermatitis** **sty** **ulcer**
verruca **wart**

heater *noun*
VARIOUS KINDS OF HEATER ARE
central heating **coal fire** **convector** **electric fire** **gas fire**
immersion heater **radiator** **stove**

heavy *adjective*
a heavy load.
ANOTHER WORD IS **weighty**
The opposite is **light**

a b c d e f g **h** i j k l m n o p q r s t u v w x y z

help *noun*
The policeman radioed for help.
OTHER WORDS YOU MIGHT USE ARE **assistance** **backing** **back-up** **support**

help *verb*
1 I help Dad with the washing up.
OTHER VERBS YOU MIGHT USE ARE **to assist** **to support**
2 I couldn't help laughing.
ANOTHER VERB IS **to stop**

helpful *adjective*
1 Our neighbours are very helpful.
OTHER WORDS YOU MIGHT USE ARE **considerate** **kind** **willing**
2 She gave me some helpful advice.
OTHER WORDS ARE **useful** **valuable**

helping *noun*
I had a big helping of pudding.
OTHER WORDS YOU MIGHT USE ARE **portion** **serving**

hesitate *verb*
Jo hesitated before diving in.
OTHER VERBS YOU MIGHT USE ARE **to delay** **to pause** **to wait** **to waver**

hide *verb*
He hid his money under the carpet.
OTHER VERBS YOU MIGHT USE ARE **to conceal** **to cover** **to put away**

high *adjective*
1 a high building.
OTHER WORDS YOU MIGHT USE ARE **lofty** **tall**
2 high prices.
ANOTHER WORD IS **expensive**
The opposite is **low**

hill *noun*
1 We climbed a hill to see the view.
OTHER WORDS YOU MIGHT USE ARE **mountain** **peak**
2 It's hard cycling up that hill.
OTHER WORDS ARE **incline** **rise** **slope**

hinder *verb*
The firemen were angry because the people watching the fire hindered them.
OTHER VERBS YOU MIGHT USE ARE **to check** **to delay** **to get in the way of** **to hamper**

hint *noun*
1 I can't guess the answer—give me a hint.
ANOTHER WORD IS **clue**
2 The expert gave us some hints on playing chess.
OTHER WORDS ARE **suggestion** **tip**

hit *verb*

VARIOUS WAYS TO HIT THINGS ARE

to bang (*informal*) **to bash** **to batter** **to beat** **to bump into** **to collide with** **to hammer** **to knock** **to rap** **to smash** **to strike** **to tap** **to thump** (*informal*) **to wallop** (*informal*) **to whack** **to whip**

A goat may **butt** you with horns.
Teachers used to **cane** pupils as a punishment.
You can **flog** someone with a whip.
You **jog** someone with your elbow.
You **kick** with your foot.
You **lash** or **thrash** someone with a whip.
You **poke** or **prod** with a stick.
You **punch** with your fist.
You can **ram** a vehicle into something.
You **slap** or **smack** or **spank** someone with your hand.
You **stub** your toe on something.
You **swat** a fly.

hoarse *adjective*

Dad's voice was hoarse because he had a cold.
OTHER WORDS YOU MIGHT USE ARE **croaking** **deep** **husky** **rough**

hobby *noun*

My hobbies are skating and chess.
OTHER WORDS YOU MIGHT USE ARE **interest** **pastime**

hold *verb*

1 I held the ladder while Dad climbed up.
OTHER VERBS YOU MIGHT USE ARE **to grasp** **to grip** **to hang on to** **to seize** **to support**

2 Sam held the baby carefully.
OTHER VERBS ARE **to carry** **to embrace** **to hug**

3 The box holds all Jo's toys.
ANOTHER VERB IS **to contain**

hole *noun*

1 a hole in the ground.
OTHER WORDS YOU MIGHT USE ARE **burrow** **cave** **crater** **pit** **pothole** **tunnel**

2 a hole in the fence.
OTHER WORDS ARE **break** **chink** **crack** **gap** **opening**

3 a hole in your jacket.
OTHER WORDS ARE **slit** **split** **tear**

4 a hole in a tyre.
OTHER WORDS ARE **leak** **puncture**

holiday *noun*

VARIOUS KINDS OF HOLIDAY ARE

adventure holiday **activity holiday** **camping holiday** **cruise** **honeymoon** **package holiday** **safari** **seaside holiday** **touring holiday**

PLACES PEOPLE STAY ON HOLIDAY ARE

bed and breakfast **camp site** **guest house** **hotel** **motel** **self-catering accommodation** **youth hostel**

a b c d e f g **h** i j k l m n o p q r s t u v w x y z

hollow *noun*
a hollow in the ground.
OTHER WORDS YOU MIGHT USE ARE **depression** **dip** **hole** **valley**

holy *adjective*
The temple is a holy place.
OTHER WORDS YOU MIGHT USE ARE **religious** **sacred**

home *noun*, see opposite page

honest *adjective*
Mum believed Sam because he is always honest.
OTHER WORDS YOU MIGHT USE ARE **sincere** **trustworthy** **truthful**
The opposite is **dishonest**

hop *verb*
Dad hopped up and down when he dropped the hammer on his foot.
OTHER VERBS YOU MIGHT USE ARE **to jump** **to leap** **to spring**

hopeful *adjective*
I'm hopeful that my cold will be better tomorrow.
OTHER WORDS YOU MIGHT USE ARE **confident** **optimistic**

hopeless *adjective*
Sam's friend is hopeless at games.
OTHER WORDS YOU MIGHT USE ARE **no good** **useless**

horizontal *adjective*
A snooker table must be perfectly horizontal.
OTHER WORDS YOU MIGHT USE ARE **flat** **level**
The opposite is **vertical**

horrible *adjective*
1 a horrible taste.
OTHER WORDS YOU MIGHT USE ARE **horrid** **nasty** **unpleasant**
2 a horrible shock.
OTHER WORDS ARE **dreadful** **frightening** **terrible**

horror *noun*
We were filled with horror when the huge beast ran towards us.
OTHER WORDS YOU MIGHT USE ARE **dread** **fear** **terror**

horse *noun*
VARIOUS WORDS FOR HORSE ARE
carthorse **nag** **piebald** **pony**
racehorse **shire-horse** **steed**
A female horse is a **mare**.
A male horse is a **stallion**.
A young horse is a **colt** or **foal**.

home *noun*

PLACES WHERE PEOPLE LIVE ARE

apartment bungalow caravan chalet cottage council house detached house farmhouse flat maisonette manor house mansion mobile home semi-detached house terrace house thatched cottage

DIFFERENT ROOMS IN A HOME ARE

attic bathroom bedroom cellar cloakroom conservatory dining room drawing room hall kitchen landing larder lavatory living room loft lounge pantry parlour passage porch scullery sitting room study toilet WC

cottage

manor house

terrace house

bungalow

a b c d e f g **h** i j k l m n o p q r s t u v w x y z

hospital *noun*
For other places where you can go if you are ill, see **health**

hostile *adjective*
I didn't like the opposing team's hostile comments.
OTHER WORDS YOU MIGHT USE ARE **aggressive** **threatening** **unfriendly**
The opposite is **friendly**

hot *adjective*
1 a hot fire.
OTHER WORDS YOU MIGHT USE ARE **blazing** **glowing** **red-hot** **roasting** **scorching** **sizzling**
2 hot weather.
ANOTHER WORD IS **sweltering**
3 hot water.
OTHER WORDS ARE **boiling** **scalding**
For other words, see **warm**
The opposite is **cold**
4 hot-tasting food.
OTHER WORDS ARE **peppery** **spicy**

hotel *noun*
For other places where people stay, see **holiday**

house *noun*
For places where people live, see **home**

hug *verb*
Granny hugged us and said goodbye.
OTHER VERBS YOU MIGHT USE ARE **to cuddle** **to embrace** **to hold**

huge *adjective*
For other words, see **big**

human *noun*
For other words, see **person**

humble *adjective*
Sam was humble about winning a prize.
ANOTHER WORD IS **modest**
The opposite is **proud**

humorous *adjective*
We laughed at her humorous remark.
OTHER WORDS YOU MIGHT USE ARE **amusing** **comic** **funny** **witty**
The opposite is **serious**

hump *noun*
They put humps in the road to make cars go slower.
OTHER WORDS YOU MIGHT USE ARE **bulge** **bump** **lump**

hunger *noun*
1 Will a sandwich satisfy your hunger?
ANOTHER WORD IS **appetite**
2 In some countries many people die of hunger.
OTHER WORDS ARE **famine** **starvation**

hungry *adjective*
I was hungry after my long walk.
OTHER WORDS YOU MIGHT USE ARE **famished** (*informal*) **peckish** **ravenous** **starved** **starving**
If you eat more food than you need you are **greedy**.

hunt *verb*
1 I think it's cruel to hunt foxes.
OTHER VERBS YOU MIGHT USE ARE **to chase** **to pursue** **to stalk** **to track down**
2 We hunted for Mum's lost purse.
OTHER VERBS ARE **to look for** **to search for** **to seek**

hurry *verb*
I hurried home from school.
OTHER VERBS YOU MIGHT USE ARE **to dash** **to hasten** **to hurtle** **to race** **to run** **to rush** **to speed**
The opposite is **dawdle**

hurt *verb*
1 The cut on my hand hurts.
OTHER VERBS YOU MIGHT USE ARE **to ache** **to be painful** **to smart** **to sting** **to throb**
2 Don't hurt the kittens!
OTHER VERBS ARE **to damage** **to harm** **to injure** **to torment** **to wound**

Ii

ice *noun*
A river of ice is a **glacier**.
A large lump of ice floating in the sea is an **iceberg**.
A finger of ice hanging down is an **icicle**.
Dangerous ice on the road is **black ice**.

idea *noun*
1 I've got an idea!
OTHER WORDS YOU MIGHT USE ARE (*informal*) **brainwave** **plan** **suggestion** **thought**
2 I have an idea that you are tired.
OTHER WORDS ARE **belief** **feeling** **impression** **opinion**

ideal *adjective*
The weather was ideal for a picnic.
OTHER WORDS YOU MIGHT USE ARE **excellent** **just right** **perfect** **suitable**

idle *adjective*
Jo is never idle, even in the holidays.
OTHER WORDS YOU MIGHT USE ARE **doing nothing** **inactive** **lazy** **unemployed** **unoccupied**
The opposite is **busy**

a b c d e f g h i j k l m n o p q r s t u v w x y z

ignorant *adjective*

1 ignorant of the truth.

ANOTHER WORD IS **unaware**

The opposite is **aware**

2 an ignorant fool.

OTHER WORDS ARE **foolish** **stupid** **unintelligent**

The opposite is **clever**

ignore *verb*

You get into trouble if you ignore what the teacher says.

OTHER VERBS YOU MIGHT USE ARE **to disobey** **to disregard** **to neglect** **to overlook** **to take no notice of**

ill *adjective*

Sam stayed away from school because he was ill.

OTHER WORDS YOU MIGHT USE ARE **indisposed** **in poor health** (*informal*) **poorly** **sick** **unwell**

The opposite is **healthy**

For other words, see **health**

illegal *adjective*

Stealing is illegal.

OTHER WORDS YOU MIGHT USE ARE **banned** **criminal** **forbidden** **unlawful**

The opposite is **legal**

illness *noun*

OTHER WORDS YOU MIGHT USE ARE **ailment** (*informal*) **bug** **complaint** **disease** **infection** **malady** **sickness**

For other words, see **health**

imaginary *adjective*

Unicorns are imaginary animals.

OTHER WORDS YOU MIGHT USE ARE **fictitious** **invented** **made-up** **non-existent** **unreal**

The opposite is **real**

imagine *verb*

You didn't really see a ghost: you only imagined it.

OTHER VERBS YOU MIGHT USE ARE **to dream** **to invent** **to make up** **to picture** **to think**

imitate *verb*

The budgie can imitate Jo's voice.

OTHER VERBS YOU MIGHT USE ARE **to copy** **to impersonate** **to reproduce**

imitation *noun*

It isn't real—it's an imitation.

OTHER WORDS YOU MIGHT USE ARE **copy** **counterfeit** **fake** **forgery** **likeness** **reproduction**

immediate *adjective*

Granny wants an immediate answer to her invitation.

OTHER WORDS YOU MIGHT USE ARE **instant** **prompt**

For more words, see **quick**

impatient *adjective*

We were impatient to begin.

OTHER WORDS YOU MIGHT USE ARE **anxious** **eager**

The opposite is **patient**

impertinent *adjective*
Teachers don't like impertinent comments from the children.
OTHER WORDS YOU MIGHT USE ARE **cheeky** **impolite** **improper** **impudent** **insolent** **rude**
The opposite is **polite**

important *adjective*
1 The important thing in swimming is to breathe properly.
OTHER WORDS YOU MIGHT USE ARE **basic** **chief** **essential** **main** **necessary**
2 an important person.
OTHER WORDS ARE **famous** **great** **notable** **powerful** **respected** **well-known**
3 an important message.
OTHER WORDS ARE **serious** **urgent**
4 an important event.
OTHER WORDS ARE **big** **major** **significant** **special**
The opposite is **unimportant**

impression *noun*
I have the impression that you are bored.
OTHER WORDS YOU MIGHT USE ARE **feeling** **idea** **opinion**

impressive *adjective*
an impressive occasion.
OTHER WORDS YOU MIGHT USE ARE **grand** **great** **magnificent** **memorable** **spectacular** **splendid** **wonderful**

improve *verb*
1 Jo's swimming has improved.
OTHER VERBS YOU MIGHT USE ARE **to develop** **to get better** **to progress**
2 Go over your work and try to improve it.
OTHER VERBS ARE **to make better** **to revise**

improvise *verb*
We improvised some music.
OTHER VERBS YOU MIGHT USE ARE **to invent** **to make up**

include *verb*
The packet includes everything you need to make a cake.
OTHER VERBS YOU MIGHT USE ARE **to consist of** **to contain**

inconvenient *adjective*
It is inconvenient to visit auntie today.
OTHER WORDS YOU MIGHT USE ARE **awkward** **troublesome**
The opposite is **convenient**

incorrect *adjective*
an incorrect answer.
OTHER WORDS YOU MIGHT USE ARE **false** **inaccurate** **mistaken** **untrue** **wrong**
The opposite is **correct**

increase *verb*
1 They increased the number of children in our class.
OTHER VERBS YOU MIGHT USE ARE **to add to** **to make bigger** **to raise**
2 The noise increased as the train got nearer.
OTHER VERBS ARE **to get louder** **to rise**
to increase in size
OTHER VERBS YOU MIGHT USE ARE **to get bigger** **to expand** **to swell**
The opposite is **decrease**

a b c d e f g h **i** j k l m n o p q r s t u v w x y z

incredible *adjective*
His story about dinosaurs was incredible.
OTHER WORDS YOU MIGHT USE ARE **far-fetched** **unbelievable** **unconvincing** **unlikely**

infectious *adjective*
an infectious disease.
ANOTHER WORD IS **catching**

inflate *verb*
to inflate a tyre.
OTHER VERBS YOU MIGHT USE ARE **to blow up** **to pump up**

influence *verb*
1 Does the weather influence the way you behave?
ANOTHER VERB IS **to affect**
2 Don't try to influence the referee!
OTHER VERBS YOU MIGHT USE ARE **to bribe** **to persuade**

inform *verb*
The teacher informed my mother that I was ill.
OTHER VERBS YOU MIGHT USE ARE **to notify** **to tell**

informal *adjective*
1 informal clothes.
OTHER WORDS YOU MIGHT USE ARE **casual** **comfortable**
2 an informal party.
OTHER WORDS ARE **easygoing** **friendly** **relaxed**
The opposite is **formal**

information *noun*
1 We rang up to get some information about the accident.
OTHER WORDS YOU MIGHT USE ARE **facts** **knowledge** **news**
2 We put the information into the computer.
ANOTHER WORD IS **data**

injure *verb*
Did you injure yourself when you fell over?
OTHER VERBS YOU MIGHT USE ARE **to damage** **to harm** **to hurt**

injury *noun*
For other words, see **wound**

innocent *adjective*
The judge declared that the accused man was innocent.
OTHER WORDS YOU MIGHT USE ARE **blameless** **guiltless**
The opposite is **guilty**

inquisitive *adjective*
It's rude to be inquisitive about other people's affairs.
OTHER WORDS YOU MIGHT USE ARE **curious** **nosy** **prying**

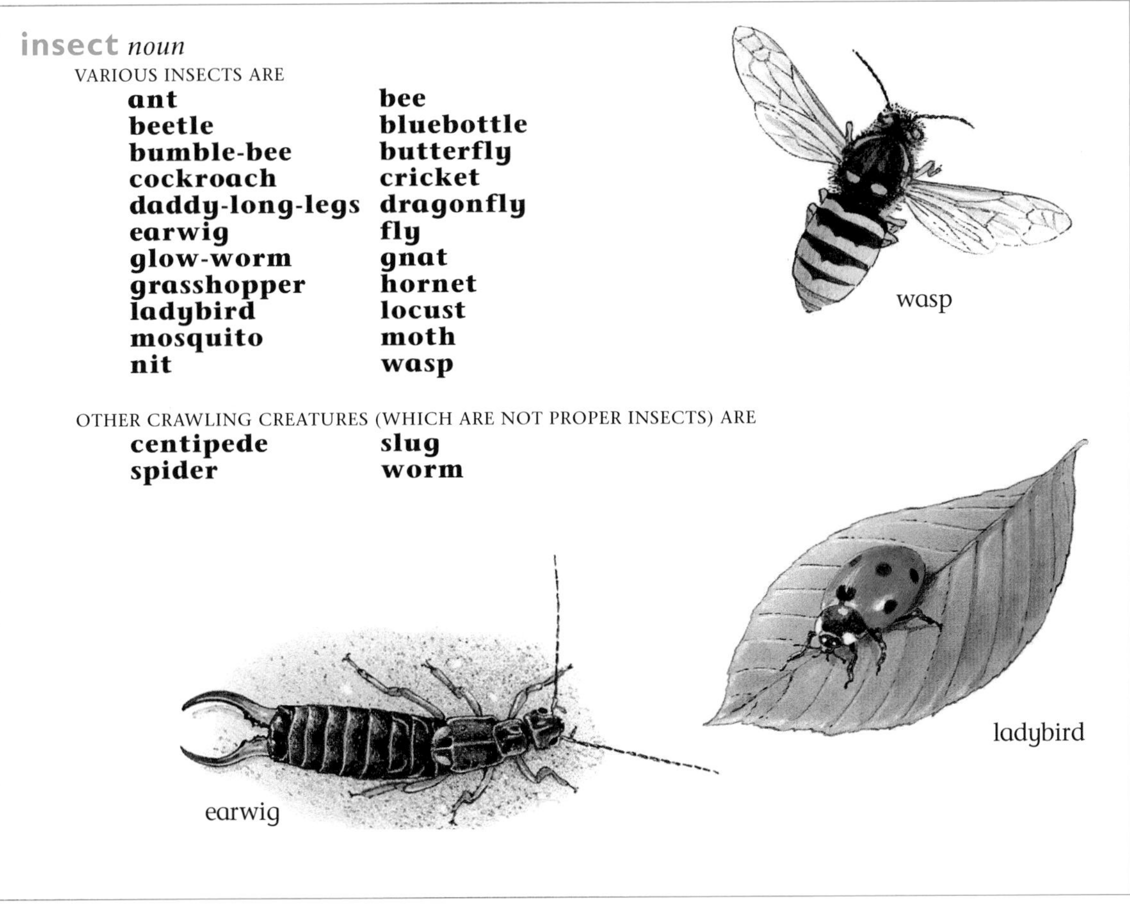

insect *noun*

VARIOUS INSECTS ARE

ant **bee** **beetle** **bluebottle** **bumble-bee** **butterfly** **cockroach** **cricket** **daddy-long-legs** **dragonfly** **earwig** **fly** **glow-worm** **gnat** **grasshopper** **hornet** **ladybird** **locust** **mosquito** **moth** **nit** **wasp**

OTHER CRAWLING CREATURES (WHICH ARE NOT PROPER INSECTS) ARE

centipede **slug** **spider** **worm**

insolent *adjective*

It is insolent to answer back to a teacher.

OTHER WORDS YOU MIGHT USE ARE **cheeky** **impertinent** **impolite** **improper** **impudent** **rude**

The opposite is **polite**

inspect *verb*

The man at the garage inspected the damage to the car.

OTHER VERBS YOU MIGHT USE ARE **to check** **to examine** **to look at**

instant *adjective*

He didn't keep us waiting, but gave us an instant reply.

OTHER WORDS YOU MIGHT USE ARE **immediate** **prompt** **quick**

instruct *verb*

1 The policeman instructed us to stay where we were.

OTHER VERBS YOU MIGHT USE ARE **to command** **to direct** **to order**

2 Our teacher instructed us in how to use the PE equipment.

OTHER VERBS ARE **to coach** **to teach** **to train**

instrument *noun*

The dentist has an interesting instrument for drilling teeth.

OTHER WORDS YOU MIGHT USE ARE **apparatus** **device** **gadget** **implement** **machine** **tool**

For musical instruments, see **music**

a b c d e f g h i j k l m n o p q r s t u v w x y z

insult *verb*
He insulted me by walking away without speaking.
OTHER VERBS YOU MIGHT USE ARE **to be rude to** **to offend** **to snub**

intelligent *adjective*
Our dog is so intelligent that she understands what we say.
OTHER WORDS YOU MIGHT USE ARE **brainy** **bright** **clever**
The opposite is **stupid**

intend *verb*
Jo intends to learn the piano next year.
OTHER VERBS YOU MIGHT USE ARE **to aim** **to plan** **to propose**

intense *adjective*
intense heat. intense pain.
OTHER WORDS YOU MIGHT USE ARE **extreme** **great** **severe** **strong**

intentional *adjective*
The player was sent off the field for an intentional foul.
OTHER WORDS YOU MIGHT USE ARE **deliberate** **intended**
The opposite is **accidental**

interest *verb*
Dad's stories always interest us.
OTHER VERBS YOU MIGHT USE ARE **to appeal to** **to attract** **to fascinate**
The opposite is **bore**

interested *adjective*
OTHER WORDS YOU MIGHT USE ARE **attentive** **curious** **keen**
IF YOU ARE TOO INTERESTED, YOU ARE **inquisitive** **nosy**
The opposite is **bored**

interfere *verb*
Don't interfere in my business!
OTHER VERBS YOU MIGHT USE ARE **to intrude** **to meddle** **to pry**
(*informal*) **to snoop**

interrupt *verb*
It's rude to interrupt when someone is talking.
OTHER VERBS YOU MIGHT USE ARE (*informal*) **to butt in** **to interfere**

interval *noun*
1 When we went to the pictures, we had ice cream in the interval.
OTHER WORDS YOU MIGHT USE ARE **break** **intermission**
2 There is an interval between the lightning and the thunder.
OTHER WORDS ARE **gap** **pause** **rest** **space**

introduce *verb*
Jo introduced me to her friend.
OTHER VERBS YOU MIGHT USE ARE **to make known** **to present**

introduction *noun*
1 an introduction to a book.
OTHER WORDS YOU MIGHT USE ARE **preface** **prologue**
2 an introduction to a ballet.
OTHER WORDS ARE **overture** **prelude**

invade *verb*
to invade a foreign country.
OTHER VERBS YOU MIGHT USE ARE **to attack** **to march into** **to occupy** **to overrun** **to raid**

invent *verb*
Who invented the first computer?
OTHER VERBS YOU MIGHT USE ARE **to create** **to devise** **to plan** **to put together** **to think up**

investigate *verb*
The police spent many weeks investigating the crime.
OTHER VERBS YOU MIGHT USE ARE **to examine** **to explore** **to inquire into** **to study**

invisible *adjective*
The door into the secret garden was invisible.
OTHER WORDS YOU MIGHT USE ARE **concealed** **hidden** **undetectable**
The opposite is **visible**

invite *verb*
Jo invited me to her party.
ANOTHER VERB IS **to ask**

irritable *adjective*
Dad gets irritable if we chatter while the football is on.
OTHER WORDS YOU MIGHT USE ARE **annoyed** **bad-tempered** **grumpy** **short-tempered** **snappy** **touchy**
For other words, see **angry**

irritate *verb*
The flies irritated the horse.
OTHER VERBS YOU MIGHT USE ARE **to anger** **to annoy** **to bother** **to upset** **to worry**

issue *verb*
The teacher issued one pencil to each child.
OTHER VERBS YOU MIGHT USE ARE **to distribute** **to give out** **to pass round**

item *noun*
Have you got any items for the jumble sale?
OTHER WORDS YOU MIGHT USE ARE **article** **object** **thing**

Jj

jab *verb*
He jabbed me with his finger.
OTHER VERBS YOU MIGHT USE ARE **to poke** **to prod** **to stab**

a b c d e f g h i **j** k l m n o p q r s t u v w x y z

jagged *adjective*
The broken plank had a jagged edge.
OTHER WORDS YOU MIGHT USE ARE **rough** **sharp** **uneven**
The opposite is **smooth**

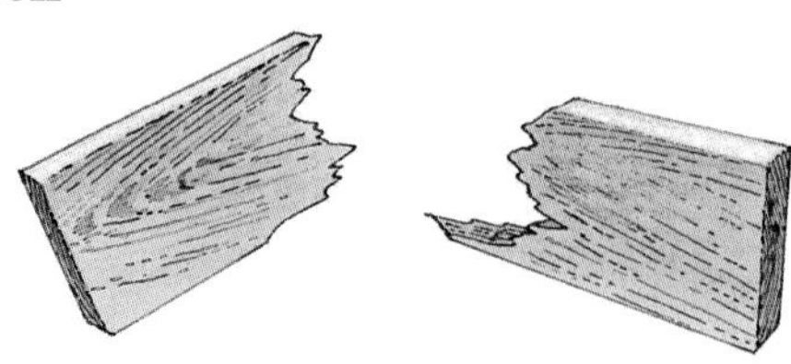

jail *noun*
see **gaol**

jam *verb*
1 I jammed my things into a box.
OTHER VERBS YOU MIGHT USE ARE **to cram** **to crush** **to squeeze**
2 Cars jammed the street.
OTHER VERBS ARE **to block** **to fill**
3 Our back door keeps jamming.
ANOTHER VERB IS **to stick**

jar *noun*
For other things to put things in, see **container**

jealous *adjective*
Jo was a bit jealous when Sam got a lot of money for his birthday.
OTHER WORDS YOU MIGHT USE ARE **bitter** **envious** **resentful**

jeer *verb*
The crowd jeered at the player who argued with the referee.
OTHER VERBS YOU MIGHT USE ARE **to laugh at** **to mock** **to sneer at** **to taunt**

jet *noun*
a jet of water.
OTHER WORDS YOU MIGHT USE ARE **fountain** **spray** **spurt** **squirt**

jewel *noun*
OTHER WORDS YOU MIGHT USE ARE
gem **precious stone**

STONES USED IN MAKING JEWELLERY ARE
amber **diamond** **emerald** **jet** **opal** **pearl** **ruby** **sapphire**

METALS USED TO MAKE JEWELLERY ARE
gold **platinum** **silver**

VARIOUS KINDS OF JEWELLERY ARE
bangle **beads** **bracelet** **brooch** **chain** **clasp**
earrings **locket** **necklace** **pendant** **ring**

job *noun*

1 I have some jobs to do for Mum before I come out to play.

OTHER WORDS YOU MIGHT USE ARE

chore **errand** **task**

2 Sam's cousin has left school and is looking for a job.

OTHER WORDS ARE

employment **occupation** **profession** **trade** **work**

SOME OF THE JOBS PEOPLE DO TO EARN THEIR LIVING ARE

accountant **actor** **architect** **artist**
barber **builder** **caretaker** **carpenter**
chef **chemist** **cleaner** **clergyman**
clerk **cook** **decorator** **dentist**
designer **detective** **driver** **doctor**
dustman **electrician** **engineer** **entertainer**
farmer **fireman** **gardener** **hairdresser**
journalist **lawyer** **lecturer** **librarian**
mechanic **midwife** **milkman** **model**
musician **nurse** **optician** **photographer**
pilot **plumber** **police officer** **postman**
receptionist **reporter** **scientist** **secretary**
shopkeeper **social worker** **teacher** **traffic warden**
typist **vet** **waiter** **writer**

join *verb*

1 to join one thing to another.

OTHER VERBS YOU MIGHT USE ARE **to attach** **to connect** **to fasten** **to fix** **to link**

For other verbs, see **fasten**

2 Two motorways join in a mile.

OTHER VERBS ARE **to come together** **to meet** **to merge**

joint *noun*

JOINTS IN YOUR BODY ARE

ankle **elbow** **hip** **knee** **knuckle** **shoulder** **wrist**

jolt *verb*

The car jolted along the rough road.

OTHER VERBS YOU MIGHT USE ARE **to bounce** **to bump** **to jerk** **to shake**

journey *noun*

KINDS OF JOURNEY ARE

excursion **expedition** **outing** **tour** **trip**

A journey in a ship is a **cruise** or a **sail** or a **voyage**.
A journey in a car is a **drive**.
A journey in a plane is a **flight**.
A journey on a horse or bicycle is a **ride**.
A journey on foot is a

hike **ramble** **trek** **walk**

A journey with a special purpose is a **mission**.
For other words, see **travel**

judge *verb*

1 The criminal was judged in a court of law.
OTHER VERBS YOU MIGHT USE ARE **to condemn** **to convict** **to punish** **to sentence**

2 The referee judged that the player was off-side.
OTHER VERBS ARE **to consider** **to decide** **to rule**

jumble *noun*

Dad wanted to know why there was a jumble of clothes on the floor.
OTHER WORDS YOU MIGHT USE ARE **assortment** **chaos** **clutter** **confusion** **mess** **muddle**

jump *verb*

1 We jumped over the fence.
OTHER VERBS YOU MIGHT USE ARE **to bound** **to hop** **to leap** **to skip** **to vault**

2 The cat jumped on the mouse.
OTHER VERBS ARE **to spring** **to pounce**

just *adjective*

The referee's decision was just.
OTHER WORDS YOU MIGHT USE ARE **fair** **honest** **lawful** **proper** **right** **unbiased**
The opposite is **unfair**

Kk

keen *adjective*

Jo is keen to learn the piano.
OTHER WORDS YOU MIGHT USE ARE **anxious** **eager** **enthusiastic**

keep *verb*

1 I'll keep some sweets for later.
OTHER VERBS YOU MIGHT USE ARE **to save** **to store**

2 If you can't do it straight away, keep trying!
OTHER VERBS ARE **to carry on** **to continue** **to persist**

3 Please keep still.
OTHER VERBS ARE **to remain** **to stay**

4 Mum says it's expensive to keep a family.
OTHER VERBS ARE **to care for** **to feed** **to look after** **to mind** **to provide for** **to support** **to tend**

kill *verb*
OTHER VERBS YOU MIGHT USE ARE
(*informal*) **to finish off** **to slay**
to kill a famous person
to assassinate
to kill a criminal
to execute or **put to death**
to kill a person
to murder
to kill a lot of people
to massacre
to kill pests
to exterminate
to kill an animal that is old or ill
to put to sleep
to kill an animal for food
to slaughter

WAYS TO KILL A PERSON ARE
to behead **to choke** **to crucify** **to drown** **to electrocute** **to gas** **to hang** **to knife** **to poison** **to shoot** **to stab** **to strangle** **to suffocate** **to throttle**

kind *adjective*
We are lucky to have kind neighbours.
OTHER WORDS YOU MIGHT USE ARE **considerate** **friendly** **good-natured** **helpful** **kind-hearted** **loving** **neighbourly** **sympathetic** **thoughtful** **unselfish**
The opposite is **unkind**

kind *noun*
1 A terrier is a kind of dog.
OTHER WORDS YOU MIGHT USE ARE **breed** **sort** **species** **type**
2 What kind of butter do you buy?
OTHER WORDS ARE **brand** **make** **variety**

kitchen *noun*, see next page

kneel *verb*
I kneeled down to tie my shoe.
OTHER VERBS YOU MIGHT USE ARE **to bend** **to crouch** **to stoop**

knife *noun*
OTHER WORDS YOU MIGHT USE ARE **carving knife** **dagger** **penknife**

knob *noun*
1 the knob on the door.
ANOTHER WORD IS **handle**
2 a knob of butter.
ANOTHER WORD IS **lump**

a b c d e f g h i j **k** l m n o p q r s t u v w x y z

kitchen *noun*

THINGS YOU USE IN A KITCHEN TO HEAT OR COOK FOOD ARE

cooker **electric plate** **gas ring** **grill** **hotplate** **kettle** **microwave** **oven** **stove** **toaster**

OTHER THINGS YOU USE IN A KITCHEN ARE

baking tin	**blender**	**bowl**	**breadboard**
breadknife	**carving knife**	**casserole**	**chip pan**
crockery	**cutlery**	**dishes**	**dish rack**
dishwasher	**draining board**	**jug**	**mincer**
mixer	**pans**	**percolator**	**pots**
rolling pin	**salt cellar**	**saucepan**	**scales**
sink	**tea towel**	**teapot**	**tin-opener**
tray	**whisk**		

PLACES WHERE YOU KEEP FOOD ARE

freezer **fridge** or **refrigerator**
larder **pantry**

knock *verb*
I knocked on the door.
OTHER VERBS YOU MIGHT USE ARE **to rap** **to tap**
For other verbs, see **hit**

know *verb*
1 Sam knows the names of all the kings and queens of England.
OTHER VERBS YOU MIGHT USE ARE **to recognize** **to remember**
2 Mum knows a bit of French.
ANOTHER VERB IS **to understand**

knowledge *noun*
1 You get a lot of knowledge from an encyclopedia.
OTHER WORDS YOU MIGHT USE ARE **facts** **information**
2 Farmers have a great knowledge of the countryside.
OTHER WORDS ARE **experience** **understanding**

Ll

lag *verb*
If we lag behind we'll miss the bus.
OTHER VERBS YOU MIGHT USE ARE **to dawdle** (*informal*) **to hang about** **to linger** **to loiter** **to straggle**

lake *noun*
For other words, see **water**

lame *adjective*
The lame man used a walking stick.
OTHER WORDS YOU MIGHT USE ARE **crippled** **disabled** **limping**

land *noun*
1 foreign lands.
OTHER WORDS YOU MIGHT USE ARE **country** **nation**
2 land to grow crops on.
OTHER WORDS ARE **earth** **ground** **soil**

land *verb*
1 The plane landed at the airport.
OTHER VERBS YOU MIGHT USE ARE **to arrive** **to come down**
2 The sailors landed on an island.
OTHER VERBS ARE **to come ashore** **to disembark**

large *adjective*
OTHER WORDS YOU MIGHT USE ARE **big** **broad** **fat** **grand** **great** **long** **roomy** **spacious** **tall** **wide**
WORDS FOR VERY LARGE THINGS ARE **colossal** **enormous** **giant** **gigantic** **huge** **immense** **infinite** **massive** **mighty** **monstrous** **tremendous** **vast**
The opposite is **small**

a b c d e f g h i j k **l** m n o p q r s t u v w x y z

last *adjective*
Our song was the last item in the concert.
OTHER WORDS YOU MIGHT USE ARE **concluding** **final**
The opposite is **first**

last *verb*
The fine weather lasted all week.
OTHER VERBS YOU MIGHT USE ARE **to continue** **to go on** **to keep on** **to persist** **to remain** **to stay**

late *adjective*
The bus is late.
OTHER WORDS YOU MIGHT USE ARE **delayed** **overdue**
Opposites are **early** or **punctual**

lately *adverb*
ANOTHER WORD IS **recently**

laugh *verb*
VARIOUS WAYS WE LAUGH ARE **to chuckle** **to giggle** **to grin** **to smile** **to titter**
TO LAUGH UNKINDLY AT SOMEONE IS **to jeer** **to sneer** **to snigger**
For other verbs, see **mock**

law *noun*
We obey the laws of the country.
OTHER WORDS YOU MIGHT USE ARE **regulation** **rule**

lay *verb*
I laid the papers on the desk.
OTHER VERBS YOU MIGHT USE ARE **to leave** **to place** **to put** **to set down** **to spread**

layer *noun*
There was a layer of ice over the playground.
OTHER WORDS YOU MIGHT USE ARE **coating** **film** **sheet** **skin** **thickness**

lazy *adjective*
That cat leads a lazy life!
ANOTHER WORD IS **idle**
The opposite is **busy**

lead *verb*
1 The teacher led the children back to the classroom.
OTHER VERBS YOU MIGHT USE ARE **to conduct** **to guide** **to take**
2 The captain led her team with great skill.
OTHER VERBS ARE **to command** **to direct** **to manage**

leak *verb*
Water leaked out of the bucket.
OTHER VERBS YOU MIGHT USE ARE **to drip** **to escape** **to ooze** **to seep** **to trickle**

lean *verb*
The sinking ship leaned to one side.
OTHER VERBS YOU MIGHT USE ARE **to heel over** **to list** **to slant** **to slope** **to tilt**

leap *verb*
Sam leaped over the fence.
OTHER VERBS YOU MIGHT USE ARE **to bound** **to jump** **to spring** **to vault**

learn *verb*

1 We learned a lot about history when we went to the castle.
OTHER VERBS YOU MIGHT USE ARE **to discover** **to find out**

2 We learned the song by heart.
ANOTHER VERB IS **to memorize**

leave *verb*

1 Don't leave your pets when you go on holiday.
OTHER VERBS YOU MIGHT USE ARE **to abandon** **to desert** **to forsake**

2 The guard blew a whistle to show that the train was ready to leave.
OTHER VERBS ARE **to depart** **to go** **to set off**

3 Leave the empty milk bottles outside the front door.
OTHER VERBS ARE **to deposit** **to place** **to put down** **to set down**

lecture *noun*

A policewoman gave us a lecture on road safety.
OTHER WORDS YOU MIGHT USE ARE **lesson** **speech** **talk**

leg *noun*

For parts of the body, see **body**

legal *adjective*

Is it legal to park on this road?
OTHER WORDS YOU MIGHT USE ARE **allowed** **lawful** **permitted**
The opposite is **illegal**

lend *verb*

Can you lend me a pen?
ANOTHER VERB IS **to loan**
If you give something to someone to use for a short time, you **lend** it.
If someone gives something to you to use, you **borrow** it.

length *noun*

OTHER WORDS YOU MIGHT USE ARE **distance** **measurement**

let *verb*

1 Sam let Jo ride his bike.
OTHER VERBS YOU MIGHT USE ARE **to allow** **to permit**

2 Aunt Jean lets her caravan to holidaymakers in the summer.
OTHER VERBS ARE **to hire** **to rent**

level *adjective*

1 You need a level field for playing rounders.
OTHER WORDS YOU MIGHT USE ARE **even** **flat** **horizontal** **smooth**

2 At half time the scores were level.
ANOTHER WORD IS **equal**

licence *noun*

You need a licence to go fishing.
ANOTHER WORD IS **permit**

lid *noun*

Put the lid back on the jam.
OTHER WORDS YOU MIGHT USE ARE **cap** **cover** **top**

lie *noun*

Don't tell lies!
OTHER WORDS YOU MIGHT USE ARE **falsehood** (*informal*) **fib**

a b c d e f g h i j k **l** m n o p q r s t u v w x y z

lie *verb*

1 Don't believe her—I think she's lying.
OTHER VERBS YOU MIGHT USE ARE **to bluff** (*informal*) **to fib**

2 Sam lay on the sofa.
OTHER VERBS ARE **to lean back** **to recline** **to sprawl**

life *noun*

Our dog is full of life.
OTHER WORDS YOU MIGHT USE ARE **energy** **liveliness** **vitality**

lifelike *adjective*

The wax models were very lifelike.
OTHER WORDS YOU MIGHT USE ARE **natural** **realistic**

lift *verb*

1 Lift the box onto the shelf.
OTHER VERBS YOU MIGHT USE ARE **to hoist** **to raise**

2 Jo lifted baby out of her pram.
ANOTHER VERB IS **to pick up**

light *adjective*

1 a light suitcase.
The opposite is **heavy**

2 a light room.
OTHER WORDS YOU MIGHT USE ARE **bright** **well-lit**
The opposite is **dark**

3 light colours.
OTHER WORDS ARE **faint** **pale**
The opposite is **strong**

light *noun*, see opposite page

like *verb*

1 We like our neighbours.
OTHER VERBS YOU MIGHT USE ARE **to approve of** **to be fond of** **to respect**
For other verbs, see **love**

2 I would like a drink, please.
OTHER VERBS ARE **to enjoy** **to fancy** **to want** **to wish for**
The opposite is **hate**

likely *adjective*

1 Rain is likely today.
ANOTHER WORD IS **probable**

2 Sam is a likely person to be captain of the team.
OTHER WORDS ARE **appropriate** **suitable**

limp *adjective*

1 limp covers on a book.
OTHER WORDS YOU MIGHT USE ARE **flexible** **soft**
The opposite is **stiff**

2 limp lettuce.
OTHER WORDS ARE **drooping** **floppy**
The opposite is **crisp**

limp *verb*

Jo limped because her shoe hurt.
ANOTHER VERB IS **to hobble**
For other words, see **lame**

light *noun*

THINGS WHICH GIVE LIGHT ARE
bulb **candle** **electric light** **floodlight** **headlight** **lamp** **lantern** **searchlight** **spotlight** **street light** **torch**

LIGHTS USED FOR DECORATION ARE
fairy lights **illuminations**

NATURAL LIGHT IS
daylight **moonlight** **starlight** **sunlight**

DIFFERENT WAYS LIGHT SHINES ARE
blaze **burn** **dazzle** **flash** **flicker** **glare** **gleam** **glimmer** **glint** **glisten** **glitter** **glow** **shine** **spark** **sparkle** **twinkle**

line *noun*

1 lines on the road.
OTHER WORDS YOU MIGHT USE ARE **dash** **mark** **streak** **stripe**

2 lines on someone's face.
OTHER WORDS ARE **crease** **furrow** **wrinkle**

3 a railway line.
OTHER WORDS ARE **rails** **route** **track**

4 We waited in a line.
OTHER WORDS ARE **column** **file** **queue** **rank** **row**

linger *verb*

Don't linger in the playground.
OTHER VERBS YOU MIGHT USE ARE **to dawdle** **to delay** (*informal*) **to hang about** **to loiter** **to remain** **to stay** **to wait about**

link *verb*

Sam can link his keyboard to a computer.
OTHER VERBS YOU MIGHT USE ARE **to attach** **to connect** **to join**

litter *noun*

We get into trouble if we leave litter round the school.
OTHER WORDS YOU MIGHT USE ARE **clutter** **junk** **rubbish**

a b c d e f g h i j k **l** m n o p q r s t u v w x y z

little *adjective*

1 Sam's got a little radio that he can put in his pocket.
OTHER WORDS YOU MIGHT USE ARE **compact** **miniature** **minute** **small** **tiny**

2 We had a little chat.
OTHER WORDS ARE **brief** **short**

3 She gave us little helpings.
OTHER WORDS ARE **mean** (*informal*) **measly** **stingy**

4 They had a little argument.
OTHER WORDS ARE **minor** **slight** **trivial** **unimportant**

The opposite is **big**

live *adjective*

There aren't any live dinosaurs.
OTHER WORDS YOU MIGHT USE ARE **existing** **living**

live *verb*

1 Plants can't live without water.
OTHER VERBS YOU MIGHT USE ARE **to exist** **to remain alive** **to survive**

2 Jo's Granny lives in a flat.
OTHER VERBS ARE **to dwell in** **to inhabit** **to occupy**

lively *adjective*

Those puppies are lively!
OTHER WORDS YOU MIGHT USE ARE **active** **energetic** **frisky**

The opposite is **lazy**

load *noun*

Can you carry that heavy load?
OTHER WORDS YOU MIGHT USE ARE **burden** **weight**

load *verb*

We loaded the trolley with food.
OTHER VERBS YOU MIGHT USE ARE **to fill** **to pack**

lock *noun*

Mum fitted a lock to the door.
OTHER WORDS YOU MIGHT USE ARE **bolt** **catch** **latch** **padlock**

lock *verb*

Did you lock the door?
OTHER VERBS YOU MIGHT USE ARE **to fasten** **to secure**

logical *adjective*

a logical argument.
OTHER WORDS YOU MIGHT USE ARE **intelligent** **reasonable** **sensible**

lonely *adjective*

1 Jo felt lonely when Sam went away.

OTHER WORDS YOU MIGHT USE ARE **alone** **forsaken** **friendless** **neglected** **solitary**

2 We heard a ghost story about a lonely farmhouse.

OTHER WORDS ARE **isolated** **remote** **secluded**

long *adjective*

It seemed a long journey.

OTHER WORDS YOU MIGHT USE ARE **endless** **lengthy**

The opposite is **short**

long *verb*

I longed for a drink.

OTHER VERBS YOU MIGHT USE ARE **to fancy** **to hanker after** **to want** **to wish for** **to yearn for**

look *verb*

1 We looked at the things we had collected on our walk.

OTHER VERBS YOU MIGHT USE ARE **to examine** **to study** **to survey** **to view**

TO LOOK AT SOMETHING QUICKLY **to glance** **to peep**

TO LOOK FOR A LONG TIME **to gaze** **to stare** **to watch**

2 The dog looked friendly.

OTHER VERBS ARE **to appear** **to seem**

3 I helped Mum look for her purse.

OTHER VERBS ARE **to hunt** **to search for** **to seek**

loose *adjective*

1 My tooth is loose.

OTHER WORDS YOU MIGHT USE ARE **shaky** **unsteady** **wobbly**

2 The animals were all loose.

OTHER WORDS ARE **at liberty** **free**

lorry *noun*

For other words, see **travel**

lose *verb*

1 Sam was upset when he lost his watch.

ANOTHER VERB IS **to mislay**

2 Our team lost on Saturday.

A PHRASE IS **to be defeated**

loud *adjective*

The neighbours complained about the loud music.

OTHER WORDS YOU MIGHT USE ARE **deafening** **noisy** **shrill**

The opposite is **quiet**

lounge *noun*

OTHER WORDS YOU MIGHT USE ARE **drawing room** **living room** **sitting room**

love *verb*

OTHER VERBS YOU MIGHT USE ARE **to adore** **to be fond of** **to be in love with** **to care for** **to idolize** **to like** **to treasure** **to worship**

lovely *adjective*

For other words, see **beautiful**

low *adjective*

The opposite is **high**

a b c d e f g h i j k l m n o p q r s t u v w x y z

loyal *adjective*
Sam is a loyal supporter of his local team.
OTHER WORDS YOU MIGHT USE ARE **devoted** **faithful** **reliable** **trustworthy**

luck *noun*
Sam found his lost watch by luck.
OTHER WORDS YOU MIGHT USE ARE **accident** **chance** **coincidence**

lucky *adjective*
I was lucky to find what I wanted.
ANOTHER WORD IS **fortunate**
The opposite is **unlucky**

luggage *noun*
The driver put our luggage in the back of the car.
DIFFERENT ITEMS OF LUGGAGE MIGHT BE
bag **box** **case** **holdall**
suitcase **trunk**

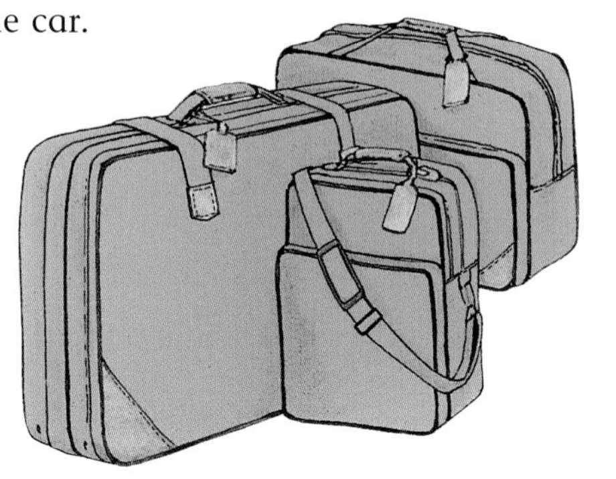

lump *noun*
1 Uncle gave Jo a lump of chocolate.
OTHER WORDS YOU MIGHT USE ARE **bar** **block** **chunk** **hunk** **piece** **slab**
2 Dad got a lump on the head where he hit himself.
OTHER WORDS YOU MIGHT USE ARE **bulge** **bump** **hump** **knob** **swelling**

luxury *noun*
That cat lives a life of luxury!
OTHER WORDS YOU MIGHT USE ARE **comfort** **ease** **pleasure** **relaxation**

Mm

machine *noun*
The workshop had a machine for doing woodwork.
OTHER WORDS YOU MIGHT USE ARE **apparatus** **instrument** **tool**
A word you might use for machines in general is **machinery**

mad *adjective*
1 He behaved so strangely that people said he was mad.
OTHER WORDS YOU MIGHT USE ARE (*informal*) **crazy** **insane** **mentally ill** **unbalanced**
2 He's mad to go out in this rain!
For other words, see **silly**

magic *noun*

1 Can witches really do magic?

OTHER WORDS YOU MIGHT USE ARE **charms** **enchantments** **sorcery** **spells** **witchcraft**

2 The conjuror did some magic.

A PHRASE YOU MIGHT USE IS **conjuring tricks**

magician *noun*

OTHER WORDS YOU MIGHT USE ARE **conjuror** **sorcerer** **wizard**

magnificent *adjective*

a magnificent palace.

OTHER WORDS YOU MIGHT USE ARE **grand** **impressive** **majestic** **noble** **splendid** **stately**

mail *noun*

For other words, see **post**

main *adjective*

The main ingredient of bread is flour.

OTHER WORDS YOU MIGHT USE ARE **basic** **chief** **essential** **important** **principal**

make *verb*, see next page

make-up *noun*

KINDS OF MAKE-UP ARE

blusher **eyeliner** **eyeshadow** **face cream** **face powder** **lipstick** **nail varnish**

THINGS PEOPLE USE TO MAKE THEMSELVES SMELL NICER ARE

aftershave **deodorant** **perfume** **scent** **talc** or **talcum powder**

male *noun*

THERE ARE SPECIAL WORDS FOR MALE AND FEMALE HUMAN BEINGS AND SOME ANIMALS.

A male human being is a **boy** or **man.**
A male goat is a **billy goat**.
A male pig is a **boar**.
A male deer is a **buck** or **stag**.
A male rabbit is a **buck**.
A male swan is a **cob**.
A male bird is a **cock**.
A male chicken is a **cockerel**.
A male duck is a **drake**.
A male goose is a **gander**.
A male sheep is a **ram**.
A male horse is a **stallion**.
A male cat is a **tom-cat**.

a
b
c
d
e
f
g
h
i
j
k
l
m
n
o
p
q
r
s
t
u
v
w
x
y
z

make *verb*

THIS VERB HAS MANY USES. HERE ARE SOME OF THE WAYS YOU CAN USE IT, AND SOME OTHER VERBS YOU COULD CHOOSE

1 I made a plan.
to form to invent to produce to think up

2 We made a den in the garden.
to build to construct to create to erect

3 They make cars in that factory.
to assemble to manufacture

4 Don't make trouble.
to bring about to cause to provoke

5 You can't make me do it.
to compel to force to oblige to order

6 The head made a speech.
to deliver to give

7 It's easy to make a P into a B.
to alter to change to convert to transform to turn

8 How can I make some money?
to earn to get to obtain to receive

9 You'll make a good player if you practise.
to become to change into to grow into to turn into

10 Will our team make the final?
to get to to reach

11 2 and 2 make 4.
to add up to to come to

12 Mum made an appointment at the doctor's.
to arrange to fix

13 I can't make out what happened.
to follow to hear to see to understand

14 She made up an excuse.
to invent to plan to think up

man *noun*

OTHER WORDS YOU MIGHT USE ARE

a polite word
gentleman
a married man
husband
a man who is not married
bachelor
a man whose wife has died
widower
a man who has children
father
a young man
boy youth

manage *verb*

1 The head manages the school.
OTHER VERBS YOU MIGHT USE ARE **to be in charge of** **to control** **to look after** **to run**

2 Can you manage a big helping?
OTHER VERBS YOU MIGHT USE ARE **to cope with** **to deal with** **to handle**

3 Could you manage to help us on Saturday?
ANOTHER VERB IS **to arrange**

manner *noun*

He spoke in a friendly manner.
OTHER WORDS YOU MIGHT USE ARE **fashion** **style** **way**

map *noun*

A simple map is a **diagram** or **plan**.
A map used by sailors is a **chart**.
A book of maps is an **atlas**.

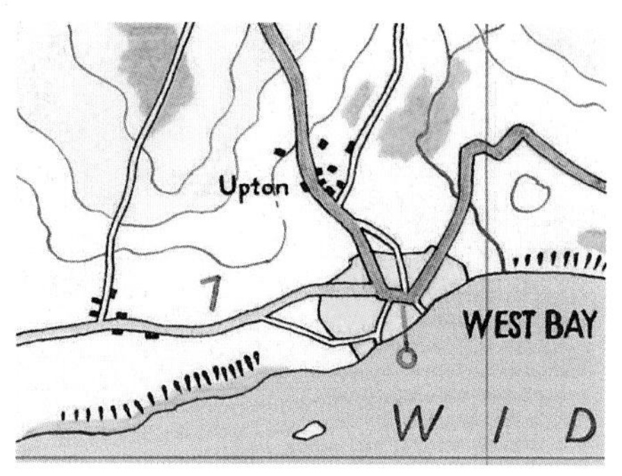

mark *noun*

There's a mark on my new dress.
OTHER WORDS YOU MIGHT USE ARE **smear** **smudge** **spot** **stain**

market *noun*

DIFFERENT KINDS OF MARKET ARE
auction **bazaar** **car boot sale** **fair** **street market**

marsh *noun*

We began to sink into the marsh.
OTHER WORDS YOU MIGHT USE ARE **bog** **swamp**

marvellous *adjective*

I had a marvellous holiday.
OTHER WORDS YOU MIGHT USE ARE **excellent** (*informal*) **fabulous** **splendid** **wonderful**

mash *verb*

We mashed the baby's dinner until it was soft.
OTHER VERBS YOU MIGHT USE ARE **to crush** **to pulp** **to purée** **to smash** **to squash**

mass *noun*

There was a mass of rubbish to clear away.
OTHER WORDS YOU MIGHT USE ARE **heap** **mound** **pile** **quantity** **stack**

match *noun*

a boxing match.
OTHER WORDS YOU MIGHT USE ARE **competition** **contest** **game**

material *noun*

1 building materials.
OTHER WORDS YOU MIGHT USE ARE **stuff** **substances** **things**

2 material to make curtains.
For other words, see **cloth**

mathematics *noun*

A short word for mathematics is **maths**.
Working with numbers is also called **arithmetic**.

WORDS FOR THINGS YOU DO IN MATHEMATICS ARE
addition or **adding** **calculation** or **calculating** **counting** **division** or **dividing** **investigating** **measuring** **multiplication** or **multiplying** **subtraction** or **subtracting** or **taking away** **sums**

VERBS YOU MIGHT USE IN MATHS ARE
to add **to add up** **to calculate** **to count** **to divide** **to investigate** **to measure** **to multiply** **to subtract** **to take away** **to work out**

OTHER WORDS YOU MIGHT USE IN MATHS ARE
angle **answer** **area** **capacity** **diagonal** **difference** **digit** **figure** **fraction** **graph** **measurement** **minus** **number** **pattern** **plus** **problem** **shape** **sum** **symmetry** **times** **total** **unit** **volume**

THINGS YOU MIGHT USE TO HELP YOU IN MATHEMATICS ARE
calculator **compasses** **computer** **ruler** **set square**

For words you might use when you measure things, see **measurement**
For names of different shapes, see **shape**

matter *noun*

1 We have some matters to discuss.
OTHER WORDS YOU MIGHT USE ARE **business** **subject** **topic**

2 What's the matter?
OTHER WORDS ARE **difficulty** **problem** **trouble**

meal *noun*

DIFFERENT MEALS ARE
breakfast **dinner** **high tea** **lunch** **supper** **tea**
A very splendid meal is a **banquet** or **feast**.
A meal where you help yourself is a **buffet**.
A small meal is a **snack**.
A meal you eat out of doors is a **picnic**.
A meal you cook out of doors is a **barbecue**.

mean *adjective*

He's mean with his money.

OTHER WORDS YOU MIGHT USE ARE **miserly** (*informal*) **stingy**

The opposite is **generous**

mean *verb*

1 What does this word mean?

OTHER VERBS YOU MIGHT USE ARE **to convey** **to indicate** **to say** **to stand for**

2 What do you mean to do?

OTHER VERBS ARE **to aim** **to intend** **to plan** **to propose**

measurement *noun*

ANOTHER WORD IS

size

OTHER WORDS YOU MIGHT USE ARE

how long something is: **length**
how wide something is: **breadth** or **width**
how tall something is: **height**

UNITS TO MEASURE LENGTH, BREADTH, OR HEIGHT ARE

centimetres **metres** **kilometres**

OLD UNITS ARE

inches **feet** **yards** **miles**

how big a surface is: **area**

UNITS TO MEASURE AREA ARE

square metres **metres**

OLD UNITS ARE

square feet **square yards** **acres**

how much something holds: **volume**

UNITS TO MEASURE VOLUME ARE

cubic centimetres or **litres**

OLD UNITS ARE

pints or **gallons**

how heavy something is: **weight**

UNITS TO MEASURE WEIGHT ARE

grams **kilograms** **tonnes**

OLD UNITS ARE

ounces **pounds** **tons**

meat *noun*

DIFFERENT KINDS OF MEAT ARE

bacon **beef** **chicken** **ham** **lamb** **pork** **turkey** **veal** **venison**

YOU CAN BUY MEAT IN THE FORM OF

burgers **chops** **joint** **mince** **sausage** **steak**

medicine *noun*

I need medicine for my cough.
For other words, see **health**

a b c d e f g h i j k l **m** n o p q r s t u v w x y z

medium *adjective*
Sam is medium height for his age.
OTHER WORDS YOU MIGHT USE ARE **average** **middling** **normal**

meet *verb*
1 Two roads meet here.
OTHER VERBS YOU MIGHT USE ARE **to come together** **to join** **to merge**
2 I met my friend in town.
OTHER VERBS ARE **to encounter** (*informal*) **to run into** **to see**
3 All the classes met in the hall.
OTHER VERBS ARE **to assemble** **to congregate** **to gather**

meeting *noun*
DIFFERENT KINDS OF MEETING ARE **assembly** **committee** **conference** **council**

melt *verb*
The ice melted in the sun.
OTHER VERBS YOU MIGHT USE ARE **to thaw** **to unfreeze**

mend *verb*
1 The garage mended the car.
OTHER VERBS YOU MIGHT USE ARE **to fix** **to put right** **to repair**
2 Dad likes mending old furniture.
OTHER VERBS ARE **to do up** **to renovate** **to restore**
3 Sam mended his jeans.
OTHER VERBS ARE **to darn** **to patch** **to sew up** **to stitch up**

mention *verb*
I mentioned that I was hungry.
OTHER VERBS YOU MIGHT USE ARE **to comment** **to remark** **to say**

merciful *adjective*
The judge was merciful and let him off with a warning.
OTHER WORDS YOU MIGHT USE ARE **forgiving** **kind** **sympathetic**
The opposite is **cruel**

mercy *noun*
The judge showed mercy.
OTHER WORDS YOU MIGHT USE ARE **forgiveness** **pity**

merry *adjective*
a merry tune.
OTHER WORDS YOU MIGHT USE ARE **cheerful** **happy** **jolly** **lively**
The opposite is **sad**

mess *noun*
Clear up this mess!
OTHER WORDS YOU MIGHT USE ARE **chaos** **clutter** **confusion** **jumble** **muddle**

message *noun*
I sent a message that I was busy.
OTHER WORDS YOU MIGHT USE ARE **letter** **note**

metal *noun*
DIFFERENT METALS ARE
aluminium **brass** **bronze** **copper** **gold** **iron** **lead** **platinum** **silver** **steel** **tin** **uranium** **zinc**

method *noun*
Our teacher showed us a good method for doing multiplication.
OTHER WORDS YOU MIGHT USE ARE **procedure** **system** **technique** **way**

middle *noun*
the middle of the earth.
OTHER WORDS YOU MIGHT USE ARE **centre** **core** **heart**

mild *adjective*
1 mild weather.
OTHER WORDS YOU MIGHT USE ARE **gentle** **pleasant** **warm**
2 a mild illness.
ANOTHER WORD IS **slight**
The opposite is **severe**

mind *noun*
Use your mind!
OTHER WORDS YOU MIGHT USE ARE **brain** **intelligence** **understanding**

mind *verb*
1 I'll mind the baby.
OTHER VERBS YOU MIGHT USE ARE **to care for** **to look after** **to tend**
2 Do you mind about missing the party?
OTHER VERBS ARE **to care** **to worry**

mine *noun*
a coal mine.
OTHER WORDS YOU MIGHT USE ARE **pit** **shaft**
A place where they dig coal from the Earth's surface is an **opencast mine**.
A place where they dig stone is a **quarry**.

mischievous *adjective*
The mischievous puppy stole Dad's slippers.
OTHER WORDS YOU MIGHT USE ARE **badly behaved** **naughty**

miserable *adjective*
1 Jo's miserable when Sam is away.
OTHER WORDS YOU MIGHT USE ARE **depressed** **gloomy** **sad** **unhappy** **wretched**
The opposite is **happy**
2 The refugees live in miserable conditions.
OTHER WORDS ARE **awful** **bad** **pitiful** **poor** **wretched**

misery *noun*
We can't imagine the misery of the refugees.
OTHER WORDS YOU MIGHT USE ARE **distress** **grief** **sadness** **sorrow** **suffering** **unhappiness**

mislead *verb*
She misled us and sent us the wrong way.
OTHER VERBS YOU MIGHT USE ARE **to deceive** **to fool** **to trick**

miss *verb*

1 If we leave now we'll miss the rush-hour traffic.
OTHER VERBS YOU MIGHT USE ARE **to avoid** **to dodge** **to steer clear of**

2 I missed the bus.
The opposite is **catch**

3 Jo missed Sam when he was away.
ANOTHER VERB IS **to pine for**

4 You can miss out the questions you don't understand.
OTHER VERBS ARE **to leave out** **to omit** **to skip**

missing *adjective*

Did you find the missing money?
ANOTHER WORD IS **lost**

mist *noun*

ANOTHER WORD IS **haze**
A thick mist is **fog**.

mistake *noun*

spelling mistakes.
OTHER WORDS YOU MIGHT USE ARE **blunder** **error** (*informal*) **slip**

misty *adjective*

a misty view.
OTHER WORDS YOU MIGHT USE ARE **blurred** **dim** **faint** **fuzzy** **hazy** **indistinct** **unclear**
The opposite is **clear**

mix *verb*

1 Mix the flour, fat, and sugar in a bowl.
OTHER VERBS YOU MIGHT USE ARE **to blend** **to combine** **to mingle** **to stir together**

2 Don't mix two packs of cards!
OTHER VERBS ARE **to confuse** **to jumble** **to muddle**

mixture *noun*

I had a mixture of sweets.
OTHER WORDS YOU MIGHT USE ARE **assortment** **variety**

moan *verb*

He moaned with pain.
OTHER VERBS YOU MIGHT USE ARE **to groan** **to wail**

mock *verb*

It's unkind to mock other people.
OTHER VERBS YOU MIGHT USE ARE **to laugh at** **to make fun of** **to ridicule** **to sneer at** **to taunt** **to tease**

moderate *adjective*

Dad drives at moderate speed.
OTHER WORDS YOU MIGHT USE ARE **medium** **middling** **normal** **ordinary** **reasonable**

modern *adjective*

1 Grandad says he doesn't understand modern inventions like computers.
OTHER WORDS YOU MIGHT USE ARE **new** **recent**
The opposite is **old**

2 Do you like modern clothes?
OTHER WORDS ARE **fashionable** **stylish** (*informal*) **trendy** **up-to-date**
The opposite is **old-fashioned**

modest *adjective*

1 She was modest about winning the prize.
ANOTHER WORD IS **humble**
The opposite is **conceited**

2 He was too modest to undress on the beach.
OTHER WORDS YOU MIGHT USE ARE **bashful** **shy**

money *noun*

Money you have in your pocket is **cash** or **change**.
IT MIGHT BE
coins (*informal*) **coppers** **notes** **silver**
People can also buy things with a **cheque** or a **credit card**.

A LOT OF MONEY IS
a fortune **wealth**

MONEY YOU GET FOR WORK YOU DO IS
earnings **income** **pay** **salary** **wages**

Money you get when you retire from work is a **pension**.
Money you save in the bank is your **savings**.
Money people have to pay to the government is **tax**.

monster *noun*
FRIGHTENING CREATURES YOU READ ABOUT IN STORIES ARE
beast **dragon** **giant** **ogre** **troll** **vampire** **werewolf**

month *noun*
THE MONTHS OF THE YEAR ARE
January **February** **March** **April** **May** **June** **July** **August** **September** **October** **November** **December**

mood *noun*
Is Dad in a good mood today?
OTHER WORDS YOU MIGHT USE ARE **humour** **temper**

moral *adjective*
a moral person.
OTHER WORDS YOU MIGHT USE ARE **good** **honest** **truthful** **virtuous**
The opposite is **immoral**

motive *noun*
What was the motive for the crime?
OTHER WORDS YOU MIGHT USE ARE **purpose** **reason**

mountain *noun*
The top of a mountain is the **summit** or **peak**.
A line of mountains is a **range** or **ridge**.
A mountain which sometimes sends out hot liquid, gases, or ash is a **volcano**.

move *verb*
THIS VERB HAS MANY USES. HERE ARE SOME OF THE WAYS YOU CAN USE IT, AND SOME OTHER VERBS YOU COULD CHOOSE

1 to move along.
to come **to fly** **to go** **to journey** **to march** **to pass** **to tour** **to travel** **to walk**

2 to move along quickly.
to canter **to dart** **to dash** **to fly** **to gallop** **to hurry** **to race** **to run** **to rush** **to shoot** **to speed** **to streak** **to tear** (*informal*) **to zoom**

3 to move along slowly.
to crawl **to dawdle** **to stroll**

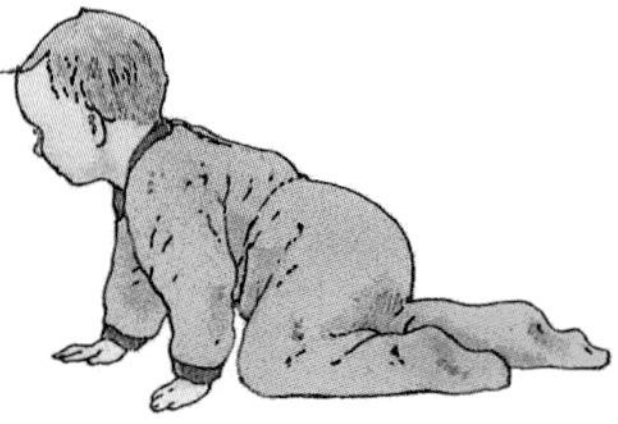

4 to move along gracefully.
to dance **to glide** **to skate** **to skim** **to slide** **to slip**

5 to move along clumsily.
to shuffle **to stagger** **to stumble** **to sway** **to totter** **to trip**

6 to move along stealthily.
to crawl **to creep** **to slink** **to slither**

7 to move away from somewhere.
to depart **to leave** **to quit**

8 to move back.
to reverse **to withdraw**

9 to move downwards.
to descend **to drop** **to fall** **to sink**

10 to move upwards.
to arise **to climb** **to mount** **to rise**

11 to move in somewhere.
to enter

12 to move round and round.
to revolve **to roll** **to rotate** **to spin** **to turn** **to twirl** **to twist** **to whirl**

13 to move towards something.
to advance **to approach**

14 to move restlessly.
to fidget **to shake** **to stir** **to toss** **to tremble** **to twist** **to twitch** **to wag** **to waggle** **to wave**

15 to move things.
to budge **to carry** **to shift** **to transport**

mud *noun*

There was some mud on the road.
OTHER WORDS YOU MIGHT USE ARE **clay** **dirt** **muck** **slime**

muddle *verb*

1 Don't muddle the library books.
OTHER VERBS YOU MIGHT USE ARE **to jumble** **to mix up**

2 You muddle me if you talk fast.
OTHER VERBS ARE **to bewilder** **to confuse**

murder *verb*

For other verbs, see **kill**

music *noun*, see next page

mysterious *adjective*

1 The doctors didn't know what to do about my mysterious illness.
OTHER WORDS YOU MIGHT USE ARE **mystifying** **puzzling** **strange**

2 The castle looked mysterious in the moonlight.
OTHER WORDS ARE **eerie** **ghostly** **magical** **weird**

mystery *noun*

The detective solved the mystery.
OTHER WORDS YOU MIGHT USE ARE **problem** **puzzle** **riddle**

music *noun*

DIFFERENT KINDS OF MUSIC ARE
classical music **music** **folk music** **jazz** **musicals** **opera** **pop music** **rap** **reggae** **rock**

KINDS OF MUSIC FOR SINGING ARE
ballad **carol** **folk song** **hymn** **lullaby** **pop song** **shanty** **spiritual**

BRASS INSTRUMENTS ARE
bugle **cornet** **horn** **trombone** **trumpet** **tuba**

OTHER INSTRUMENTS YOU PLAY BY BLOWING ARE
bagpipes **bassoon** **clarinet** **flute** **harmonica** or **mouth organ** **oboe** **pan pipes** **piccolo** **recorder** **saxophone**

INSTRUMENTS WITH STRINGS THAT YOU PLAY BY PLUCKING ARE
banjo **guitar** **harp** **sitar**

INSTRUMENTS WITH STRINGS THAT YOU CAN PLAY WITH A BOW ARE
cello **double bass** **fiddle** **viola** **violin**

violin

INSTRUMENTS YOU PLAY BY PRESSING KEYS ARE
harmonium **harpsichord** **keyboard** **organ** **piano**

PERCUSSION INSTRUMENTS ARE
castanets **chime bars** **cymbals** **drums** **glockenspiel** **gong** **kettledrum** **tambourine** **triangle** **tubular bells** **xylophone**

PEOPLE WHO MAKE MUSIC ARE
composer **conductor** **performer** **player** **singer**

PEOPLE WHO PLAY INSTRUMENTS ARE
drummer **fiddler** **guitarist** **harpist** **organist** **percussionist** **pianist** **piper** **trumpeter** **violinist**

DIFFERENT SINGING VOICES ARE
alto **bass** **soprano** **tenor** **treble**
People who play or sing on their own are **soloists**.
A singer may also be called a **vocalist**.

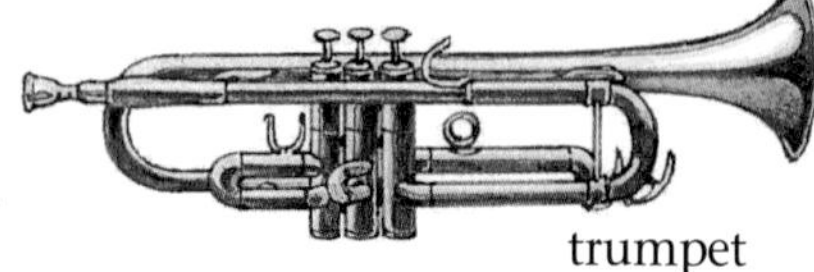
trumpet

GROUPS OF MUSICIANS ARE
band **choir** or **chorus** **ensemble** **group** **orchestra** **quartet** **quintet** **trio**

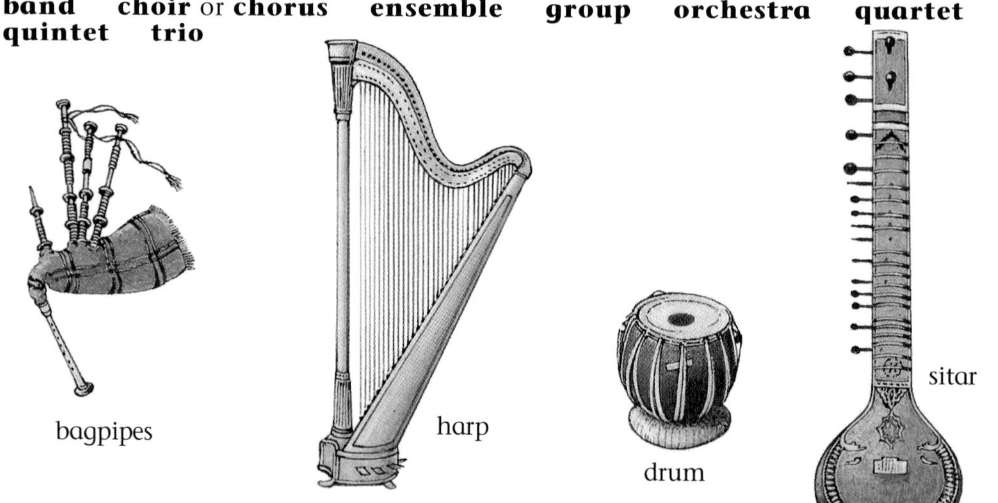
bagpipes harp drum sitar

Nn

naked *adjective*
OTHER WORDS YOU MIGHT USE ARE **bare** **nude** **unclothed** **undressed**

name *noun*
The name that you are given when you are born is your **first name**.
The name that everyone in your family has is your **surname** or **family name**.
An invented name which friends give you is a **nickname**.
A name you use instead of your real name is an **alias**.
The name of a book is the **title**.
The name of a particular make of goods is the **brand**.

narrow *adjective*
OTHER WORDS YOU MIGHT USE ARE **fine** **slim** **thin**
The opposite is **wide**

nasty *adjective*
1 nasty weather.
OTHER WORDS YOU MIGHT USE ARE **bad** **dreadful** **horrible** **unpleasant**
2 a nasty mess.
OTHER WORDS ARE **dirty** **disgusting** **filthy** **foul** **revolting**
3 a nasty person.
OTHER WORDS ARE **rude** **unfriendly** **unkind**
The opposite is **nice**

nation *noun*
People from many nations take part in the Olympic Games.
OTHER WORDS YOU MIGHT USE ARE **country** **race**

natural *adjective*
It's natural to go to sleep when you are tired.
ANOTHER WORD IS **normal**
The opposite is **unnatural**

naughty *adjective*
We punished the dog because he had been naughty.
OTHER WORDS YOU MIGHT USE ARE **bad** **disobedient** **mischievous** **wicked**
The opposite is **well-behaved**

near *adjective* and *adverb*
Our house is near to the shops.
ANOTHER WORD IS **close**

nearly *adverb*
I've nearly finished.
OTHER WORDS YOU MIGHT USE ARE **almost** **not quite** **practically**

neat *adjective*
Jo arranged her books in a neat row.
OTHER WORDS YOU MIGHT USE ARE **orderly** **smart** **tidy**
The opposite is **untidy**

necessary *adjective*
It is necessary to water plants in dry weather.
OTHER WORDS YOU MIGHT USE ARE **essential** **important** **vital**
The opposite is **unnecessary**

a b c d e f g h i j k l m n o p q r s t u v w x y z

neck *noun*
For other parts of the body, see **body**

need *verb*
1 We need some butter to make the sandwiches.
OTHER VERBS YOU MIGHT USE ARE **to require** **to want**
2 The football team needs Sam to play in goal.
OTHER VERBS ARE **to count on** **to depend on** **to rely on**

neglect *verb*
You mustn't neglect your pets when you go on holiday.
OTHER VERBS YOU MIGHT USE ARE **to forget** **to ignore** **to overlook**
The opposite is **look after**

nervous *adjective*
Our dog gets nervous when she hears thunder.
OTHER WORDS YOU MIGHT USE ARE **anxious** **edgy** **fidgety** **jumpy**
The opposite is **calm**

neutral *adjective*
The referee has to be neutral.
OTHER WORDS YOU MIGHT USE ARE **impartial** **unbiased**

new *adjective*
1 new clothes.
OTHER WORDS YOU MIGHT USE ARE **brand new** **unused**
2 new bread.
ANOTHER WORD IS **fresh**
3 a new invention.
OTHER WORDS ARE **modern** **recent** **up-to-date**
The opposite is **old**

nice *adjective*
THIS WORD HAS MANY USES. HERE ARE SOME OF THE WAYS YOU CAN USE IT, AND SOME OTHER WORDS YOU COULD CHOOSE
1 nice weather.
beautiful **fine** **good** **lovely** **pleasant**
2 nice food.
delicious **enjoyable** **tasty**
3 a nice person.
friendly **kind** **likeable**
The opposite is **nasty**

noble *adjective*
1 a noble deed.
OTHER WORDS YOU MIGHT USE ARE **brave** **gallant** **heroic** **worthy**
2 a noble palace.
OTHER WORDS ARE **grand** **majestic** **stately**

noise *noun*
Stop that noise!
OTHER WORDS YOU MIGHT USE ARE **din** **hubbub** (*informal*) **racket** **row** **rumpus** **uproar**
For kinds of noise, see **sound**

noisy *adjective*
The neighbours complained that our music was too noisy.
OTHER WORDS YOU MIGHT USE ARE **deafening** **loud** **rowdy**
The opposite is **silent**

nonsense *noun*
Don't talk nonsense!
ANOTHER WORD IS **rubbish**

normal *adjective*
1 It's quite normal for people to sweat in hot weather.
OTHER WORDS YOU MIGHT USE ARE **common** **natural** **ordinary** **usual**
2 The temperature is normal for this time of year.
ANOTHER WORD IS **average**

nosy *adjective*
The kitten was being nosy and got her head stuck in a tin.
OTHER WORDS YOU MIGHT USE ARE **curious** **inquisitive**

nothing *noun*
OTHER WORDS YOU MIGHT USE ARE **nought** **zero**
Nothing in cricket is a **duck**.
Nothing in football is **nil**.
Nothing in tennis is **love**.

notice *noun*
We put up a notice about our play.
OTHER WORDS YOU MIGHT USE ARE **advertisement** **placard** **poster** **sign**

notice *verb*
Jo noticed that Mum looked tired.
OTHER VERBS YOU MIGHT USE ARE **to detect** **to observe** **to see**

nude *adjective*
OTHER WORDS YOU MIGHT USE ARE **bare** **naked** **unclothed** **undressed**

nuisance *noun*
That dog is a nuisance!
OTHER WORDS YOU MIGHT USE ARE **bother** **pest** **trouble** **worry**

number *noun*
We had to add up the numbers.
ANOTHER WORD IS **figure**

nurse *noun*
For people who help us when we are ill, see **health**

nut *noun*
SOME NUTS YOU CAN EAT ARE
almond **brazil** **cashew** **chestnut** **coconut** **hazelnut** **peanut** **walnut**

Oo

obedient *adjective*
an obedient dog.
ANOTHER WORD IS **well-behaved**
The opposite is **disobedient**

obey *verb*
You have to obey the rules.
PHRASES YOU MIGHT USE ARE **to abide by** **to keep to**
The opposite is **disobey**

object *verb*
We object to bad language.
PHRASES YOU MIGHT USE ARE **to complain about** **to disapprove of** **to protest about**

obstinate *adjective*
The donkey was obstinate and refused to move.
OTHER WORDS YOU MIGHT USE ARE **defiant** (*informal*) **pig-headed** **stubborn** **unhelpful**
The opposite is **helpful**

obtain *verb*
For other verbs, see **get**

obvious *adjective*
Jo thought the answer to the question was obvious.
OTHER WORDS YOU MIGHT USE ARE **clear** **easy to see** **plain**

occasional *adjective*
We make occasional visits to the pictures.
OTHER WORDS YOU MIGHT USE ARE **infrequent** **rare**
The opposite is **regular**

occupation *noun*
1 What's your mother's occupation?
OTHER WORDS YOU MIGHT USE ARE **business** **employment** **job** **work**
2 Fishing is a quiet occupation.
OTHER WORDS YOU MIGHT USE ARE **activity** **hobby** **pastime**

occupy *verb*
1 Six people occupy our house.
OTHER VERBS YOU MIGHT USE ARE **to inhabit** **to live in**
2 The soldiers occupied the town.
OTHER VERBS ARE **to capture** **to conquer** **to invade** **to take over**

occur *verb*
A nasty accident occurred today.
OTHER VERBS YOU MIGHT USE ARE **to happen** **to take place**

odd *adjective*
1 Jo can't explain her dog's odd behaviour.
OTHER WORDS YOU MIGHT USE ARE **abnormal** **curious** **funny** **peculiar** **queer** **strange** **uncommon** **unusual** **weird**
The opposite is **ordinary**
2 Where did this odd sock come from?
OTHER WORDS YOU MIGHT USE ARE **extra** **single** **spare**

offend *verb*
I offended Jo because I didn't go to her party.
OTHER VERBS YOU MIGHT USE ARE **to annoy** **to displease** **to insult** **to upset**
The opposite is **please**

offensive *adjective*
1 There's an offensive smell in the kitchen.
OTHER WORDS YOU MIGHT USE ARE **disgusting** **foul** **horrible** **nasty** **unpleasant**
2 Don't use offensive language.
OTHER WORDS ARE **improper** **indecent** **rude**
The opposite is **pleasing**

offer *verb*
1 I offered some cake to Granny.
ANOTHER VERB IS **to give**
2 Sam offered to wash up.
ANOTHER VERB IS **to volunteer**

often *adverb*
OTHER WORDS YOU MIGHT USE ARE **again and again** **frequently** **regularly** **repeatedly**
The opposite is **seldom**

old *adjective*
1 an old car.
OTHER WORDS YOU MIGHT USE ARE **ancient** **old-fashioned**
2 an old man.
OTHER WORDS ARE **aged** **elderly**
3 an old magazine.
ANOTHER WORD IS **out-of-date**
4 old bread.
ANOTHER WORD IS **stale**
5 old clothes.
OTHER WORDS ARE **shabby** **worn-out**
6 valuable old furniture.
ANOTHER WORD IS **antique**
The opposite is **new**

omit *verb*
The captain omitted Sam from the team because he was injured.
OTHER VERBS YOU MIGHT USE ARE **to drop** **to exclude** **to leave out**
The opposite is **include**

open *adjective*
Leave the door open.
OTHER WORDS YOU MIGHT USE ARE **unfastened** **unlocked**
The opposite is **shut**

open *verb*
Please open the door.
OTHER VERBS YOU MIGHT USE ARE **to undo** **to unfasten** **to unlock**
The opposite is **close**

opening *noun*
1 Jo's tortoise crawled through an opening in the fence.
OTHER WORDS YOU MIGHT USE ARE **break** **crack** **gap** **hole** **space**
2 Sam looks forward to the opening of the football season.
OTHER WORDS ARE **beginning** **start**

a b c d e f g h i j k l m n **o** p q r s t u v w x y z

opinion *noun*
It's my opinion that the dog stole the sausages.
OTHER WORDS YOU MIGHT USE ARE **belief** **guess** **idea** **thought** **view**

opposite *adjective*
1 the opposite side of the road.
ANOTHER WORD IS **facing**
2 the opposite opinion.
OTHER WORDS YOU MIGHT USE ARE **contrary** **different** **opposing**

order *verb*
1 He ordered us to stand still.
OTHER VERBS YOU MIGHT USE ARE **to command** **to direct** **to instruct** **to tell**
2 We ordered fish and chips.
PHRASES YOU MIGHT USE ARE **to ask for** **to send for**

ordinary *adjective*
1 We spent the holiday doing ordinary things.
OTHER WORDS YOU MIGHT USE ARE **everyday** **normal** **typical** **unexciting** **usual**
2 Most of the birds we saw on our walk were just ordinary ones.
OTHER WORDS ARE **common** **familiar** **uninteresting** **well-known**
3 I want an ordinary portion of chips.
OTHER WORDS ARE **regular** **standard**
The opposite is **special**

organize *verb*
Our teacher organized a trip to the zoo.
ANOTHER VERB IS **to arrange**

original *adjective*
Mum said the ideas in Sam's story were very original.
OTHER WORDS YOU MIGHT USE ARE **fresh** **imaginative** **new** **unusual**

outing *noun*
We went on an outing to the country park.
OTHER WORDS YOU MIGHT USE ARE **excursion** **expedition** **trip**

oven *noun*
For things you use to heat or cook food, see **kitchen**

overgrown *adjective*
an overgrown garden.
OTHER WORDS YOU MIGHT USE ARE **tangled** **untidy**

overturn *verb*
The boat overturned.
ANOTHER VERB IS **to capsize**

own *verb*
Do you own a bike?
ANOTHER VERB IS **to possess**
to own up
ANOTHER VERB IS **to confess**

Pp

pack *verb*
We packed everything into the car.
OTHER VERBS YOU MIGHT USE ARE **to load** **to put**

packet *noun*
1 The postman brought an interesting-looking packet.
OTHER WORDS ARE **package** **parcel**
2 I bought a packet of cornflakes.
ANOTHER WORD IS **box**

page *noun*
Jo tore a page out of her notebook.
OTHER WORDS YOU MIGHT USE ARE **leaf** **sheet**

pain *noun*
OTHER WORDS YOU MIGHT USE ARE **ache** **soreness** **sting** **twinge**
VERY BAD PAIN IS **agony** **suffering** **torture**
For other words, see **hurt**

painful *adjective*
The cut on Jo's knee was painful.
OTHER WORDS YOU MIGHT USE ARE **aching** **hurting** **smarting** **sore** **stinging** **throbbing**

paint *noun*
DIFFERENT KINDS OF PAINT ARE
emulsion **enamel** **gloss** **oil paint** **varnish** **watercolour**

pale *adjective*
1 His face went pale when he heard the bad news.
OTHER WORDS YOU MIGHT USE ARE **colourless** **white**
2 Mum decorated the sitting room in pale colours.
OTHER WORDS ARE **faint** **light**

pant *verb*
We were all panting for breath at the end of the race.
OTHER VERBS YOU MIGHT USE ARE **to gasp** **to puff**

paper *noun*
DIFFERENT KINDS OF PAPER ARE
card **newspaper** **notepaper** **tissue paper** **toilet paper** **wallpaper** **wrapping paper** **writing paper**

parcel *noun*
The postman came with a parcel.
OTHER WORDS ARE **package** **packet**

pardon *verb*
The King pardoned the knight who had committed a crime.
OTHER VERBS YOU MIGHT USE ARE **to excuse** **to forgive** **to let off** **to reprieve** **to set free** **to spare**

a b c d e f g h i j k l m n o **p** q r s t u v w x y z

park *noun*
DIFFERENT KINDS OF PARK ARE **gardens** **recreation ground** **safari park** **wildlife park**

part *noun*
1 I don't want it all, only a part of it.
OTHER WORDS YOU MIGHT USE ARE **bit** **fraction** **piece** **portion** **section**
2 They sell food in a different part of the shop.
ANOTHER WORD IS **department**
3 Granny lives in a nice part of the country.
OTHER WORDS ARE **area** **district** **region**
4 Which part did you have in the nativity play?
OTHER WORDS ARE **character** **role**

particular *adjective*
1 Jo has her own particular way of writing.
OTHER WORDS YOU MIGHT USE ARE **individual** **personal**
2 Do you want a particular record, or will any music do?
ANOTHER WORD IS **special**
3 The dog is particular about what he eats.
OTHER WORDS ARE **choosy** **fussy**

partner *noun*
1 You can take a partner with you when you go to the party.
OTHER WORDS YOU MIGHT USE ARE **companion** **friend**
2 The burglar had a partner.
ANOTHER WORD IS **accomplice**

party *noun*
DIFFERENT KINDS OF PARTY ARE
ball **barbecue** **birthday party** **dance** **disco** **picnic** **social** **wedding**

pass *verb*
1 We waited for the cars to pass before we crossed the road.
OTHER VERBS YOU MIGHT USE ARE **to go by** **to move along**
2 Jo's knee hurt when she cut it, but the pain soon passed.
OTHER VERBS ARE **to disappear** **to go away** **to vanish**

passage *noun*
1 We went in through the front door and waited in the passage.
OTHER WORDS ARE **corridor** **hall**
2 They say there's a secret passage under the castle.
OTHER WORDS ARE **tunnel** **way**
3 I read my favourite passage from the book.
OTHER WORDS YOU MIGHT USE ARE **extract** **piece** **quotation**

path *noun*
We walked along the path.
DIFFERENT KINDS OF PATH ARE
bridleway **cart track** **footpath** **pavement** **towpath** **track** **trail**

patient *adjective*
Although we had to wait a long time, everyone was very patient.
ANOTHER WORD IS **calm**
The opposite is **impatient**

pattern *noun*
1 I like the patterns on the wallpaper.
OTHER WORDS YOU MIGHT USE ARE **decoration** **design** **shape**
2 Is there a pattern I can copy?
OTHER WORDS ARE **guide** **model**

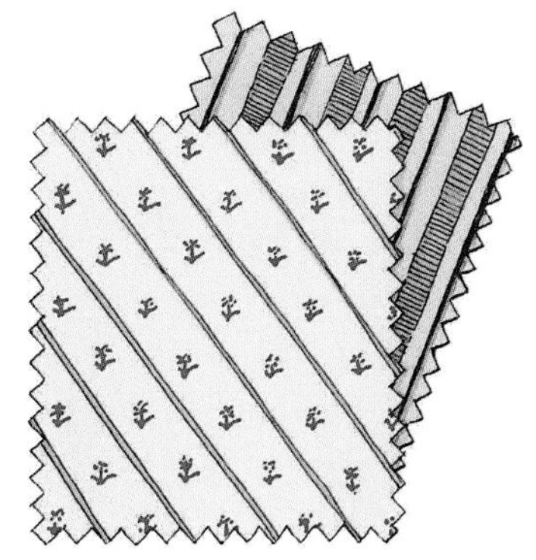

pause *noun*
There was a pause before the main film.
OTHER WORDS YOU MIGHT USE ARE **break** **delay** **gap** **intermission** **interruption** **interval**

pause *verb*
We paused to have a drink.
OTHER VERBS ARE **to rest** **to stop** **to wait**

pay *noun*
OTHER WORDS YOU MIGHT USE ARE
earnings **income** **payment**
If you are paid by the week, your pay is **wages**.
If you get a regular amount each year, your pay is a **salary**.
The pay for doing one job is a **fee**.

pay *verb*
1 Sam paid £10 for his bike.
OTHER VERBS YOU MIGHT USE ARE **to give** **to hand over** **to spend**
2 When can you pay back the money you owe me?
OTHER VERBS ARE **to refund** **to repay**

peace *noun*
1 After the war ended there was peace between the two countries.
ANOTHER WORD YOU MIGHT USE IS **agreement**
The opposite is **war**
2 We sat by the lake and enjoyed the peace of the evening.
OTHER WORDS ARE **calmness** **quiet** **stillness**
Opposites are **excitement**, **noise**

peaceful *adjective*
It seemed peaceful when the baby went to sleep.
OTHER WORDS YOU MIGHT USE ARE **calm** **quiet** **restful**
The opposite is **noisy**

pebble *noun*
ANOTHER WORD IS **stone**
A lot of pebbles are called **gravel**.
Pebbles on a beach are called **shingle**.

a b c d e f g h i j k l m n o **p** q r s t u v w x y z

peculiar *adjective*
This drink has a peculiar taste.
OTHER WORDS YOU MIGHT USE ARE **funny** **odd** **queer** **special** **strange** **unusual**

peel *noun*
the peel of an orange.
OTHER WORDS YOU MIGHT USE ARE **rind** **skin**

pen *noun*
DIFFERENT KINDS OF PEN ARE
ballpoint **Biro** **felt tip** **fountain pen** **quill pen**

people *noun*
For other words, see **person**

perfect *adjective*
1 It's a perfect day for a picnic.
OTHER WORDS YOU MIGHT USE ARE **excellent** **ideal**
2 Jo's new coat was a perfect fit.
ANOTHER WORD IS **exact**

perform *verb*
Everyone in the class performed in the concert.
OTHER VERBS YOU MIGHT USE ARE **to appear** **to take part**
DIFFERENT WAYS TO PERFORM ARE **to act** **to dance** **to play an instrument** **to sing**
For other words, see **entertainment**

perfume *noun*
Mum used some nice perfume when she went to the party.
ANOTHER WORD IS **scent**
For other words, see **smell**

period *noun*
For other words, see **time**

perish *verb*
1 Many birds perish in cold weather.
ANOTHER VERB IS **to die**
2 These pears will perish if you don't use them quickly.
OTHER VERBS YOU MIGHT USE ARE **to decay** **to go bad** **to rot**

permission *noun*
We had the teacher's permission to go home.
OTHER WORDS YOU MIGHT USE ARE **approval** **consent**

permit *noun*
You need a permit to go fishing.
OTHER WORDS YOU MIGHT USE ARE **licence** **pass** **ticket**

permit *verb*
They don't permit smoking on the bus.
OTHER VERBS YOU MIGHT USE ARE **to agree to** **to allow** **to approve of**

persist *verb*
If the pain persists you must go to the doctor.
OTHER VERBS YOU MIGHT USE ARE **to carry on** **to continue**

person *noun*

OTHER WORDS YOU MIGHT USE ARE
character **human being** **individual** **mortal**
a fully grown person
adult **grown-up**
a young person
baby **boy** **child** **girl** **infant** **toddler**
a person who is not a child but is not yet grown up
adolescent **juvenile** **teenager**
a woman who is married
wife
an unmarried woman
spinster
a woman whose husband has died
widow
the man who plays a woman in a pantomime
dame
a polite word for a woman
lady
a female child
girl
Female members of a family
aunt **daughter** **grandmother** **mother** **niece** **stepdaughter** **stepmother**
a man who is married
husband
a man who is not married
bachelor
a man whose wife has died
widower
a polite word for a man
gentleman
informal words for a man
bloke **chap** **fellow**
a young man
youth
a male child
boy or **lad**
Male members of a family
father **grandfather** **nephew** **son** **stepfather** **stepson** **uncle**

personal *adjective*

1 Jo keeps her personal belongings in a drawer in her bedroom.
ANOTHER WORD IS **private**

2 Don't make personal remarks.
OTHER WORDS ARE **cheeky** **impertinent**

persuade *verb*

We tried to persuade the cat to come down from the tree.
OTHER VERBS YOU MIGHT USE ARE **to coax** **to tempt** **to urge**

pester *verb*

Don't pester me when I'm busy!
OTHER VERBS YOU MIGHT USE ARE **to annoy** **to bother** **to nag** **to torment** **to trouble** **to worry**

a b c d e f g h i j k l m n o **p** q r s t u v w x y z

pet *noun*
ANIMALS OFTEN KEPT AS PETS ARE
budgerigar **canary** **cat** **dog** **ferret** **gerbil** **goldfish** **guinea pig** **hamster** **mouse** **parrot** **pigeon** **rabbit** **rat** **tortoise**

canary

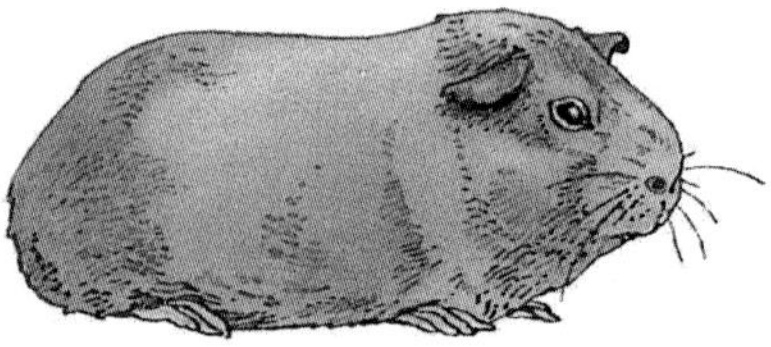

guinea pig

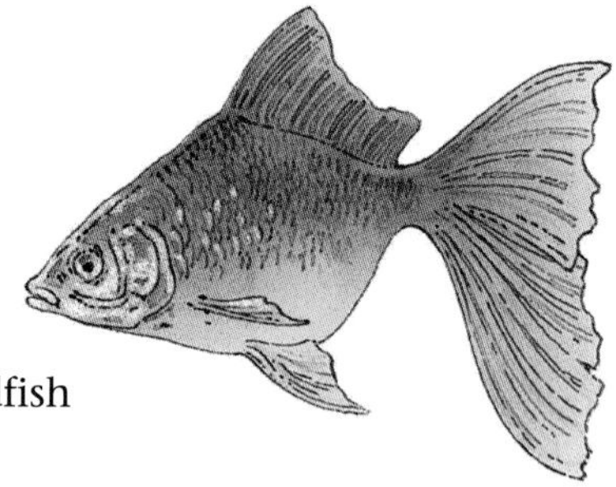

goldfish

phone *verb*
I phoned Granny to ask how she was.
OTHER VERBS YOU MIGHT USE ARE **to call** **to ring** **to telephone**

photo, **photograph** *nouns*
DIFFERENT KINDS OF PHOTOGRAPH ARE
enlargement **negative** **print** **slide** or **transparency** **snapshot**
For other words, see **camera**

pick *verb*
1 You can pick any flavour of ice cream.
OTHER VERBS YOU MIGHT USE ARE **to choose** **to decide on** **to select**
2 We picked Sam to be captain.
OTHER VERBS YOU MIGHT USE ARE **to elect** **to vote for**
3 I picked a lot of blackberries.
OTHER VERBS ARE **to collect** **to gather** **to harvest**

picture *noun*
DIFFERENT KINDS OF PICTURE ARE
cartoon **collage** **drawing** **mosaic** **mural** **painting** **photograph** **print** **sketch** **slide** or **transparency**
A picture of countryside is a **landscape**.
A picture of a person is a **portrait**.
A picture in a book is an **illustration**.

piece *noun*
1 Sam had a big piece of cake.
OTHER WORDS YOU MIGHT USE ARE **chunk** **helping** **hunk** **lump** **portion** **share** **slab** **slice**
2 Mum told Jo to pick up every single piece of the broken cup.
OTHER WORDS ARE **bit** **chip** **fragment**
3 I need a piece of cloth to clean my bike.
OTHER WORDS YOU MIGHT USE ARE **rag** **scrap**

pierce *verb*
The needle pierced my skin.
OTHER VERBS YOU MIGHT USE ARE **to go through** **to penetrate** **to prick** **to puncture**

pig *noun*
A male pig is a **boar**.
A female pig is a **sow**.
A baby pig is a **piglet**.

pile *noun*
Who dumped that pile of rubbish in the yard?
OTHER WORDS YOU MIGHT USE ARE **heap** **mound** **stack**

pillar *noun*
The roof was held up on pillars.
OTHER WORDS YOU MIGHT USE ARE **column** **post** **support**

pipe *noun*
a pipe to carry water.
OTHER WORDS YOU MIGHT USE ARE **hose** **tube**

pit *noun*
A pit where miners dig for coal is a **mine** or **coal mine**.
For other words, see **hole**

pity *noun*
The soldiers showed no pity for their enemies.
OTHER WORDS YOU MIGHT USE ARE **kindness** **mercy** **sympathy**

place *noun*
1 The map showed the place where the treasure was hidden.
OTHER WORDS YOU MIGHT USE ARE **location** **point** **position** **site** **situation** **spot**
2 This is a nice place to live.
OTHER WORDS ARE **area** **district** **neighbourhood** **region**
3 Save me a place next to you.
OTHER WORDS ARE **chair** **seat**

a b c d e f g h i j k l m n o **p** q r s t u v w x y z

place *verb*

1 Place your rubbish in the bin.
OTHER VERBS YOU MIGHT USE ARE **to deposit** **to leave** **to put**

2 Place your work on the table.
OTHER VERBS ARE **to arrange** **to lay** **to set out**

3 He placed the ladder against the wall.
OTHER VERBS ARE **to lean** **to rest** **to stand**

plain *adjective*

1 She was wearing a plain dress.
OTHER WORDS YOU MIGHT USE ARE **ordinary** **simple**
The opposite is **decorated**

2 She gave a plain signal.
OTHER WORDS ARE **clear** **definite**
The opposite is **confusing**

plan *noun*

1 Sam has a plan for making a den in the garden.
OTHER WORDS YOU MIGHT USE ARE **idea** **project** **scheme**

2 We drew a plan of the town to show where we all live.
OTHER WORDS ARE **diagram** **map**

plan *verb*

1 We plan to go to the fair on Saturday.
OTHER VERBS YOU MIGHT USE ARE **to aim** **to intend**

2 It took weeks to plan our trip.
OTHER VERBS ARE **to arrange** **to organize** **to prepare for**

plane *noun*

For other words, see **aircraft**

planet *noun*

THE PLANETS IN THE SOLAR SYSTEM ARE
Earth **Jupiter** **Mars** **Mercury** **Neptune** **Pluto** **Saturn** **Uranus** **Venus**

plant *noun*, see opposite page

play *verb*

1 I play with my friends at the weekend.
OTHER VERBS YOU MIGHT USE ARE **to amuse yourself** **to have fun**

2 Jo played a tune on the piano.
ANOTHER VERB IS **to perform**

playful *adjective*

a playful puppy.
OTHER WORDS YOU MIGHT USE ARE **frisky** **lively**

plant *noun*

DIFFERENT KINDS OF PLANT ARE
bulb **cactus** **climbing plant** **fern** **flower** **fungus** **grass** **moss** **shrub** **tree** **water plant** **weed**

PLANTS YOU CAN EAT ARE
cereals **herbs** **vegetables**
You can eat some kinds of **fungus**.
For other words, see **flower**, **tree**, **vegetable**

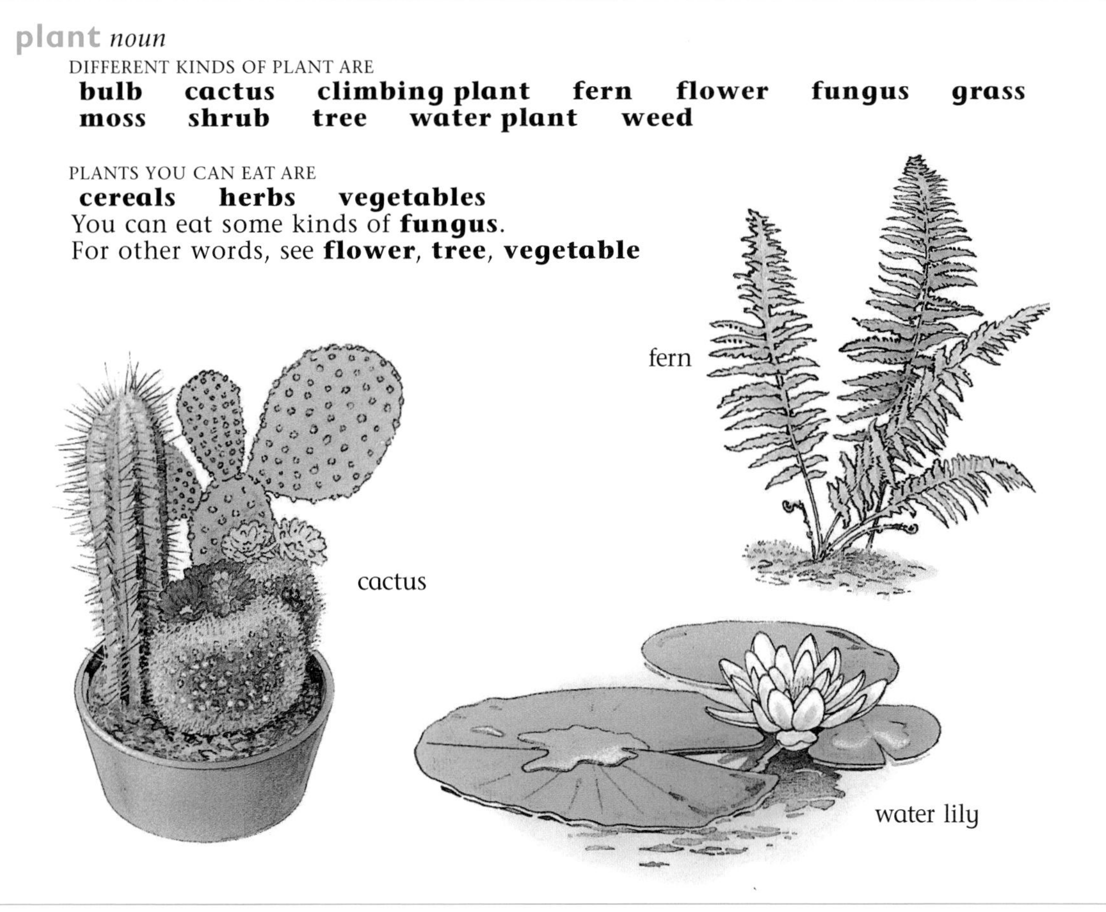

pleasant *adjective*

THIS WORD HAS MANY USES. HERE ARE SOME OF THE WAYS YOU CAN USE IT, AND SOME OTHER WORDS YOU COULD CHOOSE

1 a pleasant day out.
enjoyable **nice** **pleasing**

2 a pleasant person
friendly **kind** **likeable**

3 pleasant weather.
fine **mild** **warm**

4 pleasant countryside.
attractive **peaceful** **pretty**

The opposite is **unpleasant**

pleased *adjective*

Was Mum pleased when you gave her the present?
OTHER WORDS YOU MIGHT USE ARE **contented** **delighted** **grateful** **satisfied** **thankful**
For other words, see **happy**
The opposite is **angry**

pleasure *noun*

Jo's dog whines with pleasure when you tickle his neck.
OTHER WORDS YOU MIGHT USE ARE **contentment** **delight** **enjoyment** **happiness** **satisfaction**

plot *verb*
The robbers plotted to steal some jewels.
OTHER VERBS YOU MIGHT USE ARE **to conspire** **to plan** **to scheme**

plunge *verb*
She plunged into the water.
OTHER VERBS YOU MIGHT USE ARE **to dive** **to drop** **to jump** **to leap**

poem *noun*
OTHER WORDS YOU MIGHT USE ARE **poetry** **rhyme** **verse**

point *noun*
1 Don't hurt yourself on the sharp point.
OTHER WORDS YOU MIGHT USE ARE **spike** **tip**
2 We marked the exact point on the map.
OTHER WORDS ARE **location** **place** **position** **spot**

point *verb*
1 The signpost points the way you have to go.
OTHER VERBS YOU MIGHT USE ARE **to indicate** **to show**
2 Don't point that arrow at me!
OTHER VERBS ARE **to aim** **to direct**

pointed *adjective*
a pointed stick.
ANOTHER WORD IS **sharp**
The opposite is **blunt**

poisonous *adjective*
Some toadstools are poisonous.
OTHER WORDS YOU MIGHT USE ARE **deadly** **harmful**

poke *verb*
He poked me in the back with a stick.
OTHER VERBS YOU MIGHT USE ARE **to dig** **to jab** **to prod**

pole *noun*
We pinned our flag to a pole.
OTHER WORDS YOU MIGHT USE ARE **post** **rod** **stick**

police *noun*
DIFFERENT NAMES FOR PEOPLE WHO WORK IN THE POLICE ARE
constable **detective** **inspector** **officer** **policeman**
policewoman **sergeant**

polish *verb*
Jo helped to polish the car.
ANOTHER VERB IS **to shine**
For ways to clean things, see **clean**

polite *adjective*
a polite boy.
OTHER WORDS YOU MIGHT USE ARE **considerate** **respectful** **well-mannered**
The opposite is **rude**

pool *noun*
A large pool is a **pond** or **lake**.
A small pool is a **puddle**.
A pool made to swim in is a **swimming pool**.

poor *adjective*
1 The poor family didn't have enough to eat.
OTHER WORDS YOU MIGHT USE ARE **hard up** **needy** **penniless** **poverty-stricken**
The opposite is **rich**
2 Our teacher was angry because we had done poor work.
For other words, see **bad**

poorly *adjective*
Jo stayed at home because she was poorly.
OTHER WORDS YOU MIGHT USE ARE **ill** **sick** **unwell**
The opposite is **healthy**

popular *adjective*
We sang some popular carols at our concert.
OTHER WORDS YOU MIGHT USE ARE **famous** **favourite** **well-known**

port *noun*
The ship entered port.
For other words, see **harbour**

portion *noun*
Can I have another portion of pie?
OTHER WORDS YOU MIGHT USE ARE **helping** **piece** **share** **slice**

positive *adjective*
Are you positive you saw a ghost?
OTHER WORDS YOU MIGHT USE ARE **certain** **convinced** **definite** **sure**

possess *verb*
Sam only possesses one pair of jeans.
OTHER VERBS YOU MIGHT USE ARE **to have** **to own**

possessions *noun*
Jo keeps her personal possessions in her bedroom.
OTHER WORDS YOU MIGHT USE ARE **belongings** **property**

possible *adjective*
The opposite is **impossible**

post *noun*
1 Dad put up some posts to support the fence.
OTHER WORDS YOU MIGHT USE ARE **column** **pillar** **pole** **prop** **support**
2 The postman brought the post.
ANOTHER WORD IS **mail**
THINGS YOU GET IN THE MAIL ARE **letter** **packet** **parcel** **postcard**

poster *noun*
We put up a poster to tell people about our concert.
OTHER WORDS YOU MIGHT USE ARE **advertisement** **notice** **placard** **sign**

a b c d e f g h i j k l m n o **p** q r s t u v w x y z

postpone *verb*
They postponed sports day because it was raining.
A PHRASE IS **to put off**

pottery *noun*
OTHER WORDS YOU MIGHT USE ARE **crockery** **earthenware**
For other words, see **china**

poultry *noun*
DIFFERENT KINDS OF POULTRY ARE
chicken **cockerel** **duck** **goose** **hen** **rooster** **turkey**

pour *verb*
1 Water poured through the hole.
OTHER VERBS YOU MIGHT USE ARE **to flow** **to gush** **to run** **to stream**
2 I poured the cold tea into the sink.
OTHER VERBS ARE **to empty** **to tip**

power *noun*
1 The police have the power to arrest criminals.
OTHER WORDS YOU MIGHT USE ARE **ability** **authority** **right**
2 Those big waves have the power to knock you over.
OTHER WORDS ARE **energy** **force** **might** **strength**

powerful *adjective*
a powerful giant.
OTHER WORDS YOU MIGHT USE ARE **mighty** **strong**
The opposite is **weak**

practical *adjective*
a practical tool.
OTHER WORDS YOU MIGHT USE ARE **efficient** **handy** **useful**
The opposite is **useless**

practically *adverb*
I've practically finished.
OTHER WORDS YOU MIGHT USE ARE **almost** **nearly**

practise *verb*
If you practise for a concert, you **rehearse**.
If you practise at a sport, you **train** for it.
If you practise for a test, you **revise**.

praise *verb*
Our teacher praised us for working hard today.
OTHER VERBS YOU MIGHT USE ARE **to compliment** **to congratulate**
The opposite is **scold**

precious *adjective*
precious jewels.
OTHER WORDS YOU MIGHT USE ARE **costly** **dear** **expensive** **priceless** **valuable**
The opposite is **worthless**

precise *adjective*
What is the precise time?
OTHER WORDS YOU MIGHT USE ARE **accurate** **correct** **exact** **right**

prepare *verb*
Jo asked Sam to help her prepare for her party.
OTHER VERBS YOU MIGHT USE ARE **to get ready** **to make arrangements** **to organize** **to plan**

present *noun*
Jo got a present from Grandad.
ANOTHER WORD IS **gift**

present *verb*
1 The head presented the prizes on sports day.
OTHER VERBS YOU MIGHT USE ARE **to award** **to give** **to hand over**
2 Sam presented the songs to the audience.
ANOTHER VERB IS **to introduce**
3 We presented a nativity play at Christmas.
OTHER VERBS ARE **to act** **to perform** **to put on**

preserve *verb*
1 You can preserve food in a freezer.
OTHER VERBS YOU MIGHT USE ARE **to keep** **to save**
2 The museum put the old book in a glass case to preserve it.
OTHER VERBS ARE **to look after** **to protect**

press *verb*
1 Press the bell.
ANOTHER VERB IS **to push**
2 Sam pressed his best trousers.
OTHER VERBS YOU MIGHT USE ARE **to flatten** **to iron** **to smooth**

pretend *verb*
There are different ways of pretending.
You can **act** or **play** a part in a play.
You can **disguise** yourself as someone else.
You can **imitate** or **impersonate** someone.
You can **deceive** or **trick** someone.

pretty *adjective*
a pretty dress.
OTHER WORDS YOU MIGHT USE ARE **attractive** **beautiful** **lovely**
The opposite is **ugly**

prevent *verb*
The snow prevented us from going to Granny's.
OTHER VERBS YOU MIGHT USE ARE **to hinder** **to stop**

previously *adverb*
OTHER WORDS YOU MIGHT USE ARE **before** **earlier**

price *noun*
Before you buy anything, ask what the price is.
OTHER WORDS YOU MIGHT USE ARE **charge** **cost** **fee** **payment**
The price you pay to ride in a bus or train is the **fare**.

a b c d e f g h i j k l m n o **p** q r s t u v w x y z

prick *verb*
The doctor pricked my thumb with a needle.
OTHER VERBS YOU MIGHT USE ARE **to pierce** **to puncture**

principal *adjective*
This map only shows the principal towns.
OTHER WORDS YOU MIGHT USE ARE **chief** **important** **main**

principles *noun*
Sam taught Jo the principles of chess.
OTHER WORDS YOU MIGHT USE ARE **laws** **rules** **theory**

prison *noun*
ANOTHER WORD IS
gaol or **jail**
A small room where someone can be locked up is a **cell**.
A prison in a castle is a **dungeon**.

prisoner *noun*
ANOTHER WORD IS
captive
A person you keep prisoner until you get what you want is a **hostage**.

private *adjective*
1 Jo keeps her private things in a drawer in her bedroom.
OTHER WORDS YOU MIGHT USE ARE **personal** **secret**
2 We found a private spot for a picnic.
OTHER WORDS ARE **hidden** **quiet** **secluded**
The opposite is **public**

problem *noun*
1 If you have a problem, tell the teacher.
OTHER WORDS YOU MIGHT USE ARE **difficulty** **worry**
2 The detective had a hard problem to solve.
OTHER WORDS ARE **mystery** **puzzle** **question** **riddle**

procession *noun*
There was a big procession through the middle of town.
OTHER WORDS YOU MIGHT USE ARE **march** **parade**

prod *verb*
Someone prodded me in the back.
OTHER VERBS YOU MIGHT USE ARE **to dig** **to jab** **to poke** **to push**

produce *verb*
1 The factory down the road produces television sets.
OTHER VERBS YOU MIGHT USE ARE **to make** **to manufacture**
2 Grandad's garden produces lots of vegetables.
OTHER VERBS ARE **to grow** **to yield**
3 We produce a magazine every term.
OTHER VERBS ARE **to issue** **to publish**
4 The cat produced four kittens.
OTHER VERBS ARE **to bear** **to give birth to**
5 The conjuror produced a rabbit from a hat.
OTHER VERBS YOU MIGHT USE ARE **to bring out** **to present**

progress *noun*
to make progress
OTHER WORDS YOU MIGHT USE ARE **advance** **move** **forward** **proceed**

prohibited *adjective*
Smoking is prohibited on the bus.
OTHER WORDS YOU MIGHT USE ARE **banned** **forbidden** **illegal**
The opposite is **allowed**

promise *verb*
You promised to come to my party.
OTHER VERBS YOU MIGHT USE ARE **to agree** **to give your word** **to guarantee** **to swear** **to vow**

promptly *adverb*
1 Mum replied promptly to Granny's letter.
OTHER WORDS YOU MIGHT USE ARE **immediately** **quickly**
2 The train arrived promptly.
OTHER WORDS ARE **on time** **punctually**

prop *verb*
Jo propped her bike against the wall.
OTHER VERBS YOU MIGHT USE ARE **to lean** **to rest** **to stand** **to support**

proper *adjective*
1 Put the library books back in their proper places.
OTHER WORDS YOU MIGHT USE ARE **appropriate** **correct** **right** **suitable** **usual**
The opposite is **wrong**
2 I think it would be proper for you to apologize.
OTHER WORDS ARE **decent** **polite** **respectable**
The opposite is **rude**

protect *verb*
1 The mother bird tried to protect her babies.
OTHER VERBS YOU MIGHT USE ARE **to defend** **to guard** **to keep safe** **to look after**
2 The hedge protected us from the wind.
OTHER VERBS ARE **to screen** **to shield**

protest *verb*
We protested when they put up the bus fares.
OTHER VERBS YOU MIGHT USE ARE **to complain** **to object**

proud *adjective*
1 He was too proud to admit that he was wrong.
OTHER WORDS YOU MIGHT USE ARE **boastful** (*informal*) **cocky** **conceited** (*informal*) **stuck up** **vain**
The opposite is **modest**
2 Mum was proud when Jo won a prize.
OTHER WORDS ARE **happy** **pleased**

prove *verb*
They proved that he was guilty.
OTHER VERBS YOU MIGHT USE ARE **to demonstrate** **to show**

provide *verb*
Our teacher provided the paper for us to draw on.
OTHER VERBS YOU MIGHT USE ARE **to give** **to supply**

a b c d e f g h i j k l m n o p q r s t u v w x y z

provoke *verb*
If you provoke the dog, he may bite you.
OTHER VERBS YOU MIGHT USE ARE **to anger** **to annoy** **to tease** **to torment** **to upset** **to worry**

pry *verb*
Don't pry in my affairs!
OTHER WORDS YOU MIGHT USE ARE **to interfere** (*informal*) **to poke your nose into**

publish *verb*
We publish a magazine every term.
OTHER VERBS YOU MIGHT USE ARE **to bring out** **to issue** **to produce**

pudding *noun*
Sam ate so much first course that he didn't have room for pudding.
OTHER WORDS YOU MIGHT USE ARE (*informal*) **afters** **dessert** **sweet**

pull *verb*
1 We pulled the heavy box across the floor.
OTHER VERBS YOU MIGHT USE ARE **to drag** **to haul** **to tug**
2 The car was pulling a caravan.
ANOTHER VERB IS **to tow**
3 The horse was pulling a cart.
ANOTHER VERB IS **to draw**

punch *verb*
For other ways to hit, see **hit**

punctual *adjective*
The train was punctual.
OTHER WORDS YOU MIGHT USE ARE **on time** **prompt**
The opposite is **late**

punctuation *noun*
DIFFERENT PUNCTUATION MARKS ARE
apostrophe '
brackets ( )
colon :
comma ,
dash –
exclamation mark !
full stop .
hyphen -
question mark ?
semi-colon ;
speech marks " "

punishment *noun*
DIFFERENT KINDS OF PUNISHMENT ARE
a beating **detention** **execution** **a fine** **gaol** (or **jail**) or **prison** **an imposition** **a penalty**

pupil *noun*
OTHER WORDS YOU MIGHT USE ARE **schoolboy** **schoolgirl** **student**

pure *adjective*
pure water.
OTHER WORDS YOU MIGHT USE ARE **clean** **clear** **natural**
The opposite is **dirty**

purpose *noun*
He must have a particular purpose to go out in that storm.
OTHER WORDS YOU MIGHT USE ARE **aim** **intention** **object** **plan** **reason**

purse *noun*
Jo put her money in a purse.
OTHER THINGS YOU KEEP MONEY IN ARE
handbag **money box** **piggy bank** **pocket** **wallet**

pursue *verb*
The police pursued the robbers across the town.
OTHER VERBS YOU MIGHT USE ARE **to chase** **to follow** **to hunt**

push *verb*
1 The door will open if you push harder.
OTHER VERBS YOU MIGHT USE ARE **to press** **to shove**
2 I pushed my clothes into a drawer.
OTHER VERBS ARE **to crush** **to force** **to squeeze**

put *verb*
1 Put your dirty cups in the sink.
OTHER VERBS YOU MIGHT USE ARE **to deposit** **to leave** **to pile** **to place** **to stack**
2 We put our pictures where everyone could see them.
OTHER VERBS ARE **to arrange** **to lay** **to position** **to set out**
to put something off
ANOTHER VERB IS **to postpone**
to put up with something
ANOTHER VERB IS **to endure**

puzzle *noun*
Can you solve this puzzle?
OTHER WORDS YOU MIGHT USE ARE **mystery** **problem** **question** **riddle**

puzzle *verb*
The riddle puzzled me.
OTHER VERBS YOU MIGHT USE ARE **to bewilder** **to confuse** **to mystify** **to perplex**

Qq

quaint *adjective*
a quaint thatched cottage.
OTHER WORDS YOU MIGHT USE ARE **old-fashioned** **picturesque**

quake *verb*
Jack quaked with fear when he saw the giant.
OTHER VERBS YOU MIGHT USE ARE **to quiver** **to shake** **to shudder** **to tremble**

quality *noun*
Our butcher only sells meat of the best quality.
OTHER WORDS YOU MIGHT USE ARE **class** **grade** **standard** **value**

quantity *noun*
In hot weather the shop sells a large quantity of ice cream.
OTHER WORDS YOU MIGHT USE ARE **amount** **volume**

quarrel *verb*
Jo and Sam sometimes quarrel, but they soon make it up.
OTHER VERBS YOU MIGHT USE ARE **to argue** **to disagree** **to fall out** **to fight** **to squabble**

queer *adjective*
1 queer shapes. a queer smell.
OTHER WORDS YOU MIGHT USE ARE (*informal*) **funny** **odd** **peculiar** **strange** **unusual**
2 I feel rather queer.
For other words, see **ill**

queue *noun*
A queue of cars waited at the level crossing.
OTHER WORDS YOU MIGHT USE ARE **line** **row**

quick *adjective*
1 a quick journey.
OTHER WORDS YOU MIGHT USE ARE **fast** **rapid** **speedy** **swift**
2 a quick dance.
ANOTHER WORD IS **lively**
3 a quick reply.
OTHER WORDS ARE **instant** **prompt**
The opposite is **slow**
4 The bus came to a quick halt.
OTHER WORDS ARE **hasty** **sudden**

quiet *adjective*
1 Our teacher told us to be quiet.
ANOTHER WORD IS **silent**
2 I listened to some quiet music.
OTHER WORDS ARE **low** **soft**
The opposite is **noisy**

quite *adverb*
1 I'm not quite sure.
OTHER WORDS YOU MIGHT USE ARE **absolutely** **completely** **entirely** **totally**
2 I'm quite cold.
OTHER WORDS ARE **fairly** **moderately** (*informal*) **pretty** **rather**

quiver *verb*
For other verbs, see **quake**

Rr

radio *noun*
An old-fashioned word is **wireless**.
SOME PROGRAMMES YOU HEAR ON THE RADIO ARE
chat shows **interviews** **music** **news** **phone-in programmes** **plays** **sport** **stories** **talks** **weather forecasts**

rail *noun*
There was a rail to stop people falling into the water.
OTHER WORDS YOU MIGHT USE ARE **bar** **railing**

railway *noun*
KINDS OF RAILWAY ARE
branch line **main line** **metro** **mountain railway** **narrow gauge railway** **tramline** **underground**

KINDS OF TRAIN ARE
diesel **electric train** **express** **freight train** or **goods train** **steam train** **tram**

PARTS OF A TRAIN ARE
buffet car **carriage** **coach** **locomotive** **sleeping car** **steam engine** **wagon**

PARTS OF A RAILWAY LINE MIGHT BE
electric rail **overhead wires** **points** **sleepers** **rails**

ALONG THE RAILWAY YOU MIGHT SEE
cutting **embankment** **junction** **level crossing** **sidings** **signals** **signal box** **station** **tunnel**

THINGS YOU SEE AT A STATION ARE
booking office or **ticket office** **buffet** **platform** **timetable** **waiting room**

PEOPLE WHO WORK ON THE RAILWAY ARE
booking clerk **conductor** **driver** **guard** **porter** **signalman** **ticket collector**

rain *noun*
Very heavy rain is a **downpour**.
A short period of rain is a **shower**.
Rain coming down in very small drops is **drizzle**.
For other words, see **weather**

raise *verb*
1 A crane raised the car out of the ditch.
OTHER VERBS YOU MIGHT USE ARE **to hoist** **to lift** **to pick up**
2 We raised money for charity.
OTHER VERBS ARE **to collect** **to get** **to make**

rapid *adjective*
OTHER WORDS YOU MIGHT USE ARE **fast** **quick** **speedy** **swift**
The opposite is **slow**

a b c d e f g h i j k l m n o p q **r** s t u v w x y z

rare *adjective*
Pandas are rare animals.
OTHER WORDS YOU MIGHT USE ARE **scarce** **uncommon**
The opposite is **common**

rather *adverb*
I was rather ill yesterday.
OTHER WORDS YOU MIGHT USE ARE **fairly** **moderately** (*informal*) **pretty** **quite**

ravenous *adjective*
We were so ravenous that we ate everything!
OTHER WORDS YOU MIGHT USE ARE **famished** **hungry** **starving**

ray *noun*
A ray of light shone through the crack in the door.
OTHER WORDS YOU MIGHT USE ARE **beam** **shaft**

reach *verb*
1 I will hold you if you reach out your hand.
ANOTHER VERB IS **to stretch**
2 We can have something to eat when we reach home.
OTHER VERBS YOU MIGHT USE ARE **to arrive at** **to get to**

ready *adjective*
1 Are you ready to go?
OTHER WORDS YOU MIGHT USE ARE **prepared** **willing**
2 Have you got your money ready?
OTHER WORDS ARE **available** **handy**

real *adjective*
1 Are those real diamonds?
ANOTHER WORD IS **genuine**
The opposite is **artificial**
2 You can trust Sam: he's a real friend.
ANOTHER WORD IS **true**
The opposite is **false**

realistic *adjective*
The acting was very realistic.
OTHER WORDS YOU MIGHT USE ARE **lifelike** **natural**

realize *verb*
I suddenly realized that everyone was waiting for me.
OTHER VERBS YOU MIGHT USE ARE **to know** **to see** **to sense** **to understand**

rear *noun*
He crashed into the rear of a bus.
OTHER WORDS YOU MIGHT USE ARE **back** **end**
The opposite is **front**

rear *verb*
Our cat reared four kittens.
OTHER VERBS YOU MIGHT USE ARE **to bring up** **to care for** **to look after**

reason *noun*
Was there any reason for Sam's funny behaviour?
OTHER WORDS YOU MIGHT USE ARE **cause** **excuse** **explanation**
The reason why someone commits a crime is the **motive**.

reasonable *adjective*

1 Dad paid a reasonable price for his car.
OTHER WORDS YOU MIGHT USE ARE **fair** **moderate**

2 You can't have a reasonable argument with a tiny baby.
OTHER WORDS ARE **intelligent** **logical** **sensible**

rebel *verb*

The soldiers rebelled because they were so hungry.
OTHER VERBS YOU MIGHT USE ARE **to disobey** **to revolt**

If sailors rebel on a ship, the word is **mutiny**.

receive *verb*

1 I received ten birthday cards.
ANOTHER VERB IS **to get**

2 He received £2 for doing odd jobs.
ANOTHER VERB IS **to earn**

recent *adjective*

Have you got any recent CDs?
OTHER WORDS YOU MIGHT USE ARE **new** **up-to-date**

The opposite is **old**

reckless *adjective*

Reckless drivers can kill people.
OTHER WORDS YOU MIGHT USE ARE **careless** **thoughtless**

The opposite is **careful**

reckon *verb*

1 Jo reckoned how much the shopping cost.
OTHER VERBS YOU MIGHT USE ARE **to add up** **to calculate** **to count** **to work out**

2 I reckon our side will win.
OTHER VERBS ARE **to believe** **to feel sure** **to think**

recognize *verb*

Would you recognize that man if you saw him again?
OTHER VERBS YOU MIGHT USE ARE **to identify** **to know** **to remember**

recommend *verb*

Mum recommends the restaurant down the road.
OTHER VERBS YOU MIGHT USE ARE **to approve of** **to praise** **to speak well of**

record *noun*

1 We kept a record of the birds we saw on holiday.
OTHER WORDS YOU MIGHT USE ARE
account **description** **diary** **log**

2 Dad has lots of old pop records.
KINDS OF GRAMOPHONE RECORD ARE
album **LP** **single**
OTHER KINDS OF RECORDING ARE
cassette **compact disc** or **CD** **tape** **video**

recover *verb*

1 Mum recovered slowly after her operation.
OTHER VERBS YOU MIGHT USE ARE **to get better** **to heal** **to improve**

2 Did you recover your lost watch?
OTHER VERBS ARE **to find** **to get back** **to retrieve** **to trace**

a b c d e f g h i j k l m n o p q **r** s t u v w x y z

reduce *verb*
She reduced speed when she saw the police car.
OTHER VERBS YOU MIGHT USE ARE **to cut** **to decrease** **to lessen**

refer *verb*
1 Did Dad refer to the broken window?
OTHER VERBS YOU MIGHT USE ARE **to comment on** **to mention**
2 I referred to the dictionary to find the spelling.
OTHER VERBS ARE **to consult** **to look up** **to turn to**

refresh *verb*
The drink refreshed us.
OTHER VERBS YOU MIGHT USE ARE **to cool** **to quench the thirst** **to revive**

refuse *noun*
Put the refuse in the bin.
OTHER WORDS YOU MIGHT USE ARE **junk** **rubbish** **waste**

refuse *verb*
Why did Jo refuse to go to her friend's party?
ANOTHER VERB IS **to decline**
The opposite is **agree**

regard *verb*
We regard Sam as the best swimmer in the school.
OTHER VERBS YOU MIGHT USE ARE **to consider** **to think of**

region *noun*
The South Pole is a cold region.
OTHER WORDS YOU MIGHT USE ARE **area** **district** **place** **zone**

regret *verb*
Jo regretted saying nasty things about her friend.
OTHER VERBS YOU MIGHT USE ARE **to be sad about** **to be sorry for** **to repent**

regular *adjective*
1 Did the postman come at the regular time today?
OTHER WORDS YOU MIGHT USE ARE **customary** **normal** **usual**
2 The drummer kept a regular rhythm.
OTHER WORDS ARE **even** **steady**

rehearse *verb*
We rehearsed for the concert all afternoon.
OTHER VERBS YOU MIGHT USE ARE **to practise** **to prepare**

reject *verb*
Jo rejected the invitation to her friend's party.
OTHER VERBS YOU MIGHT USE ARE **to refuse** **to turn down**
The opposite is **accept**

rejoice *verb*
The crowd rejoiced when their team won the cup.
OTHER VERBS YOU MIGHT USE ARE **to be happy** **to celebrate**

relation *noun*
For other words, see **family**

relax *verb*
I like to relax in a hot bath.
OTHER VERBS YOU MIGHT USE ARE **to rest** **to unwind**

release *verb*
They released the animals from the cage.
OTHER VERBS YOU MIGHT USE ARE **to free** **to let loose** **to let out** **to liberate** **to set free**

reliable *adjective*
You can trust Sam: he's a reliable friend.
OTHER WORDS YOU MIGHT USE ARE **faithful** **loyal** **trustworthy**

relief *noun*
The pills gave me some relief from my headache.
OTHER WORDS YOU MIGHT USE ARE **comfort** **ease** **help**

relieved *adjective*
We were relieved to hear that Jo's accident was not serious.
OTHER WORDS YOU MIGHT USE ARE **glad** **happy** **thankful**

religion *noun*
OTHER WORDS YOU MIGHT USE ARE
belief **creed** **faith**

SOME RELIGIONS ARE
Buddhism **Christianity** **Hinduism** **Judaism** **Islam** **Sikhism**

PEOPLE WHO FOLLOW A RELIGION ARE
Buddhist **Christian** **Hindu** **Jewish** **Muslim** **Sikh**

KINDS OF RELIGIOUS SERVICE ARE
baptism or **christening** **cremation** **funeral** **Holy Communion** **mass** **prayers** **wedding** **worship**

PARTS OF A MEETING FOR WORSHIP MIGHT BE
anthem **blessing** **collection** or **offering** **confession** **devotions** **hymn** **meditation** **prayers** **psalm** **reading from scripture** **sermon**

PLACES WHERE PEOPLE WORSHIP ARE
cathedral **chapel** **church** **mosque** **pagoda** **shrine** **synagogue** **temple**

RELIGIOUS LEADERS AND TEACHERS ARE
archbishop **ayatollah** **bishop** **cardinal** **chaplain** **clergyman** **curate** **druid** **guru** **imam** **lama** **minister** **missionary** **parson** **pope** **priest** **prophet** **rabbi** **rector** **vicar**

ADJECTIVES YOU MIGHT USE TO DESCRIBE RELIGIOUS THINGS ARE
blessed **consecrated** **divine** **holy** **sacred**

ADJECTIVES YOU MIGHT USE TO DESCRIBE RELIGIOUS PEOPLE ARE
devout **pious**

A person who thinks there is no God is an **atheist**.
A person who says you can't know whether there is a God or not is an **agnostic**.

reluctant *adjective*
I was reluctant to walk home because it was raining.
OTHER WORDS YOU MIGHT USE ARE **hesitant** **unwilling**
The opposite is **enthusiastic**

a b c d e f g h i j k l m n o p q **r** s t u v w x y z

rely *verb*
You can rely on Jo to do her best.
OTHER VERBS YOU MIGHT USE ARE (*informal*) **to bank on** **to count on** **to depend on** **to trust**

remain *verb*
He told me to remain where I was.
OTHER VERBS YOU MIGHT USE ARE **to stay** **to stop**

remains *noun*
1 We explored the remains of the castle.
ANOTHER WORD IS **ruins**
2 What shall we do with the remains of this stew?
OTHER WORDS ARE (*informal*) **leftovers** **remainder** **rest**
3 His remains were buried near the church.
OTHER WORDS ARE **body** **corpse**

remark *verb*
I remarked that it was a nice day.
OTHER VERBS YOU MIGHT USE ARE **to comment** **to mention** **to say**

remarkable *adjective*
Our team had a remarkable victory.
OTHER WORDS YOU MIGHT USE ARE **amazing** **extraordinary** **special** **surprising** **unusual**

remedy *noun*
Do you know a remedy for a cold?
OTHER WORDS YOU MIGHT USE ARE **cure** **medicine** **treatment**

remember *verb*
Do you remember our holiday last year?
OTHER WORDS YOU MIGHT USE ARE **to recall** **to recollect**
The opposite is **forget**

remind *verb*
Jo reminded Mum to buy some sugar.
A PHRASE YOU MIGHT USE IS **to jog someone's memory**

remove *verb*
1 Please remove this rubbish.
OTHER VERBS YOU MIGHT USE ARE **to carry away** **to get rid of** **to move** **to shift** **to take away**
2 The dentist removed a tooth.
OTHER VERBS ARE **to extract** **to take out**
3 What removes oil from clothes?
ANOTHER VERB IS **to wash off**

repair *verb*
OTHER VERBS YOU MIGHT USE ARE (*informal*) **to fix** **to mend** **to put right**
to repair clothes **to darn** **to patch** **to sew up**
to repair something old or broken **to do up** **to renovate** **to restore**

repeat *verb*
Don't repeat everything I say!
OTHER VERBS YOU MIGHT USE ARE **to go over** **to say again**

reply *verb*
I replied to Granny's letter.
OTHER VERBS YOU MIGHT USE ARE **to answer** **to respond to**

report *verb*

1 We reported that we had finished our work.
OTHER VERBS YOU MIGHT USE ARE **to announce** **to declare** **to state**

2 I reported him to the police.
OTHER VERBS ARE **to complain about** **to inform against** (*informal*) **to tell of**

reproduce *verb*

1 Sam can reproduce a lot of bird calls.
OTHER VERBS YOU MIGHT USE ARE **to imitate** **to mimic**

2 We reproduced our work on the copier in the school office.
OTHER VERBS ARE **to copy** **to duplicate** **to photocopy**

3 Rabbits reproduce very quickly.
OTHER VERBS ARE **to breed** **to multiply**

reptile *noun*, see next page

request *verb*

When the work got too hard, we requested help from our teacher.
OTHER VERBS YOU MIGHT USE ARE **to appeal for** **to ask for** **to beg for**

require *verb*

We required 3 more runs to win.
OTHER VERBS ARE **to be short of** **to need** **to want**

rescue *verb*

Robin Hood rescued the prisoners from the Sheriff's castle.
OTHER VERBS YOU MIGHT USE ARE **to free** **to liberate** **to release** **to save** **to set free**

resemble *verb*

Sam resembles his father.
OTHER VERBS YOU MIGHT USE ARE **to be similar to** **to look like**

reserve *noun*

We have two reserves who can play on Saturday if necessary.
OTHER WORDS ARE **deputy** **stand-in** **substitute**

reserve *verb*

1 Jo reserved some sandwiches for people who came late.
OTHER VERBS YOU MIGHT USE ARE **to keep** **to save**

2 We reserved our seats on the train.
ANOTHER WORD IS **to book**

resign *verb*

The manager resigned because the team was doing so badly.
OTHER VERBS YOU MIGHT USE ARE **to give up** **to leave** (*informal*) **to quit**

resist *verb*

He made things worse because he resisted the police.
OTHER VERBS YOU MIGHT USE ARE **to defy** **to oppose** **to stand up to**

respect *noun*

We should show respect to people who work hard for us.
OTHER WORDS YOU MIGHT USE ARE **admiration** **consideration**
The respect you show towards religious things is **reverence**.

a b c d e f g h i j k l m n o p q **r** s t u v w x y z

reptile *noun*
DIFFERENT KINDS OF REPTILE ARE **alligator** **crocodile** **lizard** **snake** **tortoise** **turtle**

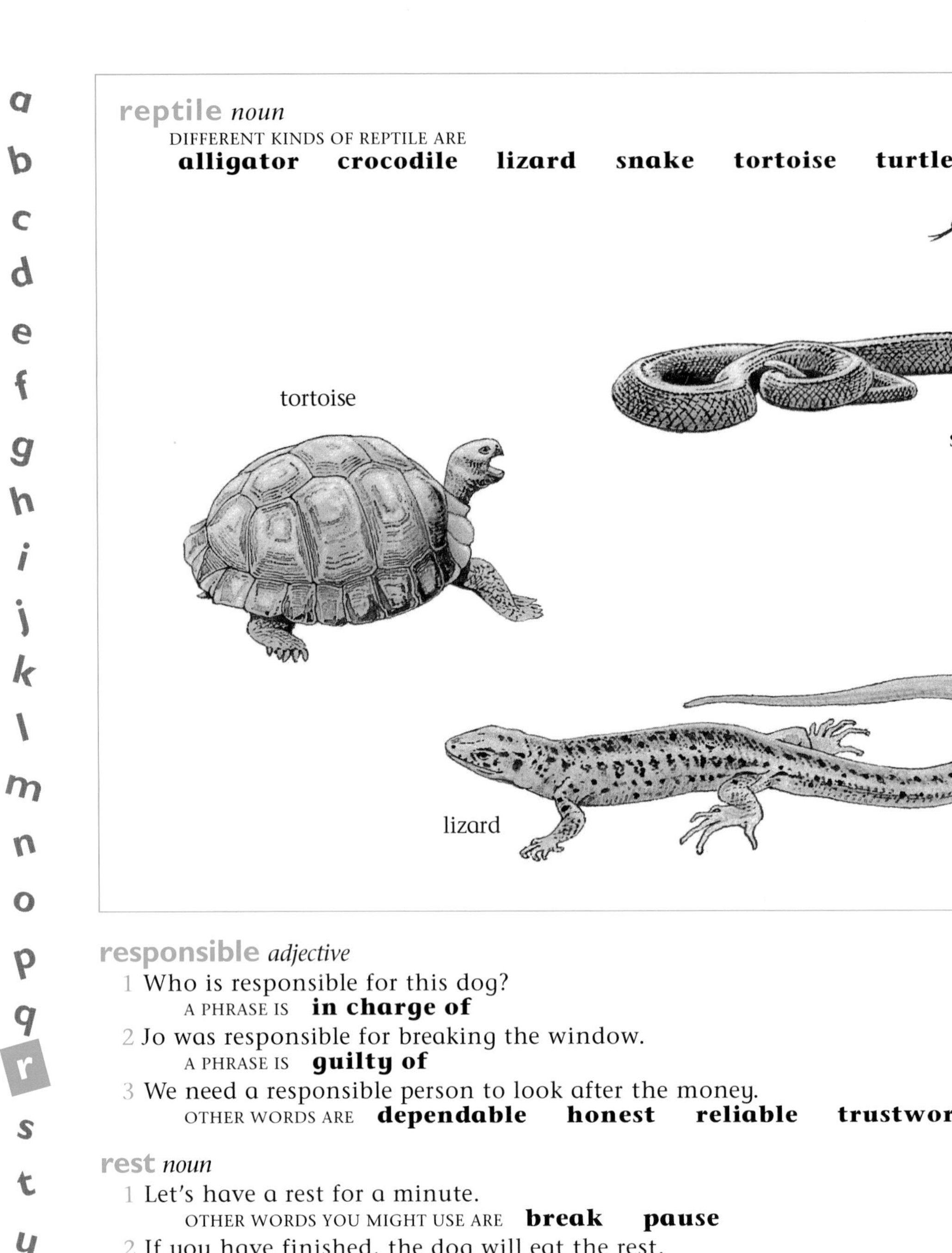

responsible *adjective*

1 Who is responsible for this dog?
A PHRASE IS **in charge of**

2 Jo was responsible for breaking the window.
A PHRASE IS **guilty of**

3 We need a responsible person to look after the money.
OTHER WORDS ARE **dependable** **honest** **reliable** **trustworthy**

rest *noun*

1 Let's have a rest for a minute.
OTHER WORDS YOU MIGHT USE ARE **break** **pause**

2 If you have finished, the dog will eat the rest.
ANOTHER WORD IS **remainder**

rest *verb*

1 Halfway up the hill we sat down to rest.
OTHER VERBS YOU MIGHT USE ARE **to relax** (*informal*) **to take it easy**
When you are resting you might **doze** **lie down** **sleep** (*informal*) **take a nap**

2 Rest the ladder against the wall.
OTHER VERBS YOU MIGHT USE ARE **to lean** **to prop** **to stand** **to support**

restore *verb*
Uncle David restores old cars.
OTHER VERBS YOU MIGHT USE ARE (*informal*) **to do up** **to mend** **to renovate** **to repair**

result *noun*
The result of getting up late was that I missed the bus.
OTHER WORDS YOU MIGHT USE ARE **consequence** **effect**

retreat *verb*
The soldiers retreated when they knew that they were losing.
OTHER VERBS YOU MIGHT USE ARE **to go back** **to move back** **to run away**

return *verb*
1 We returned at tea time.
OTHER VERBS YOU MIGHT USE ARE **to come back** **to go back**
2 Jo returned the pen I lent her.
OTHER VERBS ARE **to give back** **to repay**

reveal *verb*
1 We drew back the curtain and revealed the stage.
OTHER VERBS YOU MIGHT USE ARE **to disclose** **to show**
2 Don't ever reveal our secret!
PHRASES ARE **to let out** **to make known**

reverse *verb*
Dad damaged the car when he reversed into a wall.
OTHER VERBS ARE **to back** **to go backwards**

revolt *verb*
The players revolted because they thought the rules were not fair.
OTHER VERBS YOU MIGHT USE ARE **to disobey** **to rebel**
When sailors revolt the word is **mutiny**.

revolting *adjective*
The food was so revolting that nobody would eat it.
OTHER WORDS YOU MIGHT USE ARE **disgusting** **foul** **horrible** **nasty** **unattractive**
The opposite is **attractive**

rhythm *noun*
Sam likes music with a strong rhythm.
OTHER WORDS YOU MIGHT USE ARE **beat** **pulse**

rich *adjective*
Rich people can buy what they want.
OTHER WORDS YOU MIGHT USE ARE **prosperous** **wealthy** **well-off**
The opposite is **poor**

ride *verb*
For other verbs, see **travel**

ridiculous *adjective*
We laughed at his ridiculous hat.
OTHER WORDS YOU MIGHT USE ARE **absurd** **comic** **funny** **silly** **stupid**

a b c d e f g h i j k l m n o p q **r** s t u v w x y z

right *adjective*

1 Most people use their right hand to write with.
The opposite is **left**

2 All Jo's answers were right.
OTHER WORDS YOU MIGHT USE ARE **accurate** **correct**

3 Is that the right time?
OTHER WORDS ARE **exact** **precise** **proper** **true**

4 It's right to own up when you've been naughty.
OTHER WORDS ARE **fair** **honest** **moral**

5 A thesaurus helps you to find the right word.
OTHER WORDS ARE **appropriate** **suitable**

The opposite is **wrong**

ring *noun*

We all stood in a ring.
ANOTHER WORD IS **circle**

ring *verb*

1 I heard a bell ring.
Loud bells **peal**.
A small bell **tinkles**.
An annoying noisy bell **jangles**.
A clock **chimes**.

2 We ring Granny every Sunday.
OTHER WORDS ARE
to call **to phone** **to telephone**

riot *noun*

The police were called to control the riot.
OTHER WORDS YOU MIGHT USE ARE **disorder** **disturbance** **mutiny** **revolt**

rip *verb*

Sam ripped his jeans.
OTHER VERBS YOU MIGHT USE ARE **to split** **to tear**

rise *verb*

1 I watched the balloon rise into the sky.
OTHER VERBS YOU MIGHT USE ARE **to ascend** **to climb** **to go up** **to lift**
The opposite is **fall**

2 Bus fares are going to rise next week.
ANOTHER VERB IS **to increase**

3 We all rose when the teacher came into the room.
OTHER VERBS ARE **to get up** **to stand**

risk *noun*

There's a risk of rain today.
OTHER WORDS YOU MIGHT USE ARE **chance** **danger** **possibility**

rival *noun*

The team we played on Saturday were our old rivals.
OTHER WORDS YOU MIGHT USE ARE **enemy** **opponent**

river *noun*

For other words, see **water**

road *noun*

BIG ROADS FOR MOTOR TRAFFIC ARE

bypass **motorway** **ring road**

OTHER WORDS YOU MIGHT USE ARE

a road with houses along it is a **street**
a road with trees along it is an **avenue**
a narrow road between buildings is an **alley**
a road where you can only drive one way is a **one-way street**
a road closed at one end is a **cul-de-sac**
a road that goes up to a house is a **drive**
a narrow road in the country is a **lane**
a rough road in the country is a **track** or **cart track**
a path for horses is a **bridleway**
a path along a canal is a **towpath**

robber *noun*

ANOTHER WORD IS

thief

DIFFERENT KINDS OF ROBBER ARE

burglar **highwayman** **mugger** **pickpocket** **shoplifter**

For other words, see **steal**

rock *noun*

ANOTHER WORD IS **stone**

A big piece of rock is a **boulder**.

rock *verb*

1 The boat rocked gently in the breeze.

OTHER VERBS YOU MIGHT USE ARE **to sway** **to swing**

2 The boat rocked violently in the storm.

OTHER VERBS ARE **to roll** **to toss**

rod *noun*

The climbing frame is made of iron rods.

OTHER WORDS YOU MIGHT USE ARE **bar** **pole** **rail**

rodent *noun*

THESE ANIMALS ARE RODENTS:

gerbil **hamster** **mouse** **rat** **squirrel**

a b c d e f g h i j k l m n o p q **r** s t u v w x y z

room *noun*
For different rooms, see **home**

rope *noun*
OTHER WORDS YOU CAN USE ARE **cord** **line**

rotten *adjective*
1 rotten wood.
OTHER WORDS YOU MIGHT USE ARE **decayed** **decomposed**
2 rotten food.
OTHER WORDS ARE **bad** **mouldy** **smelly**
3 Sam is rotten at tennis!
OTHER WORDS ARE **bad** **hopeless** **incompetent** **useless**

rough *adjective*
1 We jolted along the rough road.
OTHER WORDS YOU MIGHT USE ARE **bumpy** **uneven**
The opposite is **smooth**
2 Sandpaper feels rough.
OTHER WORDS ARE **coarse** **harsh** **scratchy**
The opposite is **soft**
3 The sea was very rough.
OTHER WORDS ARE **stormy** **wild**
The opposite is **calm**
4 I don't like rough games.
OTHER WORDS ARE **bad-tempered** **boisterous** **rowdy** **violent**
The opposite is **gentle**
5 At a rough guess it will cost £100 to mend the car.
ANOTHER WORD IS **approximate**
The opposite is **exact**

round *adjective*
Most coins are round.
ANOTHER WORD IS
circular
A flat round shape is a **disc**.
A solid round shape is a **ball** or **globe** or **sphere**.

route *noun*
Sam knows a quick route into town.
ANOTHER WORD IS **way**

row *noun* (rhymes with *cow*)
1 Sam and Jo hardly ever have a row.
OTHER WORDS YOU MIGHT USE ARE **disagreement** **quarrel** **squabble**
2 What was that row in the night?
OTHER WORDS ARE **commotion** **din** **noise** **uproar**

row *noun* (rhymes with *toe*)
We stood in a straight row.
OTHER WORDS YOU MIGHT USE ARE **file** **line** **queue**

rubbish *noun*
Throw away that rubbish.
OTHER WORDS YOU MIGHT USE ARE (*informal*) **junk** **litter** **refuse** **scrap** **waste**

rude *adjective*
That rude girl shouted at us.
OTHER WORDS YOU MIGHT USE ARE **bad-mannered** **cheeky** **disrespectful** **impertinent** **impolite** **impudent** **insulting** **offensive**
The opposite is **polite**

ruin *verb*
The storm ruined the flowers in the garden.
OTHER VERBS YOU MIGHT USE ARE **to destroy** **to spoil** **to wreck**

rule *noun*
When you play a game, you must obey the rules.
OTHER WORDS YOU MIGHT USE ARE **law** **regulation**

rule *verb*
In the old days, the king used to rule the country.
OTHER VERBS YOU MIGHT USE ARE
to control **to govern** **to lead** **to manage** **to run**

DIFFERENT WORDS FOR PEOPLE WHO RULE OVER THEIR SUBJECTS MIGHT BE
dictator **emperor** **empress** **governor** **king** **monarch** **queen** **president** **prince** **princess** **rajah** **sovereign** **sultan** **tyrant** **tzar**

Some countries are ruled by a **government** with a **prime minister**.

rumour *noun*
It's not fair to spread stories that are only rumour.
ANOTHER WORD IS **gossip**

run *verb*
DIFFERENT WAYS TO RUN ARE
to jog **to race** **to scamper** **to sprint**
For other words, see **rush**

DIFFERENT WAYS A HORSE RUNS ARE
canter **gallop** **trot**

runny *adjective*
The jelly hasn't set yet—it's still runny.
OTHER WORDS YOU MIGHT USE ARE **liquid** **sloppy** **watery**

rush *verb*
Jo was hungry, so she rushed home for something to eat.
OTHER VERBS YOU MIGHT USE ARE **to dash** **to hurry** **to speed**
For other verbs, see **run**

Ss

sacred *adjective*
The Bible and the Koran are sacred books.
OTHER WORDS YOU MIGHT USE ARE **holy** **religious**

sad *adjective*
1 a sad look on someone's face.
OTHER WORDS YOU MIGHT USE ARE **depressed** **disappointed** **gloomy** **heartbroken** **melancholy** **miserable** **mournful** **sorrowful** **tearful** **troubled** **unhappy** **wretched**
2 sad news.
OTHER WORDS YOU MIGHT USE ARE **depressing** **disappointing** **distressing** **tragic** **upsetting**
The opposite is **happy**

safe *adjective*
1 When we got indoors, we felt safe from the storm.
OTHER WORDS YOU MIGHT USE ARE **protected** **secure**
2 We were glad to get home safe.
ANOTHER WORD IS **unharmed**
3 Is the dog safe?
OTHER WORDS YOU MIGHT USE ARE **harmless** **tame**

sailor *noun*
ANOTHER WORD IS **seaman**
The sailors who sail a ship are the **crew**.

salad *noun*
THINGS YOU EAT IN SALAD ARE
beetroot **celery** **cress** **cucumber** **lettuce** **mustard and cress** **onion** **potato** **radish** **tomato** **watercress**

sample *noun*
Jo showed Dad samples of her work.
OTHER WORDS YOU MIGHT USE ARE **example** **specimen**

satisfactory *adjective*
We can go out to play if our work is satisfactory.
OTHER WORDS YOU MIGHT USE ARE **acceptable** **all right** **good enough**

satisfy *verb*
He's always grumpy: nothing satisfies him.
OTHER VERBS YOU MIGHT USE ARE **to content** **to make happy** **to please**

savage *adjective*
a savage attack.
OTHER WORDS YOU MIGHT USE ARE **bloodthirsty** **brutal** **cruel** **fierce** **heartless** **ruthless** **vicious** **violent**
The opposite is **gentle**

save *verb*
1 Robin Hood saved the prisoners.
OTHER VERBS YOU MIGHT USE ARE **to free** **to liberate** **to release** **to rescue** **to set free**
2 I saved some sweets for later.
OTHER VERBS ARE **to keep** **to preserve** **to put aside**

say *verb*
For other verbs, see **talk**

saying *noun*
'I don't believe it' is a common saying.
OTHER WORDS YOU MIGHT USE ARE **expression** **phrase** **remark**
A saying that is supposed to teach a moral, like 'Many hands make light work', is a **proverb**.

scarce *adjective*
1 Water is scarce in the desert.
A PHRASE IS **in short supply**
The opposite is **plentiful**
2 Snakes are scarce in England.
OTHER WORDS ARE **rare** **uncommon**
The opposite is **common**

scarcely *adverb*
I could scarcely believe my eyes!
OTHER WORDS YOU MIGHT USE ARE **barely** **hardly** **only just**

scare *verb*
The sudden noise scared me.
OTHER VERBS ARE **to alarm** **to frighten** **to shock** **to startle** **to terrify** **to upset**

scatter *verb*
The baby always scatters her toys round the room.
OTHER VERBS YOU MIGHT USE ARE **to spread** **to throw about**

scent *noun*
the scent of roses.
OTHER WORDS YOU MIGHT USE ARE **fragrance** **perfume** **smell**

school *noun*
DIFFERENT KINDS OF SCHOOL ARE
boarding school **comprehensive school** **first school** **infant school** **junior school** **kindergarten** **middle school** **nursery school** **play group** **primary school** **secondary school**
For other words, see **educate**, **teach**

a b c d e f g h i j k l m n o p q r **s** t u v w x y z

science *noun*
DIFFERENT KINDS OF SCIENCE ARE
astronomy **biology** **botany** **chemistry** **electronics** **engineering** **geology** **physics** **psychology** **technology** **zoology**

scold *verb*
Jo scolded the dog for eating her chocolate.
OTHER VERBS YOU MIGHT USE ARE **to reprimand** (*informal*) **to tell off** (*informal*) **to tick off**

scramble *verb*
I scrambled over the rocks.
OTHER VERBS YOU MIGHT USE ARE **to clamber** **to climb** **to crawl**

scrap *noun*
1 We put scraps of food out for the birds.
OTHER WORDS YOU MIGHT USE ARE **bit** **crumb** **piece**
2 Dad took some scrap to the tip.
OTHER WORDS YOU MIGHT USE ARE (*informal*) **junk** **rubbish** **waste**

scrape *verb*
1 I scraped my knee on the stones.
OTHER VERBS YOU MIGHT USE ARE **to graze** **to scratch**
2 Jo scraped the mud off her shoe.
OTHER VERBS ARE **to clean** **to rub** **to scrub**

scratch *verb*
Dad scratched the car on the gate.
OTHER VERBS YOU MIGHT USE ARE **to damage** **to graze** **to scrape**

scream *verb*
Everyone screamed when the ride went faster and faster.
OTHER VERBS ARE **to cry out** **to howl** **to screech** **to shriek** **to squeal** **to yell**

sculpture *noun*
OTHER WORDS ARE **carvings** **statues**

sea *noun*
ANOTHER WORD IS **ocean**

seal *verb*
Remember to seal the envelope.
OTHER VERBS YOU MIGHT USE ARE **to close** **to fasten** **to stick down**

search *verb*
I was searching for my watch.
OTHER VERBS YOU MIGHT USE ARE **to hunt for** **to look for**

seaside *noun*
We had a trip to the seaside.
OTHER WORDS YOU MIGHT USE ARE
beach **coast**
Another word for beach is **shore**.

THINGS YOU MIGHT SEE AT THE SEASIDE ARE
breakwater **cliffs** **pier** **promenade** **rocks** **rock pools** **sand** **sand dunes** **shingle** **waves**

THINGS YOU MIGHT FIND ARE
pebbles **seaweed** **shellfish** **shells**

season *noun*
THE SEASONS OF THE YEAR ARE
spring **summer** **autumn** **winter**

seat *noun*
DIFFERENT THINGS YOU SIT ON ARE
armchair **bench** **chair** **deckchair** **pew** **pouffe** **rocking chair** **settee** **sofa** **stool**
The seat a king or queen sits on for official occasions is a **throne**.

secret *adjective*
1 a secret diary.
OTHER WORDS YOU MIGHT USE ARE **intimate** **personal** **private**
2 a secret place.
OTHER WORDS ARE **concealed** **hidden** **unknown**
The opposite is **public**

secure *adjective*
Make sure the ladder is secure before you climb it.
OTHER WORDS YOU MIGHT USE ARE **firm** **fixed** **safe** **steady**
The opposite is **loose**

a b c d e f g h i j k l m n o p q r **s** t u v w x y z

see *verb*

1 Did you see anyone you know?

OTHER VERBS YOU MIGHT USE ARE **to make out** **to notice** **to recognize** **to spot**

To see someone or something very briefly is to **glimpse** it.

2 We saw a good film.

OTHER VERBS ARE **to look at** **to view** **to watch**

3 If you see an accident, tell the police.

ANOTHER VERB IS **to witness**

seem *verb*

Granny seems better today.

OTHER VERBS YOU MIGHT USE ARE **to appear** **to look**

seize *verb*

1 I seized the end of the rope.

OTHER VERBS YOU MIGHT USE ARE (*informal*) **to grab** **to hold** **to snatch**

2 The police seized the thief.

OTHER VERBS ARE **to arrest** **to capture** **to catch**

seldom *adverb*

It seldom snows in May.

ANOTHER WORD IS **rarely**

The opposite is **often**

select *verb*

1 You can select some sweets from the tin.

OTHER VERBS YOU MIGHT USE ARE **to choose** **to pick**

2 We selected Jo to be captain.

OTHER VERBS ARE **to appoint** **to decide on** **to vote for**

selfish *adjective*

It's selfish to keep the best sweets for yourself.

OTHER WORDS YOU MIGHT USE ARE **greedy** **mean** **thoughtless**

The opposite is **generous**

send *verb*

We sent a parcel to Grandad.

OTHER VERBS YOU MIGHT USE ARE **to dispatch** **to post**

sense *noun*

1 If you've got any sense, you won't go out in the rain.

OTHER WORDS YOU MIGHT USE ARE

intelligence **wisdom**

2 We use our five senses to recognize things.

OUR FIVE SENSES ARE

hearing **sight** **smell** **taste** **touch**

sensible *adjective*

Sensible people stay in when it rains.

OTHER WORDS YOU MIGHT USE ARE **reasonable** **thoughtful** **wise**

The opposite is **silly**

sensitive *adjective*

Jo has a sensitive skin.

OTHER WORDS YOU MIGHT USE ARE **delicate** **soft** **tender**

separate *adjective*
1 They kept the sick children separate from the rest of us.
OTHER WORDS ARE **apart** **divided** **isolated** **segregated**
2 The infants are in a separate building from the juniors.
OTHER WORDS ARE **detached** **different** **distinct**

series *noun*
We had a series of accidents.
OTHER WORDS ARE **row** **sequence** **string** **succession**

serious *adjective*
1 Sam takes a serious interest in his work.
OTHER WORDS YOU MIGHT USE ARE **careful** **sincere** **thoughtful**
2 She had a serious look on her face.
OTHER WORDS ARE **grave** **sad** **solemn**
3 Several people were hurt in the serious accident.
OTHER WORDS ARE **awful** **bad** **dreadful** **severe** **terrible**

service *noun*
KINDS OF RELIGIOUS SERVICE ARE
baptism or **christening** **funeral** **Holy Communion** **mass** **prayers** **wedding service** **worship**
For other words, see **religion**

set *verb*
1 Has the glue set yet?
ANOTHER VERB IS **to harden**
2 We set out our work for the parents to see.
OTHER VERBS YOU MIGHT USE ARE **to arrange** **to lay out** **to put out**
3 We set off at breakfast time.
OTHER VERBS ARE **to depart** **to start**

settle *verb*
Have you settled on what to do?
OTHER VERBS YOU MIGHT USE ARE **to agree** **to decide** **to fix**

severe *adjective*
1 a severe teacher.
OTHER WORDS YOU MIGHT USE ARE **stern** **strict**
2 a severe illness.
OTHER WORDS ARE **bad** **serious**
The opposite is **mild**

sew *verb*
ANOTHER WORD IS **to stitch**
To sew up a hole is **to darn**.
To sew with loose stitches is **to tack**.

sewing *noun*
OTHER WORDS ARE **embroidery** **needlework**

shabby *adjective*
shabby clothes.
OTHER WORDS YOU MIGHT USE ARE **faded** **old** **ragged** (*informal*) **scruffy** **worn**
The opposite is **smart**

a
b
c
d
e
f
g
h
i
j
k
l
m
n
o
p
q
r
s
t
u
v
w
x
y
z

shade *noun*

1 We sat in the shade of a tree.
ANOTHER WORD IS **shadow**

2 My coat is a pretty shade of red.
OTHER WORDS YOU MIGHT USE ARE **colour** **hue** **tinge**

shady *adjective*

We sat down in a shady place.
OTHER WORDS YOU MIGHT USE ARE **shaded** **shadowy**

shaggy *adjective*

The dog had a shaggy coat.
OTHER WORDS YOU MIGHT USE ARE **hairy** **rough** **woolly**

shake *verb*

1 I shook with fear.
OTHER VERBS YOU MIGHT USE ARE **to quake** **to quiver** **to shiver** **to shudder** **to tremble**

2 The house shook in the earthquake.
OTHER VERBS ARE **to rock** **to sway** **to vibrate** **to wobble**

shallow *adjective*

The opposite is **deep**

shame *noun*

We'll never forget the shame of losing 14–0!
OTHER WORDS YOU MIGHT USE ARE **disgrace** **embarrassment**

shape *noun*, see opposite page

share *noun*

1 We all had a share of the money.
OTHER WORDS YOU MIGHT USE ARE **fraction** **part**

2 Mum made sure that everyone had a fair share of the pudding.
OTHER WORDS ARE **helping** **portion** **ration**

share *verb*

We shared the food between us.
OTHER VERBS YOU MIGHT USE ARE **to deal out** **to distribute** **to divide** **to split**

sharp *adjective*

1 a sharp stick.
ANOTHER WORD IS **pointed**

2 a sharp knife.
OTHER WORDS YOU MIGHT USE ARE **keen** **razor-sharp**
The opposite is **blunt**

3 a sharp bend in the road.
ANOTHER WORD IS **sudden**

4 a sharp girl.
OTHER WORDS ARE **bright** **clever** **intelligent** **quick** **smart**
The opposite is **dull**

shed *verb*

A lorry shed its load on the motorway.
OTHER VERBS ARE **to drop** **to scatter**

shape *noun*

OTHER WORDS YOU MIGHT USE ARE **form** **outline**

DIFFERENT SHAPES ARE

circle **heptagon** **hexagon** **oblong** **octagon** **oval** **pentagon** **rectangle** **semicircle** **spiral** **square** **triangle**

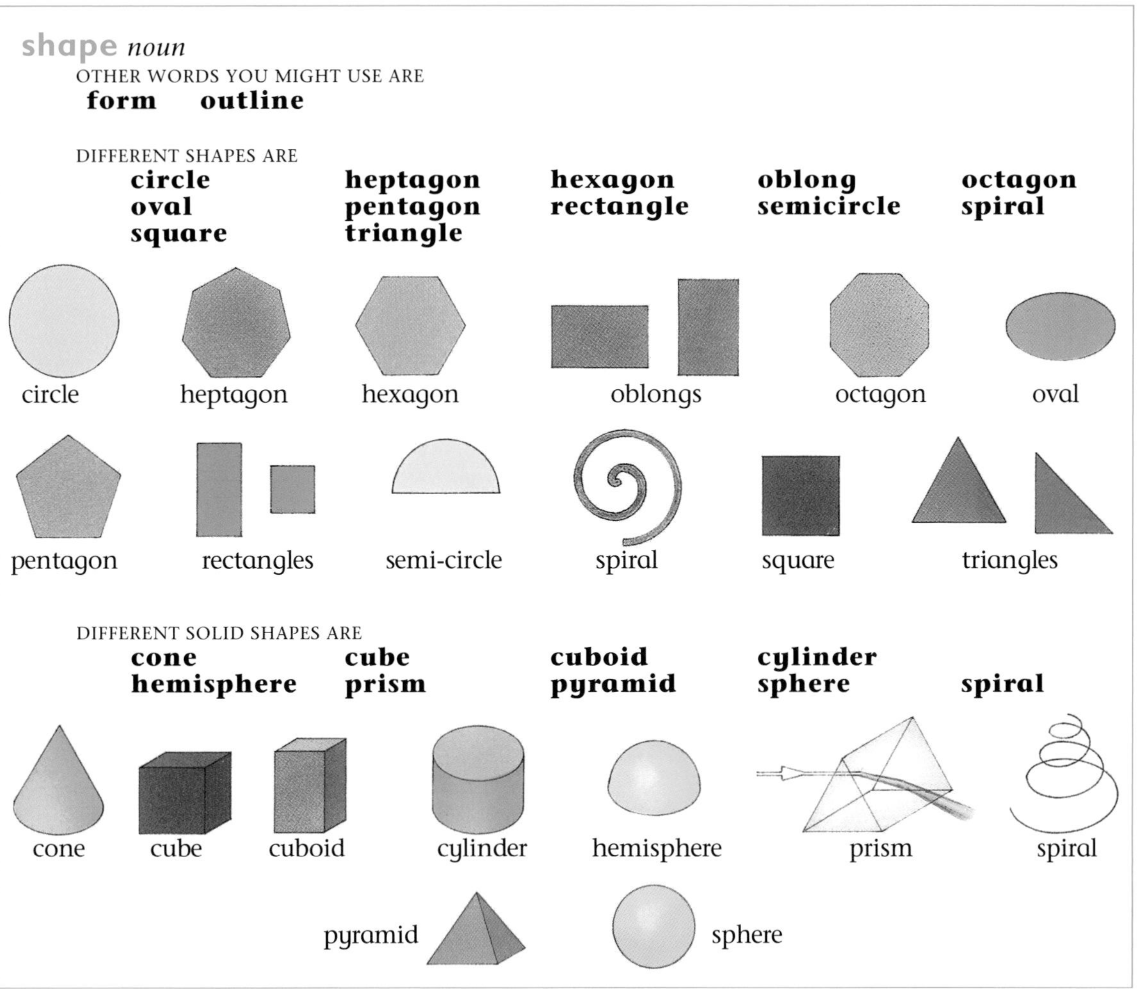

DIFFERENT SOLID SHAPES ARE

cone **cube** **cuboid** **cylinder** **hemisphere** **prism** **pyramid** **sphere** **spiral**

cone cube cuboid cylinder hemisphere prism spiral

pyramid sphere

sheet *noun*

1 a sheet on a bed.

For things you have on a bed, see **bed**

2 a sheet of paper.

OTHER WORDS YOU MIGHT USE ARE **leaf** **page**

shelter *noun*

The animals looked for shelter from the storm.

OTHER WORDS ARE **cover** **protection** **refuge** **safety**

shelter *verb*

The hedge sheltered us from the wind.

OTHER VERBS YOU MIGHT USE ARE **to guard** **to hide** **to protect** **to shield**

shift *verb*

For other verbs, see **move**

shine *verb*

Things shine in different ways.

THEY CAN:

blaze **burn** **dazzle** **flash** **flicker** **glare** **gleam** **glimmer** **glint** **glisten** **glitter** **glow** **shine** **sparkle** **twinkle**

a b c d e f g h i j k l m n o p q r s t u v w x y z

shiny *adjective*

a shiny new coin.

OTHER WORDS YOU MIGHT USE ARE **bright** **gleaming** **glossy** **polished** **shining**

The opposite is **dull**

shiver *verb*

I was shivering with cold.

OTHER VERBS YOU MIGHT USE ARE **to quiver** **to shake** **to shudder** **to tremble**

shock *verb*

1 The explosion shocked everyone.

OTHER VERBS YOU MIGHT USE ARE **to alarm** **to frighten** **to startle** **to stun** **to surprise**

2 The swearing shocked us.

OTHER VERBS ARE **to disgust** **to offend** **to upset**

shoe *noun*

THINGS YOU WEAR ON YOUR FEET ARE

boots **clogs** **plimsolls** **sandals** **slippers** **trainers** **wellingtons**

shoot *verb*

He shot at the target.

OTHER VERBS YOU MIGHT USE ARE **to aim** **to fire**

shop *noun*

ANOTHER WORD IS

store

BIG SHOPS THAT SELL ALL KINDS OF GOODS ARE

department store **hypermarket** **supermarket**

DIFFERENT KINDS OF SHOP ARE

baker	**bank**	**barber**	**book shop**
butcher	**chemist**	**clothes shop**	**dairy**
delicatessen	**DIY shop**	**fishmonger**	**florist**
greengrocer	**grocer**	**hairdresser**	**ironmonger**
jeweller	**launderette**	**newsagent**	**off-licence**
post office	**shoe shop**		

short *adjective*

1 a short poem.
ANOTHER WORD IS **brief**
The opposite is **long**

2 a short person.
OTHER WORDS ARE **little** **small**
The opposite is **tall**

shout *verb*

Sam shouted so loud that the people next door heard him.
OTHER VERBS YOU MIGHT USE ARE **to call** **to cry out** **to roar** **to scream** **to shriek** **to yell**

show *noun*

an art show.
OTHER WORDS ARE **display** **exhibition**

show *verb*

1 We showed our work to the visitors.
OTHER VERBS YOU MIGHT USE ARE **to display** **to exhibit** **to present**

2 She showed me how to do it.
OTHER VERBS ARE **to explain** **to teach** **to tell**

3 We drew pictures to show how people used to dress in Victorian times.
OTHER VERBS ARE **to illustrate** **to portray** **to represent**

shrill *adjective*

a shrill whistle.
OTHER WORDS YOU MIGHT USE ARE **high** **piercing** **sharp**

shrivel *verb*

The plants shrivelled in the heat.
OTHER VERBS YOU MIGHT USE ARE **to dry up** **to shrink** **to wither**

shudder *verb*

I shuddered when I thought of the monster.
OTHER VERBS YOU MIGHT USE ARE **to quake** **to quiver** **to shake** **to tremble**

shut *verb*

Shut the door.
OTHER VERBS ARE **to close** **to fasten** **to lock** **to seal**
To shut a door loudly is to **slam** it.
The opposite is **open**

shy *adjective*

He was too shy to say that he knew the answer.
OTHER WORDS YOU MIGHT USE ARE **bashful** **modest** **nervous** **timid**
The opposite is **bold**

sick *adjective*

Jo was away from school because she was sick.
OTHER WORDS YOU MIGHT USE ARE **ill** (*informal*) **poorly** **unwell**

to be sick
OTHER WORDS ARE (*informal*) **throw up** **vomit**
For other words, see **health**

a b c d e f g h i j k l m n o p q r s t u v w x y z

side *noun*

1 A cube has six sides.
OTHER WORDS ARE **face** **surface**

2 I stood at the side of the road.
ANOTHER WORD IS **edge**

A grassy side of a road is a **verge**

sight *noun*

1 The optician says that Sam has good sight.
OTHER WORDS YOU MIGHT USE ARE **eyesight** **vision**

2 The hills are a lovely sight.
OTHER WORDS ARE **scene** **spectacle**

sign *noun*

1 He gave a sign that it was my turn.
OTHER WORDS YOU MIGHT USE ARE **hint** **reminder** **signal**

2 The doctor said that spots might be a sign of measles.
OTHER WORDS ARE **indication** **symptom**

silent *adjective*

1 During the night the house is completely silent.
OTHER WORDS YOU MIGHT USE ARE **quiet** **soundless**

The opposite is **noisy**

2 Sam was silent when he heard the bad news.
OTHER WORDS ARE **dumb** **speechless**

silky *adjective*

The cat has a silky coat.
OTHER WORDS YOU MIGHT USE ARE **sleek** **smooth** **soft**

The opposite is **rough**

silly *adjective*

It's silly to go out in the rain.
OTHER WORDS ARE (*informal*) **daft** **foolish** **ridiculous** **senseless** **stupid**

The opposite is **sensible**

similar *adjective*

The two girls had similar dresses.
ANOTHER WORD IS **matching**

The opposite is **different**

simple *adjective*

1 a simple problem.
OTHER WORDS YOU MIGHT USE ARE **clear** **easy** **straightforward**

The opposite is **complicated**

2 a simple dress.
ANOTHER WORD IS **plain**

sincere *adjective*

He was sincere when he said he was glad to see us.
OTHER WORDS YOU MIGHT USE ARE **genuine** **honest** **truthful**

The opposite is **dishonest**

singer *noun*
ANOTHER WORD IS
vocalist
A group of singers is a **choir** or a **chorus**.
Someone who sings on their own is a **soloist**.
SINGERS WITH DIFFERENT KINDS OF VOICE ARE
alto **bass** **contralto** **soprano** **tenor** **treble**
For other words to do with music, see **music**

single *adjective*
There wasn't a single sweet left!
ANOTHER WORD IS **solitary**

site *noun*
We found a nice site to put up the tent.
OTHER WORDS YOU MIGHT USE ARE **plot** **position** **situation** **spot**

situation *noun*
1 My house is in a nice situation.
OTHER WORDS YOU MIGHT USE ARE **place** **position** **spot**
2 I was in an awkward situation when I lost my money.
ANOTHER WORD IS **position**

size *noun*
For other words, see **measurement**

skate *verb*
He skated gracefully over the ice.
OTHER VERBS YOU MIGHT USE ARE **to glide** **to skim** **to slide**

skeleton *noun*
For other parts of the body, see **body**

skid *verb*
The car skidded on the ice.
OTHER VERBS YOU CAN USE ARE **to slide** **to slip**

skilful *adjective*
a skilful player.
OTHER WORDS YOU MIGHT USE ARE **clever** **expert** **talented**

skill *noun*
Sam admired the player's skill.
OTHER WORDS YOU MIGHT USE ARE **ability** **cleverness** **talent**

skin *noun*
WORDS FOR ANIMALS' SKIN ARE **fur** **hide**
Words for the skin of an orange are **peel** or **rind**.

skip *verb*
The lambs skipped about the field.
OTHER VERBS ARE **to dance** **to frisk** **to hop** **to jump** **to leap** **to prance** **to spring**

slanting *adjective*
a slanting line.
OTHER WORDS ARE **sloping** **tilting**

a b c d e f g h i j k l m n o p q r s t u v w x y z

sledge *noun*
OTHER WORDS ARE **sleigh** **toboggan**

sleep *verb*
DIFFERENT WAYS TO GO TO SLEEP ARE
to doze (*informal*) **to drop off** **to nod off** **to slumber** **to snooze** (*informal*) **to take a nap**
When animals sleep for a long time in the winter, they **hibernate**.

sleepy *adjective*
I was sleepy so I went to bed.
OTHER WORDS YOU MIGHT USE ARE **drowsy** **tired** **weary**

slender *adjective*
She has a slender figure.
ANOTHER WORD IS **graceful**
For other words, see **slim**

slide *verb*
We slid on the ice.
OTHER VERBS YOU MIGHT USE ARE **to glide** **to skate** **to skid** **to slip**

slight *adjective*
a slight accident.
OTHER WORDS YOU MIGHT USE ARE **minor** **small** **unimportant**
The opposite is **serious**

slim *adjective*
He could get through the hole in the fence because he was so slim.
OTHER WORDS YOU MIGHT USE ARE **lean** **slender** **slight** **thin**
The opposite is **fat**

slip *verb*
Sam slipped and fell over.
OTHER VERBS YOU MIGHT USE ARE **to skid** **to slide**

slippery *adjective*
Take care: the floor is slippery.
OTHER WORDS ARE **greasy** **icy** **oily** **slimy** **slithery** **smooth**

slope *noun*
It's hard to run up a steep slope.
OTHER WORDS ARE **bank** **gradient** **hill** **ramp** **rise**

slope *verb*
The beach slopes down to the sea.
ANOTHER VERB IS **to slant**

slot *noun*
I put a coin in the slot.
OTHER WORDS YOU MIGHT USE ARE **groove** **opening** **slit**

slow *adjective*
1 There was a slow change in the weather.
ANOTHER WORD IS **gradual**
2 I'm sorry I'm late, but my watch is slow.
The opposite is **fast**

sly *adjective*
They say the fox is a sly animal.
OTHER WORDS ARE **crafty** **cunning** (*informal*) **sneaky** **wily**

smack *verb*
For other verbs, see **hit**

small *adjective*
1 The book was small enough to put in my pocket.
OTHER WORDS YOU MIGHT USE ARE **compact** **little** **minute** **tiny**
2 Sam made a small model of the castle.
ANOTHER WORD IS **miniature**
3 She gave us small helpings.
OTHER WORDS ARE **mean** (*informal*) **measly** **stingy**
4 We had a small problem.
OTHER WORDS ARE **minor** **slight** **unimportant**
The opposite is **big**

smart *adjective*
1 He looked smart in his new clothes.
OTHER WORDS YOU MIGHT USE ARE **neat** **posh** **tidy** **well-dressed**
The opposite is **untidy**
2 That's a smart dog if he understands what you say.
OTHER WORDS YOU MIGHT USE ARE **bright** **clever** **intelligent**
The opposite is **stupid**

smart *verb*
The wasp sting made Sam's hand smart.
OTHER VERBS YOU MIGHT USE ARE **to hurt** **to sting** **to throb**

smear *verb*
I smeared ointment on the sore place.
OTHER VERBS YOU MIGHT USE ARE **to rub** **to spread** **to wipe**

smell *noun*
ANOTHER WORD IS **odour**
WORDS FOR A NICE SMELL ARE **aroma** **fragrance** **perfume** **scent**
A word for a nasty smell is **stink**.
A word for a slight smell is **whiff**.

smile *verb*
For other verbs, see **laugh**

smoke *noun*
the smoke from an engine.
OTHER WORDS YOU MIGHT USE ARE **exhaust** **fumes**

smooth *adjective*
1 a smooth surface.
OTHER WORDS YOU MIGHT USE ARE **even** **flat** **level**
The opposite is **rough**
2 a smooth sea.
ANOTHER WORD IS **calm**
The opposite is **stormy**

smudge *verb*
I smudged the wet paint.
OTHER WORDS YOU MIGHT USE ARE **to smear** **to streak**

a b c d e f g h i j k l m n o p q r **s** t u v w x y z

snatch *verb*
The dog snatched the sandwich out of my hand.
OTHER VERBS YOU MIGHT USE ARE **to grab** **to seize** **to take**

sneak *verb*
She sneaked up behind me and made me jump.
OTHER VERBS YOU MIGHT USE ARE **to creep** **to steal**

soft *adjective*
1 The baby cuddled a soft toy.
OTHER WORDS TO DESCRIBE SOFT THINGS ARE **flexible** **floppy** **limp** **spongy** **springy** **squashy**
The opposite is **hard**
2 Jo's dress is made of soft material.
OTHER WORDS YOU MIGHT USE ARE **silky** **smooth** **velvety**
The opposite is **rough**
3 They played soft music when we went into church.
OTHER WORDS YOU MIGHT USE ARE **gentle** **low** **quiet** **restful**
The opposite is **loud**

soil *noun*
Sam planted his seeds in the soil.
OTHER WORDS YOU MIGHT USE ARE **earth** **ground**

soldier *noun*
ANOTHER WORD IS
serviceman or **servicewoman**
Soldiers who go on horseback are the **cavalry**.
Soldiers who go on foot are the **infantry**.
A soldier trained for specially daring raids is a **commando**.
A soldier trained to fight on land or at sea is a **marine**.
A soldier who goes into battle by parachute is a **paratrooper**.

WORDS FOR A LOT OF SOLDIERS ARE
army **troops**

For other fighters, see **fight**

solemn *adjective*
They looked solemn when they heard the news.
OTHER WORDS YOU MIGHT USE ARE **grave** **serious** **thoughtful**

solid *adjective*
1 Cricket balls are solid.
The opposite is **hollow**
2 We were glad to get out of the mud onto solid ground.
OTHER WORDS YOU MIGHT USE ARE **firm** **hard**
The opposite is **soft**

solution *noun*
Did you get the solution to the puzzle?
OTHER WORDS YOU MIGHT USE ARE **answer** **explanation**

solve *verb*
Jo solved the puzzle in a couple of minutes.
OTHER VERBS YOU MIGHT USE ARE **to answer** **to explain** **to work out**

song *noun*
DIFFERENT KINDS OF MUSIC FOR SINGING ARE
ballad **carol** **folk song** **hymn** **lullaby** **pop song** **shanty**
For other words to do with music, see **music**

soothe *verb*
Quiet music soothes your nerves.
OTHER VERBS YOU MIGHT USE ARE **to calm** **to comfort** **to relax**
The opposite is **disturb**

sore *adjective*
Jo had a sore place on her knee.
OTHER WORDS YOU MIGHT USE ARE **aching** **inflamed** **painful** **raw** **red** **tender**

sorrow *noun*
Jo was full of sorrow when her cat died.
OTHER WORDS YOU MIGHT USE ARE **grief** **misery** **sadness** **unhappiness**

sorry *adjective*
1 He was sorry when he saw the damage he had done.
OTHER WORDS ARE **apologetic** **ashamed** **regretful** **repentant**
2 Jo was sorry for the sick boy.
OTHER WORDS ARE **sad** **sympathetic**

sort *noun*
1 Which sort of cake do you like?
OTHER WORDS YOU MIGHT USE ARE **brand** **kind** **type** **variety**
2 What sort of dog is that?
OTHER WORDS ARE **breed** **species**

sort *verb*
Sam sorted the library books.
OTHER VERBS YOU MIGHT USE ARE **to arrange** **to classify** **to organize**

sound *adjective*
1 Jo's dog is in a sound condition.
OTHER WORDS YOU MIGHT USE ARE **healthy** **strong**
2 The teacher said we had done sound work.
OTHER WORDS YOU MIGHT USE ARE **correct** **good** **reasonable**

sound *noun*, see next page

sour *adjective*
a sour taste.
OTHER WORDS YOU MIGHT USE ARE **acid** **sharp** **tangy** **tart**
The opposite is **sweet**

source *noun*
the source of a river.
OTHER WORDS ARE **beginning** **origin** **starting point**

a b c d e f g h i j k l m n o p q r **s** t u v w x y z

sound *noun* and *verb*

DIFFERENT SOUNDS WE CAN MAKE ARE
bawl **boo** **clap** **cry** **groan**
hiccup **hiss** **jeer** **lisp** **moan**
scream **shout** **shriek** **sigh** **sniff**
snore **sob** **wail** **whistle** **yell**

For other sounds we make, see **talk**

DIFFERENT SOUNDS ANIMALS MAKE ARE
bark **bellow** **bleat** **bray** **croak**
growl **grunt** **howl** **jabber** **low**
miaow **moo** **neigh** **purr** **roar**
screech **snarl** **snort** **squeak** **squeal**
whine **whinny** **yap**

SOUNDS DIFFERENT BIRDS MAKE ARE
cackle **chirp** **cluck** **coo** **crow**
hoot **quack** **screech** **squawk** **twitter**
warble

SOUNDS INSECTS MAKE ARE
buzz **drone** **hum** **murmur**

DIFFERENT SOUNDS THINGS MAKE ARE
bang **blare** **bleep** **boom** **chime**
clang **clank** **clash** **clatter** **click**
clink **crack** **crackle** **crash** **creak**
jangle **jingle** **peal** **ping** **plop**
pop **rattle** **ring** **rumble** **rustle**
sizzle **slam** **snap** **splutter** **swish**
throb **thud** **thunder** **tick** **tinkle**
twang **whiz**

For other words, see **music**, **noise**

space *noun*

1 Give me a bit of space.
ANOTHER WORD IS **room**

2 Write your answer in the space.
ANOTHER WORD IS **blank**

3 What goes in that empty space?
OTHER WORDS YOU MIGHT USE ARE **gap** **hole** **opening**

spacecraft *noun*

DIFFERENT KINDS OF SPACECRAFT ARE **rocket** **spaceship** **space shuttle**

spare *adjective*

Take some spare socks in case you get your feet wet.
OTHER WORDS YOU MIGHT USE ARE **additional** **extra**

spare *verb*

The cruel soldier would not spare his enemy.
OTHER VERBS YOU MIGHT USE ARE **to be merciful to** **to forgive** **to let off** **to pardon** **to reprieve** **to save**

sparkle *verb*

The firework sparkled in the dark.
OTHER VERBS YOU MIGHT USE ARE **to flash** **to spark**

speak *verb*
For other verbs, see **talk**

spear *noun*
A spear used by knights in old times was a **lance**.
A spear used to kill whales is a **harpoon**.
A spear you throw as a sport is a **javelin**.

special *adjective*
1 Your birthday is a special day.
ANOTHER WORD IS **important**
2 Petrol has a special smell.
OTHER WORDS ARE **different** **distinct**
3 Jo has tea in her special mug.
OTHER WORDS YOU MIGHT USE ARE **individual** **particular** **personal**

specimen *noun*
Show me a specimen of your work.
OTHER WORDS YOU MIGHT USE ARE **example** **illustration** **sample**

speck *noun*
a speck of dust.
OTHER WORDS ARE **bit** **dot** **grain** **spot**

speckled *adjective*
a speckled pattern.
OTHER WORDS ARE **dotted** **mottled** **spotty**

spectacular *adjective*
a spectacular fireworks display.
OTHER WORDS YOU MIGHT USE ARE **big** **exciting** **impressive**

speech *noun*
We listened to the speech.
OTHER WORDS YOU MIGHT USE ARE **lecture** **talk**

speed *noun*
We walked at an ordinary speed.
OTHER WORDS YOU MIGHT USE ARE **pace** **rate**

spell *noun*
a magic spell.
OTHER WORDS YOU MIGHT USE ARE **charm** **enchantment**

a b c d e f g h i j k l m n o p q r **s** t u v w x y z

spend *verb*

1 How much money did you spend?

OTHER VERBS YOU MIGHT USE ARE **to pay** **to use**

2 We spent a nice day by the sea.

ANOTHER VERB IS **to pass**

spike *noun*

There were spikes along the top of the railings.

OTHER WORDS YOU MIGHT USE ARE **point** **prong**

spill *verb*

Who spilt the milk on the carpet?

OTHER VERBS YOU MIGHT USE ARE **to drop** **to slop** **to tip** **to upset**

spin *verb*

The top spun round and round.

OTHER VERBS ARE **to revolve** **to turn** **to twirl** **to whirl**

spirit *noun*

Another word for your spirit is your **soul**.

SPIRITS YOU READ ABOUT IN STORIES ARE

demon **devil** **fairy** **genie**
ghost **gremlin** **imp** **phantom**
poltergeist (*informal*) **spook**

spiteful *adjective*

Jo doesn't like people who make spiteful remarks.

OTHER WORDS YOU MIGHT USE ARE (*informal*) **catty** **hurtful** **nasty** **unkind**

The opposite is **kind**

splash *verb*

The car splashed water over us.

OTHER VERBS YOU MIGHT USE ARE **to shower** **to slop** **to spatter**

splendid *adjective*

1 The soldiers wore splendid uniforms.

OTHER WORDS YOU MIGHT USE ARE **brilliant** **gorgeous** **grand** **impressive** **magnificent**

2 We had a splendid holiday.

For other words, see **good**

split *verb*

1 He split the log with an axe.

OTHER VERBS YOU MIGHT USE ARE **to chop** **to crack** **to cut** **to slice**

2 We split into two teams.

OTHER VERBS ARE **to divide** **to separate**

spoil *verb*

The stain has spoilt my new dress.

OTHER VERBS YOU MIGHT USE ARE **to damage** (*informal*) **to mess up** **to ruin** **to wreck**

sport *noun*

DIFFERENT SPORTS ARE

athletics **baseball** **basketball** **boxing**
climbing **cricket** **cycling** **darts**
fishing **football** **golf** **gymnastics**
hockey **ice hockey** **rounders** **rugby**
running **sailing** **showjumping** **skating**
skiing **snooker** **soccer** **squash**
surfing **swimming** **table tennis** **tennis**
volleyball **water-skiing** **windsurfing** **wrestling**
yachting

spot *noun*

1 You've got a dirty spot on your new trousers.
OTHER WORDS YOU MIGHT USE ARE
blot **dot** **mark** **speck** **stain**

2 I've got spots on my face.
DIFFERENT KINDS OF SPOTS ARE
boil **freckle** **mole** **pimple**
A spot on your eyelid is a **sty**.
A large number of spots is a **rash**.

3 Here's a nice spot for a picnic.
OTHER WORDS ARE
place **position** **situation**

spray *verb*
The bus sprayed us with water when it went through the puddle.
OTHER VERBS YOU MIGHT USE ARE **to scatter** **to shower** **to spatter** **to splash** **to sprinkle**

spread *verb*
We spread the map on the table.
OTHER VERBS YOU MIGHT USE ARE **to lay out** **to open out** **to unfold**

spring *verb*
1 The cat crouched, ready to spring on the mouse.
OTHER VERBS YOU MIGHT USE ARE **to jump** **to leap** **to pounce**
2 Weeds sprang up all over the garden.
OTHER VERBS ARE **to grow** **to shoot**

sprout *verb*
The seeds began to sprout.
OTHER VERBS YOU MIGHT USE ARE **to grow** **to shoot up** **to spring up**

squabble *verb*
Those boys are always squabbling.
OTHER VERBS YOU MIGHT USE ARE **to argue** **to fight** **to quarrel**

squeeze *verb*
1 I squeezed an orange to make some juice.
OTHER VERBS YOU MIGHT USE ARE **to crush** **to press**
2 They squeezed us into a little room.
OTHER VERBS ARE **to crowd** **to push** **to shove** **to squash**

squirt *verb*
Water squirted out of the hole.
OTHER VERBS YOU MIGHT USE ARE **to pour** **to spout** **to spurt** **to stream**

stack *noun*
a stack of books.
OTHER WORDS ARE **heap** **mound** **pile**

stage *noun*
1 We stood on the stage to sing.
ANOTHER WORD IS **platform**
2 The baby is at the crawling stage.
OTHER WORDS ARE **period** **phase**

stain *noun*
What's that stain on your shirt?
OTHER WORDS ARE **blot** **mark** **smudge** **spot**

stairs *noun*
OTHER WORDS YOU MIGHT USE ARE **staircase** **steps**

stale *adjective*
1 stale bread.
OTHER WORDS YOU MIGHT USE ARE **dry** **old**
2 stale news.
ANOTHER WORD IS **out-of-date**
The opposite is **fresh**

stalk *noun*
a flower on a stalk.
ANOTHER WORD IS **stem**

stand *verb*
1 We all stood when the visitors arrived.
OTHER VERBS YOU MIGHT USE ARE **to get up** **to rise**
2 I stood my books on the shelf.
OTHER VERBS ARE **to arrange** **to place** **to position**

standard *noun*
Our teacher expects a high standard of work.
OTHER WORDS YOU MIGHT USE ARE **level** **quality**

stare *verb*
For other verbs, see **look**

start *verb*
1 What time does the film start?
OTHER VERBS YOU MIGHT USE ARE **to begin** **to commence**
2 Our teacher has started a chess club.
OTHER VERBS ARE **to create** **to introduce** **to set up**
3 They started on their journey at dawn.
OTHER VERBS ARE **to depart** **to embark** **to set off** **to set out**

startle *verb*
The explosion startled us.
OTHER VERBS YOU MIGHT USE ARE **to alarm** **to frighten** **to shock** **to surprise** **to upset**

starving *adjective*
For other words, see **hungry**

state *verb*
Dad stated that he had no money.
OTHER VERBS YOU MIGHT USE ARE **to announce** **to declare** **to report** **to say**

statement *noun*
The police issued a statement about the burglary.
OTHER WORDS YOU MIGHT USE ARE **announcement** **communication**

statue *noun*
We saw some statues in the museum.
OTHER WORDS YOU MIGHT USE ARE **carving** **figure** **sculpture**

a
b
c
d
e
f
g
h
i
j
k
l
m
n
o
p
q
r
s
t
u
v
w
x
y
z

stay *verb*

1 Stay here until I come back.
OTHER VERBS YOU MIGHT USE ARE **to remain** **to stop** **to wait**

2 Stay on the path.
OTHER VERBS ARE **to carry on** **to continue** **to keep on**

3 Jo went to stay with Granny.
ANOTHER WORD IS **to visit**

steady *adjective*

1 Make sure the ladder is steady.
OTHER WORDS YOU MIGHT USE ARE **firm** **secure** **solid**

2 The music had a steady rhythm.
OTHER WORDS ARE **constant** **continuous** **even** **regular**

steal *verb*

OTHER VERBS YOU MIGHT USE ARE
(*informal*) **to pinch** **to take**
Someone who steals things is a **robber** or a **thief**.
Someone who steals things from someone's house is a **burglar**.
Someone who steals things in a riot is a **looter**.
Someone who steals things from a shop is a **shoplifter**.
Someone who steals by attacking people in the street is a **mugger**.
Someone who steals things out of your pocket is a **pickpocket**.
Someone who used to steal things from travellers was a **highwayman**.

step *noun*

1 We all moved forwards one step.
OTHER WORDS YOU MIGHT USE ARE **pace** **stride**

2 I climbed up the steps.
ANOTHER WORD IS **stair**

stern *adjective*

She had a stern look on her face.
OTHER WORDS YOU MIGHT USE ARE **angry** **grim** **severe** **strict**

stick *noun*

DIFFERENT KINDS OF STICK ARE:
a long straight stick
pole **rod**
a stick that is part of a plant
branch **stalk** **twig**
a stick used in a relay race or by the conductor of a band
baton
a stick used to support plants
bamboo **cane**
a stick used as a weapon
club **truncheon**
a stick used to help someone walk
crutch **walking stick**
a magician's stick
wand

stick *verb*

1 The door has stuck.
ANOTHER VERB IS **to jam**

2 This glue will stick plastic.
OTHER VERBS YOU MIGHT USE ARE **to fasten** **to fix** **to glue**

3 She stuck a pin in me!
OTHER VERBS ARE **to jab** **to stab**

stiff *adjective*

1 stiff cardboard.
OTHER WORDS YOU MIGHT USE ARE **hard** **rigid**

2 stiff paste.
ANOTHER WORD IS **thick**

still *adjective*

It was a very still evening.
OTHER WORDS ARE **calm** **peaceful** **quiet**

stir *verb*

1 Sam stirred the cake mixture.
OTHER VERBS YOU MIGHT USE ARE **to beat** **to mix** **to whisk**

2 Mum called Jo and said it was time to stir.
OTHER VERBS ARE **to get going** **to get up** **to move**

stomach *noun*

AN INFORMAL WORD IS **tummy**
A word some people think is impolite is **belly**.

stone *noun*

DIFFERENT KINDS OF STONE ARE **boulder** **cobble** **gravel** **jewel** **pebble** **rock**

stoop *verb*

I stooped down to pull up my sock.
OTHER VERBS YOU MIGHT USE ARE **to bend** **to bow** **to crouch** **to kneel**

stop *verb*

1 The policeman stopped the traffic.
OTHER VERBS YOU MIGHT USE ARE **to check** **to halt** **to hold up**

2 The bus stopped.
OTHER VERBS ARE **to draw up** **to halt** **to pull up**

3 The noise suddenly stopped.
OTHER VERBS ARE **to cease** **to end** **to finish**

4 You can stop for tea.
ANOTHER VERB IS **to stay**

store *verb*

We store food in the fridge.
OTHER VERBS YOU MIGHT USE ARE **to keep** **to put away** **to save**

a b c d e f g h i j k l m n o p q r **s** t u v w x y z

storm *noun*
DIFFERENT KINDS OF STORM:
a violent storm
tempest
a snow storm
blizzard
a storm with a lot of wind
gale **hurricane** **tornado** **whirlwind**
a storm with a lot of rain
deluge **downpour** **rainstorm**
a storm with thunder and lightning
thunderstorm
For other words, see **weather**

story *noun*
OTHER WORDS YOU MIGHT USE ARE
narrative **tale**

DIFFERENT KINDS OF STORY ARE
adventure story **comedy** **fable** **fairy tale** **fantasy** **folk tale** **legend** **love story** **myth** **novel** **parable** **romance**

stout *adjective*
a stout person.
OTHER WORDS YOU MIGHT USE ARE **fat** **overweight** **plump** (*informal*) **tubby**
The opposite is **thin**

straight *adjective*
a straight line. a straight road.
ANOTHER WORD IS **direct**
The opposite is **crooked**

strain *verb*
1 He strained to escape from the monster's grip.
OTHER VERBS YOU MIGHT USE ARE **to make an effort** **to struggle** **to try hard**
2 Jo strained a muscle when she was running.
OTHER VERBS ARE **to damage** **to hurt** **to injure**
3 Don't strain yourself!
OTHER VERBS ARE **to exhaust** **to tire out** **to wear out**

strange *adjective*
1 When I woke up I was in a strange place.
OTHER WORDS YOU MIGHT USE ARE **different** **foreign** **new** **unfamiliar** **unknown**
The opposite is **familiar**
2 A strange thing happened.
OTHER WORDS ARE **curious** **extraordinary** **funny** **mysterious** **odd** **peculiar** **puzzling** **queer** **surprising** **unusual**
The opposite is **ordinary**

stranger *noun*
Please show me the way, because I am a stranger here.
A stranger might be a **foreigner** or a **visitor**.

stray *verb*
Whatever you do, don't stray in the forest.
OTHER VERBS YOU MIGHT USE ARE **to get lost** **to roam about** **to wander**

streak *noun*
The plane left a white streak in the sky.
OTHER WORDS YOU MIGHT USE ARE **line** **stripe**

stream *noun*
We paddled across a stream.
ANOTHER WORD IS **brook**
A big stream is a **river**.
For other words, see **water**

strength *noun*
Have you got the strength to lift this box?
OTHER WORDS ARE **force** **might** **power**

strengthen *verb*
Dad put in some posts to strengthen the fence.
OTHER VERBS YOU MIGHT USE ARE **to reinforce** **to support**
The opposite is **weaken**

stretch *verb*
You can stretch elastic.
OTHER VERBS YOU MIGHT USE ARE **to lengthen** **to pull out**

strict *adjective*
a strict teacher.
OTHER WORDS YOU MIGHT USE ARE **firm** **severe** **stern**

string *noun*
OTHER THINGS YOU MIGHT USE TO TIE THINGS UP ARE
cord **lace** **line** **ribbon** **rope** **wire**

strip *verb*
We stripped off our clothes to go swimming.
OTHER VERBS YOU MIGHT USE ARE **to peel off** **to remove** **to take off**

stripe *noun*
Sam's football shirt has red and white stripes.
OTHER WORDS ARE **band** **line** **strip**

a b c d e f g h i j k l m n o p q r **s** t u v w x y z

strong *adjective*

1 a strong person.
OTHER WORDS YOU MIGHT USE ARE **healthy** **muscular** **sturdy** **tough** **wiry**

2 a strong rope. strong walking shoes.
OTHER WORDS ARE **sound** **stout** **thick**

The opposite is **weak**

struggle *verb*

1 The thief struggled to get away.
OTHER VERBS YOU MIGHT USE ARE **to fight** **to wrestle**

2 We struggled to put the tent up.
OTHER VERBS ARE **to exert yourself** **to make an effort** **to strive** **to try**

stubborn *adjective*

The stubborn animal refused to move.
OTHER WORDS YOU MIGHT USE ARE **defiant** **disobedient** **obstinate**

study *verb*

1 Mum is studying for an exam.
OTHER VERBS YOU MIGHT USE ARE **to learn** **to revise** (*informal*) **to swot**

2 The police studied the evidence.
OTHER VERBS ARE **to analyse** **to consider** **to examine** **to investigate** **to think about**

stuff *noun*

1 What's this stuff in the jar?
ANOTHER WORD IS **substance**

2 What's that stuff in the attic?
OTHER WORDS ARE **articles** **odds and ends** **things**

3 I put my stuff in a box.
OTHER WORDS ARE **belongings** **possessions**

stuffy *adjective*

a stuffy room.
OTHER WORDS YOU MIGHT USE ARE **close** **muggy** **stifling** **warm**

stumble *verb*

I stumbled over a big stone.
OTHER VERBS YOU MIGHT USE ARE **to blunder** **to stagger** **to trip**

stun *verb*

1 The hit on the head stunned her.
OTHER VERBS YOU MIGHT USE ARE **to daze** **to knock out**

2 The unexpected news stunned us.
OTHER VERBS ARE **to amaze** **to astonish** **to shock** **to surprise**

stupid *adjective*

1 a stupid idea.
OTHER WORDS YOU MIGHT USE ARE **crazy** **foolish** **idiotic** **silly**

2 a stupid person.
OTHER WORDS ARE **dense** **dim** **dull** **slow** (*informal*) **thick**

The opposite is **clever**

style *noun*

Jo likes the new style of dancing.
OTHER WORDS YOU MIGHT USE ARE **fashion** **way**

subject *noun*
Sam chose an interesting subject for his project.
OTHER WORDS YOU MIGHT USE ARE **theme** **topic**

submit *verb*
1 The wrestler submitted to his opponent.
OTHER VERBS YOU MIGHT USE ARE **to give in** **to surrender** **to yield**
2 We must submit our work today.
OTHER VERBS ARE **to give in** **to hand in** **to present**

substance *noun*
What's this sticky substance?
OTHER WORDS YOU MIGHT USE ARE **material** **stuff**

subtract *verb*
Our teacher subtracts marks for untidy work.
OTHER VERBS YOU MIGHT USE ARE **to deduct** **to take away**

succeed *verb*
1 Jo succeeded in winning the race.
OTHER VERBS YOU MIGHT USE ARE **to be successful** **to do well**
2 Did your plan succeed?
ANOTHER VERB IS **to work**

sudden *adjective*
The car came to a sudden halt.
OTHER WORDS YOU MIGHT USE ARE **abrupt** **hasty** **quick** **unexpected**
The opposite is **gradual**

suffer *verb*
I hate to see animals suffer pain.
OTHER VERBS YOU MIGHT USE ARE **to bear** **to endure** **to go through** **to put up with** **to stand**

suffering *noun*
For other words, see **pain**

sufficient *adjective*
Have you got sufficient money for your journey?
OTHER WORDS YOU MIGHT USE ARE **adequate** **enough**

suggest *verb*
What do you suggest we should do?
OTHER VERBS YOU MIGHT USE ARE **to advise** **to propose** **to recommend**

suitable *adjective*
Is this dress suitable for a wedding?
OTHER WORDS YOU MIGHT USE ARE **appropriate** **proper** **right**

sulky *adjective*
After Mum told him off he was sulky for hours.
OTHER WORDS ARE **bad-tempered** **cross** **gloomy** **moody** **sullen**
The opposite is **cheerful**

sunny *adjective*
sunny weather.
OTHER WORDS YOU MIGHT USE ARE **bright** **clear** **cloudless** **fine**

supply *noun*
There's a supply of paper in the cupboard.
OTHER WORDS YOU MIGHT USE ARE **reserve** **stock**

a b c d e f g h i j k l m n o p q r **s** t u v w x y z

supply *verb*
We took our own sandwiches, and our teacher supplied the drinks.
OTHER VERBS YOU MIGHT USE ARE **to contribute** **to give** **to provide**

support *verb*
1 Those pillars support the roof.
OTHER VERBS YOU MIGHT USE ARE **to bear** **to hold up** **to prop up**
2 Our friends supported us when we were in trouble.
OTHER VERBS ARE **to aid** **to assist** **to encourage** **to help** **to stand up for**

supporter *noun*
Sam is a supporter of the local team.
OTHER WORDS ARE **fan** **follower**

suppose *verb*
Let's suppose that Jo's the queen.
OTHER VERBS YOU MIGHT USE ARE **to assume** **to believe** **to imagine** **to pretend**

sure *adjective*
1 I'm sure he will come.
OTHER WORDS YOU MIGHT USE ARE **certain** **confident** **convinced** **definite** **positive**
2 He's sure to come.
ANOTHER WORD IS **bound**

surprise *verb*
The unexpected news surprised us.
OTHER VERBS YOU MIGHT USE ARE **to amaze** **to astonish** **to shock** **to startle** **to stun**

surrender *verb*
After a long fight, the army surrendered.
OTHER VERBS YOU MIGHT USE ARE **to give in** **to submit** **to yield**

survey *noun*
We did a survey to find out who comes to school by car.
OTHER WORDS YOU MIGHT USE ARE **investigation** **study**

survive *verb*
Some plants don't survive through the winter.
OTHER VERBS YOU MIGHT USE ARE **to keep going** **to last** **to live**

suspect *verb*
Mum suspects that I broke her mug.
OTHER VERBS ARE **to guess** **to have a feeling** **to think**

swamp *noun*
The lorry got stuck in the swamp.
OTHER WORDS ARE **bog** **marsh**

swear *verb*
1 Do you swear that you'll tell the truth?
OTHER VERBS YOU MIGHT USE ARE **to give your word** **to promise** **to vow**
2 He swore when he hit his finger.
ANOTHER VERB IS **to curse**

sweep *verb*
I swept the floor.
ANOTHER VERB IS **to brush**
For ways to clean things, see **clean**

sweet *adjective*
For other words to describe how things taste, see **taste**
The opposite is **sour**

swell *verb*
You can see the tyre swell while you pump it up.
OTHER VERBS ARE **to blow up** **to bulge** **to get bigger** **to grow** **to puff up**

swelling *noun*
I got a nasty swelling where the wasp stung me.
OTHER WORDS YOU MIGHT USE ARE **bulge** **bump** **lump**

swift *adjective*
a swift journey.
OTHER WORDS YOU MIGHT USE ARE **fast** **quick** **rapid** **speedy**
The opposite is **slow**

swindle *verb*
He swindled us and made us pay too much.
OTHER VERBS YOU MIGHT USE ARE **to cheat** **to deceive** **to fool** **to trick**

swing *verb*
The branches swung to and fro in the wind.
ANOTHER VERB IS **to sway**

switch *verb*
I switched places with my friend.
OTHER VERBS YOU MIGHT USE ARE **to change** **to exchange** **to swap**

swoop *verb*
The owl swooped down on its prey.
OTHER VERBS ARE **to dive** **to pounce**

sympathy *noun*
He didn't have much sympathy when I was ill!
OTHER WORDS YOU MIGHT USE ARE **consideration** **feeling** **mercy** **pity**

symptom *noun*
Spots might be a symptom of measles.
OTHER WORDS ARE **indication** **sign**

Tt

take *verb*

1 Take my hand.
OTHER VERBS YOU MIGHT USE ARE **to clasp** **to get hold of** **to grasp** **to hold** **to seize**

2 The bus takes you into town.
OTHER VERBS ARE **to bring** **to carry** **to transport**

3 The army took many prisoners.
OTHER VERBS ARE **to capture** **to catch** **to seize**

4 The burglar took the jewels.
OTHER VERBS ARE **to remove** **to steal**

5 The dentist took out one of my teeth.
OTHER VERBS ARE **to extract** **to remove**

talent *noun*

Sam has great talent in football.
OTHER WORDS YOU MIGHT USE ARE **ability** **skill**

talented *adjective*

Jo is a talented musician.
OTHER WORDS YOU MIGHT USE ARE **clever** **expert** **gifted** **skilful**

talk *noun*

1 I had a nice talk with Granny.
OTHER WORDS YOU MIGHT USE ARE **chat** **conversation** **discussion**

2 The head gave us a long talk.
OTHER WORDS ARE **address** **lecture** **speech**

talk *verb*

OTHER VERBS YOU MIGHT USE ARE
to communicate **to express yourself** **to say something** **to speak**

THERE ARE DIFFERENT WAYS OF TALKING. YOU CAN
call out **chat** **chatter** **exclaim**
gossip **have a conversation** **lisp**
mumble **murmur** **mutter** **prattle**
recite a poem **scream** **screech** **shout**
shriek **snap at someone** **snarl**
splutter **stammer** **stutter** **whisper**
yell

tall *adjective*

a tall tower.
ANOTHER WORD IS **high**
The opposite is **low** or **short**

tame *adjective*

These animals are very tame.
OTHER WORDS YOU MIGHT USE ARE **gentle** **meek** **obedient** **safe**
The opposite is **dangerous** or **wild**

tangled *adjective*

tangled string.
OTHER WORDS YOU MIGHT USE ARE **knotted** **muddled** **twisted**

tank *noun*
A tank to keep fish in is an **aquarium**.

tap *verb*
She tapped on the door.
OTHER VERBS YOU MIGHT USE ARE **to knock** **to rap**

task *noun*
OTHER WORDS YOU MIGHT USE ARE **job** **work**

taste *noun*
1 Do you like the taste of this?
ANOTHER WORD IS
flavour
2 Can I have a taste of your ice cream?
OTHER WORDS YOU MIGHT USE ARE
bit **lick** **mouthful** **nibble** **piece**

WORDS TO DESCRIBE THINGS THAT TASTE NICE ARE
appetizing **delicious** **luscious** **tasty**

WORDS TO DESCRIBE THINGS THAT TASTE NASTY ARE
bad (*informal*) **off** **stale** **uneatable**

OTHER WORDS TO DESCRIBE HOW THINGS TASTE ARE
acid **bitter** **creamy** **fruity** **hot** **meaty** **peppery** **salty** **savoury** **sharp** **sour** **spicy** **sugary** **sweet** **tangy**

taste *verb*
Taste a bit of this!
OTHER VERBS YOU MIGHT USE ARE **to nibble** **to sample** **to sip** **to try**

teach *verb*
OTHER WORDS YOU MIGHT USE ARE
to teach someone in school **educate**
to teach someone to do a job **instruct** **train**
to teach someone to be good at a sport **coach**

teacher *noun*
DIFFERENT KINDS OF TEACHER ARE **lecturer** **professor** **schoolteacher** **tutor**
a person who teaches us to play games properly **coach** **trainer**
a person who teaches you how to do a particular thing **instructor**

team *noun*
a football team.
ANOTHER WORD IS **side**

tear *verb*
Sam tore his jeans.
OTHER VERBS ARE **to rip** **to slit** **to split**

tease *verb*
If you tease the cat she'll scratch.
OTHER VERBS YOU MIGHT USE ARE **to annoy** **to laugh at** **to make fun of** **to pester** **to torment**

a b c d e f g h i j k l m n o p q r s t u v w x y z

telephone *verb*

I telephoned Grandad to ask him to come to tea.

OTHER VERBS YOU MIGHT USE ARE **to call** **to dial** **to phone** **to ring**

television *noun*

DIFFERENT KINDS OF TV PROGRAMME ARE

cartoons **chat shows** **comedy** **commercials** **films** **interviews** **music** **nature programmes** **news** **plays** **quiz shows** **serials** **sport**

tell *verb*

1 He told me he'd be home for tea.

OTHER VERBS YOU MIGHT USE ARE **to inform** **to promise**

2 Our teacher told the story.

OTHER VERBS ARE **to narrate** **to relate**

3 I told the police what happened.

OTHER VERBS ARE **to describe to someone** **to explain to someone**

4 Mum told us to stop shouting.

OTHER VERBS ARE **to command** **to instruct** **to order**

to tell someone off

OTHER VERBS YOU MIGHT USE ARE **to reprimand** **to scold** (*informal*) **to tick off**

temper *noun*

1 Is Dad in a good temper?

ANOTHER WORD IS **mood**

2 Baby yells when she's in a temper.

OTHER WORDS YOU MIGHT USE ARE **rage** **tantrum**

to lose your temper

A PHRASE IS **get angry**

tend *verb*

1 Grandad tends to fall asleep in the evening.

A PHRASE YOU MIGHT USE IS **to be liable to**

2 Nurses tend sick people.

OTHER VERBS YOU MIGHT USE ARE **to care for** **to look after** **to mind**

tender *adjective*

1 I gave the baby a tender smile.

OTHER WORDS YOU MIGHT USE ARE **affectionate** **fond** **gentle** **kind** **loving**

The opposite is **cruel**

2 The baby has tender skin.

OTHER WORDS ARE **delicate** **soft**

The opposite is **tough**

3 I had a tender place where I hit my head.

OTHER WORDS ARE **sensitive** **sore**

terrible *adjective*

There was a terrible storm.

OTHER WORDS YOU MIGHT USE ARE **alarming** **awful** **bad** **dreadful** **frightening** **horrible** (*informal*) **scary** **terrific**

terrific *adjective*

1 I had a terrific idea.

For other words, see **good**

2 There was a terrific storm.

For other words, see **terrible**

terrify *verb*
The dog terrified the baby.
OTHER VERBS YOU MIGHT USE ARE **to alarm** **to frighten** **to scare** **to upset**

terror *noun*
People ran away from the fire in terror.
OTHER WORDS YOU MIGHT USE ARE **alarm** **fear** **fright** **panic**

test *noun*
1 a spelling test. a driving test.
ANOTHER WORD IS **exam** OR **examination**
2 a scientific test.
OTHER WORDS YOU MIGHT USE ARE **experiment** **research** **trial**

thankful *adjective*
I was thankful it wasn't raining.
OTHER WORDS YOU MIGHT USE ARE **grateful** **pleased**

thaw *verb*
The snow thawed when the sun came out.
OTHER VERBS YOU MIGHT USE ARE **to melt** **to unfreeze**
The opposite is **freeze**

theatre *noun*
We went to the theatre for a Christmas treat.
OTHER WORDS YOU MIGHT USE ARE
performance **show**
THINGS YOU SEE IN A THEATRE ARE
ballet **comedy** **drama** **musical** **opera** **pantomime** **play**

For other words, see **entertainment**

thick *adjective*
1 a thick line.
OTHER WORDS YOU MIGHT USE ARE **broad** **wide**
2 a thick slice of cake.
AN INFORMAL WORD IS **chunky**
The opposite is **thin**
3 thick gravy.
The opposite is **runny**

thief *noun*
For different kinds of thief, see **steal**

thin *adjective*
1 a thin line.
OTHER WORDS YOU MIGHT USE ARE **fine** **narrow**
The opposite is **thick**
2 a thin person.
KIND WORDS YOU MIGHT USE ARE **lean** **slender** **slim**
AN UNKIND WORD IS **skinny**
The opposite is **fat**
3 thin gravy.
OTHER WORDS ARE **runny** **watery**
The opposite is **thick**

a b c d e f g h i j k l m n o p q r s t u v w x y z

thing *noun*

1 What are these things in the cupboard?
OTHER WORDS YOU MIGHT USE ARE **article** **item** **object**

2 I've got several things on my mind.
OTHER WORDS ARE **idea** **thought** **worry**

3 I saw a funny thing today.
ANOTHER WORD IS **happening**

think *verb*

1 If you think, you won't make a mistake.
OTHER VERBS YOU MIGHT USE ARE **to attend** **to concentrate**

2 We thought about what to do.
OTHER VERBS ARE **to consider** **to reflect**

3 I think you are right.
OTHER VERBS ARE **to believe** **to feel** **to guess** **to suppose**

thorough *adjective*

1 a thorough job.
OTHER WORDS YOU MIGHT USE ARE **careful** **proper**

2 a thorough mess.
OTHER WORDS ARE **absolute** **complete** **utter**

thoughtful *adjective*

1 You look thoughtful today.
OTHER WORDS YOU MIGHT USE ARE **serious** **solemn**

2 It's thoughtful of you to wash up.
OTHER WORDS ARE **considerate** **friendly** **helpful** **unselfish**

threaten *verb*

For other verbs, see **frighten**

thrilling *adjective*

The band played thrilling music.
OTHER WORDS ARE **exciting** **rousing** **stirring**

throw *verb*

She threw a stone and broke the glass.
OTHER VERBS YOU MIGHT USE ARE **to bowl** **to cast** (*informal*) **to chuck** **to fling** **to hurl** **to lob** **to pitch** **to sling** **to toss**

tidy *adjective*

Mum asked Jo to make her room tidy.
OTHER WORDS YOU MIGHT USE ARE **neat** **orderly** **smart** **trim**

tie *verb*

1 Can you tie this string?
ANOTHER VERB IS **to knot**

2 I tied a bandage round my leg.
OTHER VERBS YOU MIGHT USE ARE **to bind** **to fasten** **to fix** **to wind**

3 They tied up the boat.
OTHER VERBS ARE **to anchor** **to moor**

4 The farmer tied up the bull.
ANOTHER VERB IS **to tether**

tight *adjective*

1 Make sure the lid is tight.
OTHER WORDS YOU MIGHT USE ARE **firm** **fixed** **secure**

2 These shoes are a bit tight.
OTHER WORDS ARE **close-fitting** **small**

The opposite is **loose**

tilt *verb*

The boat tilted to one side.
OTHER VERBS ARE **to lean** **to slant** **to slope** **to tip**

time *noun*

1 Is this a good time to ring Granny?
OTHER WORDS YOU MIGHT USE ARE
moment **opportunity**

2 Shakespeare lived in the time of Elizabeth I.
OTHER WORDS ARE
age **era** **period**

UNITS USED TO MEASURE TIME ARE
centuries **days** **fortnights** **hours** **minutes** **months** **seconds** **weeks** **years**

DIFFERENT TIMES OF THE DAY ARE
afternoon **bedtime** **dawn** **dusk** **evening** **midday** **midnight** **morning** **night** **noon** **sunrise** **sunset** **twilight**

THE SEASONS OF THE YEAR ARE
spring **summer** **autumn** **winter**

SPECIAL TIMES OF THE YEAR ARE
an anniversary **your birthday** **Christmas** **Diwali** **Easter** **Hallowe'en** **Hogmanay** **Midsummer** **New Year** **Passover** **Ramadan** **St Valentine's Day** **Yom Kippur**

THINGS WE USE TO MEASURE TIME ARE
calendar **clock** **digital watch** **hourglass** **sundial** **watch**

timid *adjective*

He was too timid to ask for more.
OTHER WORDS ARE **cowardly** **fearful** **nervous** **shy**

The opposite is **brave**

tiny *adjective*

Some insects are tiny.
OTHER WORDS ARE **little** **microscopic** **minute** **small**

The opposite is **big**

tip *noun*

1 the tip of a pencil.
OTHER WORDS ARE **end** **point**

2 the tip of an iceberg.
OTHER WORDS ARE **head** **top**

tip *verb*

A big wave tipped the boat over.
OTHER VERBS YOU MIGHT USE ARE **to capsize** **to overturn** **to turn over** **to upset**

tired *adjective*

1 We were tired after our walk.
OTHER WORDS YOU MIGHT USE ARE **exhausted** **weary** **worn out**

2 Go to bed: you look tired.
OTHER WORDS ARE **drowsy** **sleepy**

tiring *adjective*

tiring work.
OTHER WORDS YOU MIGHT USE ARE **exhausting** **hard**
The opposite is **easy**

toilet *noun*

OTHER WORDS YOU MIGHT USE ARE **lavatory** (*informal*) **loo** **WC**

token *noun*

I've got a token for a free drink.
OTHER WORDS ARE **counter** **coupon** **voucher**

tomb *noun*

OTHER WORDS ARE **grave** **gravestone** **memorial** **monument** **tombstone**

tone *noun*

Her voice had a gentle tone.
OTHER WORDS YOU MIGHT USE ARE **expression** **note** **sound**

tool *noun*

Dad has tools for every job.

OTHER WORDS YOU MIGHT USE ARE
device **gadget** **implement** **instrument**

TOOLS USED FOR WOODWORK ARE
chisel **clamp** **drill** **hammer**
pincers **plane** **saw** **vice**

TOOLS YOU MIGHT USE ON THE CAR ARE
jack **lever** **oil can** **pliers**
screwdriver **spanner**

TOOLS USED IN THE GARDEN ARE
broom **fork** **hoe** **lawnmower**
rake **shears** **spade** **trowel**
watering can

OTHER TOOLS PEOPLE USE ARE
axe **chopper** **crowbar** **file**
ladder **pick** **shovel** **sledgehammer**
wrench

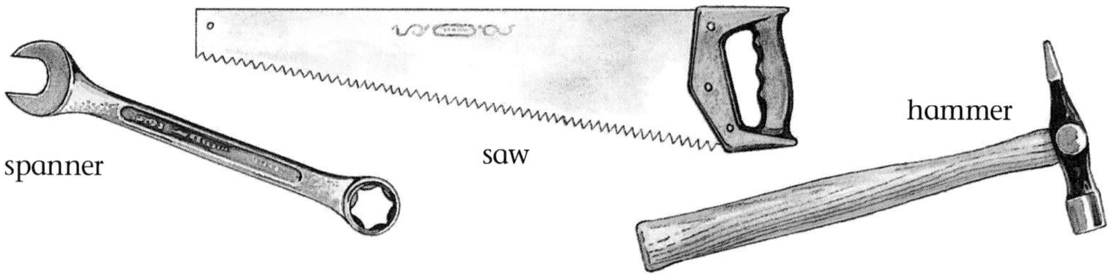

spanner
saw
hammer

top *noun*

1 the top of a hill.

OTHER WORDS YOU MIGHT USE ARE **head** **peak** **summit** **tip**

The opposite is **bottom**

2 the top of a jar.

OTHER WORDS ARE **cap** **cover** **lid**

topic *noun*

We all wrote about different topics.

OTHER WORDS YOU MIGHT USE ARE **subject** **theme**

torment *verb*

1 I hate it when people torment animals.

OTHER VERBS YOU MIGHT USE ARE **to annoy** **to distress** **to tease**

2 Sam saw a big boy tormenting some little ones.

OTHER VERBS ARE **to bully** **to victimize**

torture *verb*

It's horrible to think of people torturing each other.

OTHER VERBS ARE **to be cruel to** **to hurt**

total *adjective*

Because it rained, the picnic was a total disaster.

OTHER WORDS YOU MIGHT USE ARE **absolute** **complete**

total *noun*

Count the money and tell me the total.

OTHER WORDS ARE **amount** **answer** **sum**

touch *verb*

OTHER VERBS YOU MIGHT USE ARE

to contact **to feel** **to handle**

DIFFERENT WAYS TO TOUCH PEOPLE OR ANIMALS ARE

to caress **to cuddle** **to embrace** **to fondle** **to kiss** **to pat** **to rub** **to stroke** **to tickle**

DIFFERENT WAYS TO TOUCH THINGS ARE

to fiddle with **to fidget with** **to finger** **to handle** **to hold**

tough *adjective*

You need tough shoes to walk in the hills.

OTHER WORDS YOU MIGHT USE ARE **hard-wearing** **stout** **strong** **sturdy**

tour *verb*

We toured the castle before we had our picnic.

OTHER VERBS ARE **to go round** **to visit**

tow *verb*

The car was towing a caravan.

OTHER VERBS YOU MIGHT USE ARE **to haul** **to pull**

a b c d e f g h i j k l m n o p q r s **t** u v w x y z

town *noun*
A big town is a **city**.
A small town is a **village**.
The areas at the edge of a town are the **outskirts** or **suburbs**.

THINGS YOU OFTEN FIND IN A TOWN ARE

bank	**bus station**	**café**	**car park**
church	**cinema**	**college**	**factory**
flats	**hotel**	**leisure centre**	**library**
museum	**offices**	**park**	**police station**
post office	**railway station**	**school**	**shopping centre**
supermarket	**theatre**	**town hall**	

For other words, see **shop**

IN THE OUTSKIRTS OF A TOWN YOU MIGHT FIND
housing estate **industrial estate** **retail park**

track *verb*
The hounds tracked the fox across the fields.
OTHER VERBS YOU MIGHT USE ARE **to chase** **to follow** **to hunt** **to pursue** **to trail**

traffic *noun*
TRAFFIC YOU SEE ON THE ROADS INCLUDES
bicycles **buses** **cars** **coaches** **lorries**
motorbikes or **motorcycles** **taxis** **vans**
For other words, see **travel**

tragedy *noun*
The plane crash was a terrible tragedy.
OTHER WORDS YOU MIGHT USE ARE **calamity** **catastrophe** **disaster** **misfortune**

trail *noun*
For other words, see **path**

trail *verb*
1 The police trailed him for miles.
For other verbs, see **track**
2 Jo's scarf is so long that it trails in the mud.
ANOTHER VERB IS **to drag**

train *noun*
We went to London on the train.
For other words, see **railway**

train *verb*
1 Jo's Dad trains the school team.
OTHER VERBS YOU MIGHT USE ARE **to coach** **to instruct** **to teach**
2 The team trains every Thursday.
OTHER VERBS ARE **to exercise** **to practise**

trainer *noun*

1 Sam's feet are too big for his old trainers.
For other things you wear on your feet, see **shoe**

2 Our team has a new trainer.
ANOTHER WORD IS **coach**

transfer *verb*

1 A bus transferred us from the airport to the hotel.
OTHER VERBS YOU MIGHT USE ARE **to carry** **to take** **to transport**

2 The goalkeeper was transferred to another team.
OTHER VERBS ARE **to move** **to switch**

transform *verb*

The fairy transformed the pumpkin into a coach.
OTHER VERBS YOU MIGHT USE ARE **to change** **to turn**

transport *noun*

For different kinds of transport, see **travel**

trap *verb*

We trapped the mouse in a box.
OTHER VERBS YOU MIGHT USE ARE **to capture** **to catch** **to corner**

travel *noun*, see next page

treacherous *adjective*

Take care: that dog's treacherous.
OTHER WORDS YOU MIGHT USE ARE **dangerous** **untrustworthy**
The opposite is **loyal**

tread *verb*

Don't tread on the flowers.
OTHER VERBS YOU MIGHT USE ARE **to step** **to trample** **to walk**

treat *verb*

1 Treat your pets well.
OTHER VERBS YOU MIGHT USE ARE **to care for** **to look after**

2 How shall we treat this problem?
OTHER VERBS ARE **to attend to** **to deal with** **to tackle**

tree *noun*, see next page

tremble *verb*

I trembled with fear.
OTHER VERBS YOU MIGHT USE ARE **to quake** **to quiver** **to shake** **to shiver** **to shudder**

tremendous *adjective*

1 We heard a tremendous explosion.
OTHER WORDS ARE **alarming** **awful** **fearful** **frightful** **terrible** **terrific**

2 Granny gave us tremendous helpings of dinner.
OTHER WORDS ARE **big** **enormous** **huge** **large**

travel *verb*

DIFFERENT WAYS TO TRAVEL ARE

cruise **cycle** **drive** **fly**
hitch-hike **ride** **sail** **walk**

DIFFERENT KINDS OF JOURNEY ARE

cruise **drive** **expedition** **flight**
hike **outing** **pilgrimage** **ramble**
ride **safari** **tour** **trek**
trip **voyage** **walk**

A person who travels is a **traveller**.

OTHER WORDS FOR PEOPLE WHO TRAVEL ARE

a person who drives a car: **motorist**
a person who travels while someone else drives: **passenger**
a person who goes on foot
hiker **pedestrian** **rambler** **walker**
a person who travels to work every day: **commuter**
a traveller to a holy place: **pilgrim**
a person who travels on holiday
holidaymaker **tourist**
a person who travels in a boat
sailor **yachtsman** **yachtswoman**
a person who travels to find somewhere new: **explorer**
people who travel about because that's how they like to live
gypsies **nomads** **tramps** **travellers**
Something you travel in is a **vehicle**.

DIFFERENT VEHICLES THAT PEOPLE TRAVEL IN ON THE ROADS ARE

bus **car** **coach** **jeep**
minibus **motorbike** or **motorcycle** **taxi**
tram

OTHER FORMS OF TRANSPORT FOR PASSENGERS ARE

aeroplane **bicycle** **ferry** **railway**
underground

WAYS PEOPLE USED TO TRAVEL ARE

carriage **horse** **stagecoach**

VEHICLES THAT CARRY GOODS ARE

articulated lorry **cart** **lorry**
pick-up truck **truck** **van** **wagon**

OTHER KINDS OF TRANSPORT FOR GOODS ARE

aircraft **goods train** **ship**

VEHICLES MADE TO DO SPECIAL JOBS ARE

ambulance **bulldozer** **caravan** **digger**
dustcart **fire engine** **horsebox** **milk float**
police car **steamroller** **tanker** **tractor**

For other words, see
aircraft, **boat**, **car**,
railway

tree *noun*

DIFFERENT KINDS OF TREE ARE

ash **beech** **birch** **cedar** **chestnut**
elm **fir** **holly** **larch** **lime**
maple **oak** **palm tree** **pine** **plane**
poplar **sycamore** **willow** **yew**

a b c d e f g h i j k l m n o p q r s t u v w x y z

trick *noun*

1 That was a nasty trick!
OTHER WORDS YOU MIGHT USE ARE **cheat** **deception** **fraud** **hoax**

2 The dolphins did some amazing tricks.
ANOTHER WORD IS **stunt**

trick *verb*

He tricked us into buying rubbish.
OTHER VERBS YOU MIGHT USE ARE **to cheat** **to fool** **to hoax** **to mislead** **to swindle**

trickle *verb*

Water trickled out of the crack.
OTHER VERBS YOU MIGHT USE ARE **to dribble** **to drip** **to leak** **to ooze** **to run** **to seep**

trip *noun*

a trip to the seaside.
OTHER WORDS YOU MIGHT USE ARE **excursion** **expedition** **outing** **visit**
For other words, see **travel**

trouble *noun*

1 Mum has had a lot of trouble lately.
OTHER WORDS YOU MIGHT USE ARE **distress** **grief** **hardship** **misery** **misfortune** **problems** **sadness** **worry**

2 There was some trouble in the playground at dinner time.
OTHER WORDS ARE **bother** **commotion** **disorder** **fighting** **fuss** **row**

3 Sam takes trouble with his work.
OTHER WORDS ARE **care** **effort**

trouble *verb*

Do wasps trouble you?
OTHER VERBS YOU MIGHT USE ARE **to annoy** **to bother** **to upset** **to worry**

trousers *noun*

For other words, see **clothes**

true *adjective*

1 Is that story true?
OTHER WORDS YOU MIGHT USE ARE **correct** **factual** **genuine** **real**

2 Jo is a true friend.
OTHER WORDS ARE **faithful** **loyal** **reliable** **trustworthy**

trust *verb*

You can trust Jo to do her best.
PHRASES YOU MIGHT USE ARE (*informal*) **to bank on** **to be sure of** **to count on** **to depend on** **to have faith in** **to rely on**

try *verb*

1 Sam tried to swim ten lengths.
OTHER VERBS ARE **to aim** **to attempt** **to endeavour** **to exert yourself** **to make an effort** **to strive**

2 Can I try the cake?
ANOTHER VERB IS **to sample**

3 Try the brakes before you ride your bike.
OTHER VERBS ARE **to experiment with** **to test**

tube *noun*

ANOTHER WORD IS **pipe**
A tube to take water from the tap to where you want it is a **hose**.

tune *noun*
Jo played a well-known tune.
ANOTHER WORD IS **melody**

tunnel *noun*
A tunnel that a rabbit makes is a **burrow**.
A tunnel under a road is a **subway** or **underpass**.

turn *noun*
It's your turn to play next.
OTHER WORDS ARE **chance** **go** **opportunity**

turn *verb*
1 The wheel began to turn.
OTHER VERBS YOU MIGHT USE ARE **to revolve** **to rotate** **to spin** **to twirl** **to whirl**
For other verbs, see **twist**
2 Tadpoles turn into frogs.
OTHER VERBS ARE **to become** **to change into**
3 We turned the attic into a playroom.
OTHER VERBS ARE **to convert** **to transform**

twinkle *verb*
The lights twinkled in the distance.
OTHER VERBS ARE **to flicker** **to shine** **to sparkle**
For other verbs, see **light**

twist *verb*
1 The road twisted up the hill.
OTHER VERBS YOU MIGHT USE ARE **to bend** **to curve** **to zigzag**
2 I twisted the wires round each other.
OTHER VERBS ARE **to coil** **to curl** **to loop** **to turn** **to wind**

type *noun*
1 What type of music do you like?
OTHER WORDS YOU MIGHT USE ARE **kind** **sort**
2 What type of dog is that?
OTHER WORDS ARE **breed** **species** **variety**

typical *adjective*
In England, showers are typical April weather.
OTHER WORDS YOU MIGHT USE ARE **common** **normal** **ordinary** **usual**
The opposite is **unusual**

Uu

ugly *adjective*
We screamed when we saw the ugly monster.
OTHER WORDS YOU MIGHT USE ARE **foul** **frightful** **hideous** **monstrous** **repulsive** **unattractive**
The opposite is **beautiful**

a b c d e f g h i j k l m n o p q r s t u v w x y z

uncommon *adjective*
Eagles are uncommon in this country.
OTHER WORDS YOU MIGHT USE ARE **infrequent** **rare** **unusual**
The opposite is **common**

unconscious *adjective*
If you are unconscious, you may be **knocked out** or you may have **fainted**.
The opposite is **conscious**

understand *verb*
Do you understand what I mean?
OTHER VERBS YOU MIGHT USE ARE **to follow** **to grasp** **to know** **to realize** **to see**

undo *verb*
Jo undid the parcel.
OTHER VERBS YOU MIGHT USE ARE **to unfasten** **to untie**

unemployed *adjective*
PHRASES ARE **on the dole** **out of work**

uneven *adjective*
1 We jolted along the uneven road.
OTHER WORDS YOU MIGHT USE ARE **bumpy** **rough**
The opposite is **smooth**
2 The music had an uneven beat.
ANOTHER WORD IS **irregular**
The opposite is **regular**

unfair *adjective*
1 It's unfair if she gets more than me.
OTHER WORDS YOU MIGHT USE ARE **unjust** **unreasonable** **wrong**
2 We complained that the referee was unfair.
OTHER WORDS YOU MIGHT USE ARE **biased** **prejudiced**
The opposite is **fair**

unfriendly *adjective*
Mum was upset by our neighbour's unfriendly remarks.
OTHER WORDS YOU MIGHT USE ARE **aggressive** **angry** **disagreeable** **hostile** **nasty** **offensive** **rude**
For other words, see **unkind**
The opposite is **friendly**

unhappy *adjective*
He was unhappy after his dog died.
OTHER WORDS ARE **depressed** **gloomy** **glum** **heartbroken** **miserable** **sorrowful** **tearful** **troubled** **wretched**
The opposite is **happy**

unite *verb*
We united to sing the last song.
OTHER VERBS YOU MIGHT USE ARE **to combine** **to join together**

unkind *adjective*
Jo hates to see people being unkind to animals.
OTHER WORDS ARE **cruel** **heartless** **spiteful** **thoughtless**
For other words, see **unfriendly**
The opposite is **kind**

unlikely *adjective*
I don't believe his unlikely story.
OTHER WORDS YOU MIGHT USE ARE **far-fetched** **improbable** **incredible** **unconvincing**
The opposite is **likely**

unlucky *adjective*
We were unlucky to miss the bus.
ANOTHER WORD IS **unfortunate**
The opposite is **lucky**

unpleasant *adjective*
1 The accident was an unpleasant experience.
OTHER WORDS YOU MIGHT USE ARE **awful** **dreadful** **frightening** **painful** **terrible** **upsetting**
2 I hate touching unpleasant things.
OTHER WORDS ARE **disgusting** **horrible** **nasty** **objectionable**
3 The noisy neighbours were very unpleasant.
OTHER WORDS ARE **rude** **unfriendly**
The opposite is **pleasant**

untidy *adjective*
1 Our teacher hates untidy work.
OTHER WORDS YOU MIGHT USE ARE **careless** **disorganized** **scruffy**
2 Everything was in an untidy pile on the floor.
OTHER WORDS ARE **confused** **disorderly** **jumbled** **muddled**
The opposite is **tidy**

unusual *adjective*
It's unusual to have snow in May.
OTHER WORDS YOU MIGHT USE ARE **extraordinary** **odd** **peculiar** **strange** **surprising** **uncommon**
The opposite is **common**

upset *verb*
1 The thunder upset the dog.
OTHER VERBS YOU MIGHT USE ARE **to alarm** **to bother** **to distress** **to frighten** **to trouble** **to worry**
2 Sam upset the milk.
OTHER VERBS ARE **to knock over** **to overturn** **to spill**

urge *noun*
I had an urge to giggle.
OTHER WORDS ARE **desire** **wish**

urge *verb*
Mum urged us to be quick.
OTHER VERBS YOU MIGHT USE ARE **to appeal to** **to beg** **to encourage** **to entreat** **to plead with**

use *verb*
1 They used the most up-to-date machines to dig the tunnel.
ANOTHER VERB IS **to employ**
2 Have we used all the milk?
OTHER VERBS YOU MIGHT USE ARE **to consume** **to finish**

a b c d e f g h i j k l m n o p q r s t u v w x y z

useful *adjective*

1 Dad's penknife is a useful tool.
OTHER WORDS YOU MIGHT USE ARE **convenient** **handy** **practical**

2 Sam is a useful member of the team.
OTHER WORDS ARE **helpful** **valuable**

The opposite is **useless**

useless *adjective*

1 A car is useless without petrol.
ANOTHER WORD IS **unusable**

2 He was a useless goalkeeper.
OTHER WORDS ARE **incompetent** **worthless**

The opposite is **useful**

usual *adjective*

1 Ten o'clock is my usual bedtime.
OTHER WORDS YOU MIGHT USE ARE **normal** **ordinary** **regular**

2 It's usual to put milk in tea.
OTHER WORDS ARE **common** **expected** **typical**

The opposite is **unusual**

Vv

vague *adjective*

1 He made some vague comments, but nothing definite.
OTHER WORDS YOU MIGHT USE ARE **broad** **general**

2 He was a vague sort of person.
OTHER WORDS ARE **absent-minded** **forgetful** **scatterbrained**

The opposite is **definite**

vain *adjective*

He's so vain that he's always looking in the mirror.
OTHER WORDS ARE **boastful** **conceited** **proud**

The opposite is **modest**

valuable *adjective*

1 valuable jewels.
OTHER WORDS YOU MIGHT USE ARE **expensive** **precious** **priceless**

The opposite is **worthless**

2 He gave me some valuable advice.
OTHER WORDS ARE **helpful** **useful** **worthwhile**

The opposite is **useless**

vanish *verb*

The robber vanished into the crowd.
ANOTHER VERB IS **to disappear**

variety *noun*

1 There's a variety of things to eat.
OTHER WORDS YOU MIGHT USE ARE **assortment** **mixture**

2 Mum grows many varieties of flowers.
OTHER WORDS ARE **kind** **sort** **type**

various *adjective*
We made various sandwiches.
OTHER WORDS YOU MIGHT USE ARE **assorted** **different** **mixed**

vary *verb*
The date of Easter varies each year.
OTHER VERBS YOU MIGHT USE ARE **to alter** **to change**

vegetable *noun*
VEGETABLES PEOPLE EAT INCLUDE

asparagus	**beans**
Brussels sprouts	**cabbage**
carrot	**cauliflower**
greens	**leek**
marrow	**onion**
parsnip	**pea**
potato	**pumpkin**
spinach	**swede**
turnip	

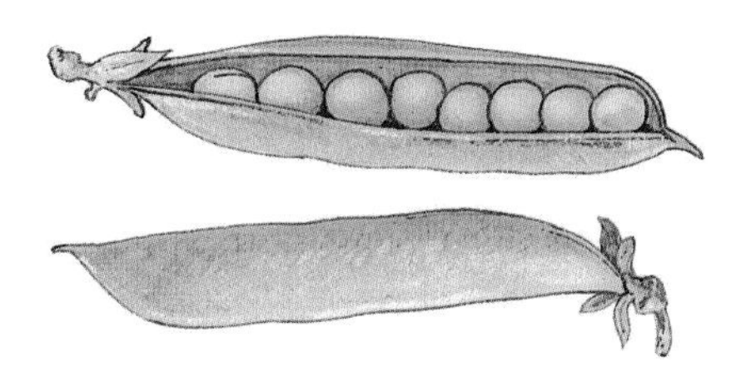

vehicle *noun*
For other words, see **travel**

version *noun*
1 Jo's version of the accident is different from Sam's.
OTHER WORDS YOU MIGHT USE ARE **account** **description** **story**
2 Mum makes a vegetarian version of shepherd's pie.
OTHER WORDS ARE **kind** **sort** **type**

vertical *adjective*
The opposite is **horizontal**

vibrate *verb*
When the engine started we felt the boat vibrate.
OTHER VERBS YOU MIGHT USE ARE **to quiver** **to shake** **to shudder** **to throb**

victory *noun*
We celebrated our team's victory.
OTHER WORDS YOU MIGHT USE ARE **success** **triumph** **win**
The opposite is **defeat**

view *verb*
We viewed the the stars through a telescope.
OTHER VERBS YOU MIGHT USE ARE **to look at** **to watch**

villain *noun*
I guessed he was the villain at the very beginning of the film.
OTHER WORDS ARE (*informal*) **baddy** **rascal** **scoundrel**
The opposite is **hero**

violent *adjective*
1 a violent attack.
OTHER WORDS ARE **cruel** **ferocious** **fierce** **savage**
2 a violent storm.
OTHER WORDS ARE **rough** **severe** **strong**
The opposite is **gentle**

a b c d e f g h i j k l m n o p q r s t u **v** w x y z

visible *adjective*
Is the ink stain still visible?
OTHER WORDS ARE **clear** **noticeable** **obvious** **plain**
The opposite is **invisible**

visit *verb*
Granny visited us on Sunday.
OTHER VERBS YOU MIGHT USE ARE **to call** (*informal*) **to drop in**

visitor *noun*
Are you expecting a visitor?
OTHER WORDS ARE **caller** **guest**

vivid *adjective*
1 vivid colours.
OTHER WORDS YOU MIGHT USE ARE **bright** **brilliant** **colourful**
2 a vivid imagination.
ANOTHER WORD IS **lively**
3 a vivid dream.
OTHER WORDS ARE **clear** **lifelike**
The opposite is **dull**

voice *noun*
For different ways you can use your voice, see **talk**

volume *noun*
1 The tank holds a large volume of oil.
OTHER WORDS ARE **amount** **mass** **quantity**
2 How many volumes are there in the library?
ANOTHER WORD IS **book**

volunteer *verb*
Sam volunteered to wash up.
ANOTHER VERB IS **to offer**

vote *verb*
Who did you vote for?
OTHER VERBS YOU MIGHT USE ARE **to choose** **to pick** **to select**

vow *verb*
He vowed never to do it again.
OTHER VERBS YOU MIGHT USE ARE **to give your word** **to guarantee** **to promise** **to swear**

voyage *noun*
For other words, see **travel**

vulgar *adjective*
We don't like vulgar language.
OTHER WORDS YOU MIGHT USE ARE **bad-mannered** **coarse** **impolite** **improper** **indecent** **rude**
The opposite is **polite**

wait *verb*

1 Wait there!

OTHER VERBS YOU MIGHT USE ARE **to halt** **to keep still** **to remain** **to rest** **to stay** **to stop**

2 Don't wait: get on with it!

OTHER VERBS ARE **to delay** **to hesitate** **to pause**

wake *verb*

I asked Mum to wake me early.

OTHER VERBS YOU MIGHT USE ARE **to call** **to rouse**

walk *verb*

DIFFERENT WAYS TO WALK ARE

to creep **to hobble** **to limp** **to march** **to plod** **to prowl** **to shuffle** **to stagger** **to stride** **to strut** **to stumble** **to totter** **to trot** **to trudge**

to go for a gentle walk: **to stroll**

to go for a long country walk

to hike **to ramble** **to trek**

When a baby tries to walk it **crawls**.

DIFFERENT WORDS FOR A WALKER ARE

a person who walks in the street: **pedestrian**

a person who goes for a walk in the country

hiker **rambler**

wander *verb*

The sheep wander about the hills.

OTHER VERBS YOU MIGHT USE ARE **to ramble** **to roam** **to stray**

want *verb*

You can't always have what you want.

OTHER VERBS YOU MIGHT USE ARE **to desire** **to fancy** **to long for** **to wish for** **to yearn for**

war *noun*

THINGS THAT HAPPEN IN WAR ARE:

ambush **attack** **battle** **fighting** **invasion** **retreat** **siege** **surrender**

For other words, see **weapon**

warm *adjective*

If something is very warm it is **hot**.

If something is slightly warm it is **lukewarm** or **tepid**.

WORDS TO DESCRIBE WARM WEATHER ARE **close** **humid** **sultry**

warn *verb*

The policeman warned him not to do it again.

ANOTHER VERB IS **to caution**

a b c d e f g h i j k l m n o p q r s t u v w x y z

wash *verb*

DIFFERENT WAYS TO WASH THINGS ARE
to bath **to mop** **to rinse** **to scrub** **to shampoo** **to sponge down** **to swill** **to wipe**

waste *noun*

Put the waste in the bin.
OTHER WORDS YOU MIGHT USE ARE **junk** **litter** **refuse** **rubbish**

watch *verb*

1 I watched the ducks on the lake.
OTHER VERBS ARE **to gaze at** **to look at** **to observe** **to stare at**

2 Will you watch my things while I go for a swim?
OTHER VERBS YOU MIGHT USE ARE **to guard** **to look after** **to mind**

water *noun*

KINDS OF WATER YOU CAN DRINK ARE
mineral water **spring water** **tap water**

OTHER KINDS OF WATER ARE
big stretches of water
lake **ocean** **reservoir** **sea**
small areas of water
pond **puddle**
water that spreads over land that is usually dry
flood
water which goes along a channel
brook **canal** **ditch** **river** **stream** **waterway**
water which rushes over rocks
cascade **cataract** **rapids** **waterfall**
places where water comes out of the ground
spring **well**
water which spurts out of a hole
fountain **jet** **spray**
A place where water seems to spin round and round is a **whirlpool**.

wave *noun*

Big waves are **breakers** or **surf**.
Small waves are **ripples**.

wave *verb*

The flags waved in the breeze.
OTHER VERBS YOU MIGHT USE ARE **to flap** **to flutter** **to shake**

way *noun*

1 Sam thinks his way of building a den is the best.
OTHER WORDS YOU MIGHT USE ARE **method** **technique**

2 She does her hair in a pretty way.
OTHER WORDS ARE **fashion** **manner** **style**

3 What is the best way home?
ANOTHER WORD IS **route**

weak *adjective*

1 a weak person.

OTHER WORDS YOU MIGHT USE ARE **delicate** **feeble** **frail**

For other words, see **ill**

2 a weak branch.

OTHER WORDS YOU MIGHT USE ARE **brittle** **flimsy** **fragile** **thin**

3 weak tea.

OTHER WORDS YOU MIGHT USE ARE **tasteless** **watery**

The opposite is **strong**

wealthy *adjective*

a wealthy businessman.

OTHER WORDS YOU MIGHT USE ARE **prosperous** **rich** **well-off**

The opposite is **poor**

weapon *noun*

WEAPONS WHICH FIRE THINGS ARE

airgun **bow and arrow** **cannon**
catapult **crossbow** **machine-gun**
musket **pistol** **revolver**
rifle **shotgun**

WEAPONS WHICH BLOW UP ARE

bomb **grenade** **mine**
missile **nuclear weapons** **time bomb**
torpedo

WEAPONS WHICH CUT WITH A SHARP EDGE ARE

cutlass **dagger** **sabre**
sword

WEAPONS WITH A SHARP POINT ARE

bayonet **harpoon** **javelin**
lance **spear**

weary *adjective*

I was weary after the long walk.

OTHER WORDS YOU MIGHT USE ARE **exhausted** **tired** **worn out**

weather *noun*, see next page

weep *verb*

He wept when his dog died.

OTHER VERBS YOU MIGHT USE ARE **to cry** **to shed tears** **to sob**

weird *adjective*

1 What a weird thing to do!

OTHER WORDS YOU MIGHT USE ARE **curious** **funny** **odd** **peculiar** **queer** **strange**

2 There was a weird atmosphere in the castle.

OTHER WORDS ARE (*informal*) **creepy** **ghostly** (*informal*) **scary**

welcome *verb*

We welcomed the guests at the door.

OTHER VERBS YOU MIGHT USE ARE **to greet** **to receive**

a b c d e f g h i j k l m n o p q r s t u v **w** x y z

weather *noun*

WORDS TO DO WITH DIFFERENT KINDS OF WEATHER ARE
cloud **drought** **fog** **frost**
hail **heatwave** **ice** **lightning**
mist **rain** **rainbow** **snow**
storm **sunshine** **thaw** **thunder**
wind

WORDS FOR DIFFERENT KINDS OF RAIN
a short fall of rain **shower**
very heavy rain **downpour**
very fine light rain **drizzle**
mixed rain and snow **sleet**

DIFFERENT KINDS OF WIND
a very strong wind **gale**
a gentle wind **breeze**
a sudden puff of wind **gust**

DIFFERENT KINDS OF STORM
a violent storm **tempest**
a snow storm **blizzard**
a storm with a lot of wind
gale **hurricane** **tornado** **whirlwind**
a storm with a lot of rain
deluge **rainstorm**
a storm with thunder and lightning **thunderstorm**

WORDS YOU MIGHT USE TO DESCRIBE THE WEATHER ARE
blustery **bright** **clear** **cloudless**
cloudy **cold** **drizzly** **dull**
fair **fine** **foggy** **freezing**
frosty **hazy** **hot** **icy**
misty **rainy** **showery** **snowy**
stormy **sultry** **sunny** **thundery**
wet **windy** **wintry**

well *adjective*
I hope you are well.
OTHER WORDS ARE **fit** **healthy**
The opposite is **ill**

well-known *adjective*
a well-known pop star.
OTHER WORDS YOU MIGHT USE ARE **familiar** **famous**

wet *adjective*
1 I got wet in the storm.
OTHER WORDS YOU MIGHT USE ARE **drenched** **soaked**
2 The field is too wet to play on.
OTHER WORDS ARE **muddy** **soggy** **waterlogged**
3 It was a wet day.
OTHER WORDS ARE **drizzly** **rainy** **showery**
If something is slightly wet it is **damp** or **moist**.
The opposite is **dry**

whip *verb*
For other verbs, see **hit**

whirl *verb*
The wheel whirled round.
OTHER VERBS YOU MIGHT USE ARE **to revolve** **to rotate** **to spin** **to turn** **to twirl**

whiskers *noun*
OTHER WORDS ARE **hairs** **bristles**

whisper *verb*
For other verbs, see **talk**

whole *adjective*
1 We ate the whole cake.
OTHER WORDS YOU MIGHT USE ARE **complete** **entire**
2 Yasmin dropped the cake but it stayed whole.
OTHER WORDS ARE **intact** **undamaged**

wicked *adjective*
It's wicked to take food from starving people.
OTHER WORDS YOU MIGHT USE ARE **bad** **evil** **immoral** **sinful** **wrong**
The opposite is **good**

wide *adjective*
1 The stream was too wide to jump.
ANOTHER WORD IS **broad**
2 There's a wide gap between the two scores.
ANOTHER WORD IS **large**

wild *adjective*
1 wild animals.
OTHER WORDS YOU MIGHT USE ARE **free** **natural** **untamed**
The opposite is **tame**
2 wild weather.
OTHER WORDS ARE **rough** **stormy** **violent** **windy**
The opposite is **calm**
3 wild behaviour.
OTHER WORDS ARE **boisterous** **disorderly** **excited** **noisy** **rowdy** **unruly**
The opposite is **orderly**

willing *adjective*
1 Sam is willing to help us.
OTHER WORDS YOU MIGHT USE ARE **happy** **prepared** **ready**
2 Jo is a willing worker, too.
OTHER WORDS ARE **cooperative** **helpful** **obliging**
The opposite is **reluctant**

win *verb*
1 Jo won first prize.
OTHER VERBS YOU MIGHT USE ARE **to earn** **to gain** **to receive**
2 The better team won.
OTHER VERBS ARE **to come first** **to succeed** **to triumph**
The opposite is **lose**

a b c d e f g h i j k l m n o p q r s t u v w x y z

wind (rhymes with *tinned*) *noun*
KINDS OF WIND
a very strong wind is a **gale**.
a gentle wind is a **breeze**.
a sudden puff of wind is a **gust**.
A **whirlwind** blows round and round and can do a lot of damage.

For other words, see **weather**
A kind of wind you feel if someone leaves a door open indoors is a **draught**.

wind (rhymes with *find*) *verb*
I wound the string into a ball.
OTHER VERBS YOU MIGHT USE ARE **to coil** **to curl** **to loop** **to turn** **to twist**

windy, **wintry** *adjectives*
For other words, see **weather**

wipe *verb*
DIFFERENT WAYS TO WIPE THINGS ARE **to dry** **to dust** **to mop** **to polish** **to rub** **to scour** **to sponge** **to wash**

wire *noun*
an electric wire.
OTHER WORDS YOU MIGHT USE ARE **cable** **flex** **lead**

wise *adjective*
If you're wise you won't go out in the rain.
OTHER WORDS YOU MIGHT USE ARE **intelligent** **reasonable** **sensible** **thoughtful**
The opposite is **silly**

wish *verb*
For other verbs, see **want**

wither *verb*
The plants withered in the dry weather.
OTHER VERBS YOU MIGHT USE ARE **to dry up** **to shrink** **to shrivel** **to wilt**

wobble *verb*
1 Jo wobbled a bit when she first rode a bike.
OTHER VERBS YOU MIGHT USE ARE **to be unsteady** **to sway** **to waver**
2 The jelly wobbles when you move the plate.
OTHER VERBS ARE **to shake** **to tremble**

woman *noun*
OTHER WORDS YOU MIGHT USE
a polite word is a **lady**.
a married woman is a **wife**.
a woman who is not married is a **spinster**.
a woman whose husband has died is a **widow**.
a woman who has children is a **mother**.
a young woman is a **girl**.
The man who plays a woman in a pantomime is the **dame**.

wonder *verb*
I wonder if it will be fine tomorrow.
ANOTHER VERB IS **to ask yourself**

wonderful *adjective*
We had a wonderful time.
OTHER WORDS YOU MIGHT USE ARE **amazing** **excellent** (*informal*) **fabulous** **marvellous** **special**
The opposite is **dreadful**

wood *noun*
1 Dad bought some wood to make a table.
ANOTHER WORD IS
timber
KINDS OF TIMBER ARE
beams **boards** **planks** **posts**
2 We went for a walk in the wood.
ANOTHER WORD IS
woodland
A large wood is a **forest**.
A small wood is a **copse** or **grove** or **thicket.**
A place where fruit trees are growing is an **orchard**.

word *noun*, see next page

work *noun*
1 Keeping a garden tidy takes a lot of work.
OTHER WORDS YOU MIGHT USE ARE **effort** **exertion** **labour** **toil**
2 What kind of work does Dad do?
OTHER WORDS ARE **job** **occupation** **profession** **trade**
3 Our teacher set us work to do.
OTHER WORDS ARE **assignment** **project** **task**

work *verb*
1 We worked hard all morning.
OTHER VERBS YOU MIGHT USE ARE **to labour** (*informal*) **to slave away** **to toil**
2 Does your watch work?
ANOTHER VERB IS **to go**
3 Can you work this machine?
ANOTHER VERB IS **to operate**

worry *verb*
1 Don't worry; everything will be all right.
PHRASES YOU MIGHT USE ARE **to be anxious** **to be concerned** **to be troubled** **to feel uneasy**
2 Don't worry the cat when she's sleeping.
OTHER VERBS ARE **to annoy** **to bother** **to disturb** **to pester** **to trouble** **to upset**

a b c d e f g h i j k l m n o p q r s t u v w x y z

word *noun*

Different words do different jobs and so they belong to different groups called parts of speech.

THE EIGHT PARTS OF SPEECH ARE

adjective **adverb** **conjunction**
interjection or **exclamation** **noun**
preposition **pronoun** **verb**

Words which are the names of people, things, or ideas are nouns. For example: *girl*, *animal*, and *happiness* are all nouns.

A word which you use instead of a noun is a pronoun. For example: *I*, *you*, *she*, and *it* are pronouns.

A word which describes a noun is an adjective. In the phrase *'an old green car' old* and *green* are adjectives.

A word which goes in front of a noun to make a phrase is a preposition. In the phrases *'near my house'* and *'under the table' near* and *under* are prepositions.

Words which show what someone does or what happens are verbs. In the sentences *'Jo ran home'* and *'The rain stopped' ran* and *stopped* are verbs.

A word which tells you how, when, or where something happens is an adverb. For example: in the sentences *'Jo ran home quickly'* and *'Put it here' quickly* and *here* are adverbs.

Words like *and* or *but* which we use to join words or ideas are conjunctions.

A word like *Hello!* or *Well!* is an interjection or exclamation.

worship *verb*

Jo worships her Grandad.

OTHER VERBS YOU MIGHT USE ARE **to adore** **to love**

worthless *adjective*

worthless rubbish.

ANOTHER WORD IS **useless**

The opposite is **valuable**

wound *verb*

Was anyone wounded in the accident?

OTHER VERBS YOU MIGHT USE ARE

to harm **to hurt** **to injure**

THERE ARE DIFFERENT WAYS YOU CAN BE WOUNDED

An animal can **bite** you.
A knock or fall can **bruise** you.
Something very hot **burns** you.
A knife will **cut** you.
You can **break** or **fracture** a bone.
You can **graze** your skin on something rough.
A gun can **shoot** you.
You can **sprain** a joint by twisting it.
A dagger can **stab** you.
Some insects can **sting** you.

wrap *verb*
I wrapped the parcel in paper.
OTHER VERBS YOU MIGHT USE ARE **to cover** **to enclose**

wreck *verb*
The accident wrecked the car.
OTHER VERBS YOU MIGHT USE ARE **to break up** **to destroy** **to ruin** **to shatter** **to smash**

write *verb*
THERE ARE DIFFERENT WAYS TO WRITE THINGS
Musicians **compose** music.
When you are bored, you **doodle**.
You **jot** down rough notes.
People **print** books and newspapers.
When you are in a hurry you **scrawl** or **scribble**.
You can **type** things or use a word processor.

DIFFERENT KINDS OF WRITING
articles for a magazine or paper
diary **essays** **films** **letters** **novels** **plays** **poems** **stories**
programmes for radio and TV

Another word for a writer is **author**.
DIFFERENT KINDS OF WRITER
a writer of novels is a **novelist**.
a writer for a newspaper is a **journalist**.
a person who writes poetry is a **poet**.
a person who writes for radio or TV is a **scriptwriter**.
a person who writes plays is a **dramatist** or **playwright**.
Someone who writes music is a **composer**.

wrong *adjective*
1 I gave a wrong answer.
OTHER WORDS YOU MIGHT USE ARE **false** **inaccurate** **incorrect** **mistaken** **untrue**
2 It is wrong to steal.
OTHER WORDS ARE **dishonest** **illegal** **immoral**
3 Cruelty to animals is wrong.
OTHER WORDS ARE **evil** **wicked**
The opposite is **right**

Xx

xylophone *noun*
For other musical instruments, see **instrument**

Yy

yell *verb*
He yelled angrily at me.
OTHER VERBS YOU MIGHT USE ARE **to call** **to shout**

young *adjective*
SOMETIMES THERE ARE SPECIAL WORDS FOR YOUNG THINGS
A person who is not a child but is not yet grown up **adolescent** **juvenile** **teenager**
A young person **baby** **boy** **child** **girl** **infant** **toddler**
A young cow or whale is a **calf**.
A young hen is a **chick** or **pullet**.
A young bear is a **cub**.
A young swan is a **cygnet**.
A young duck is a **duckling**.
A young deer is a **fawn**.
A young bird is a **fledgling** or **nestling**.
A young horse is a **foal**.
A young goose is a **gosling**.
A young goat is a **kid**.
A young cat is a **kitten**.
A young sheep is a **lamb**.
A young pig is a **piglet**.
A young dog is a **puppy**.
A young tree is a **sapling**.
A young plant is a **seedling**.

Zz

zero *noun*
OTHER WORDS YOU MIGHT USE ARE **nil** **nothing** **nought**

zigzag *noun*
a zigzag line.
OTHER WORDS YOU MIGHT USE ARE **bendy** **crooked**

a b c d e f g h i j k l m n o p q r s t u v w x y z